WHY THEY KILLED GANDHI

UNMASKING THE IDEOLOGY AND THE CONSPIRACY

Ashok Kumar Pandey

SPEAKING TIGER

SPEAKING TIGER BOOKS LLP
125A, Ground Floor, Shahpur Jat, near Asiad Village,
New Delhi 110049

First published in Hindi by Rajkamal Prakashan in 2020
This English edition published by Speaking Tiger in 2022

ISBN: 978-93-5447-001-1
eISBN: 978-93-5447-009-7

10 9 8 7 6 5 4 3 2 1

Typeset in Minion Regular by SÜRYA, New Delhi
Printed at Shree Maitrey Printech Pvt. Ltd., Noida

For Nana,
who went to jail during
the Quit India movement,
and in whom
I most closely saw Gandhi

CONTENTS

Preface

Gandhi's life has never been a mystery. He bared open every aspect of his life as seen in the ninety-two volumes of the *Collected Works of Mahatma Gandhi* and various other books/booklets written by him or people like Mahadev Desai and Pyarelal, who accompanied him as friends and personal assistants, and kept track of every activity of his. Most of the derogatory WhatsApp forwards in vogue these days claim to 'reveal' what Gandhi has already told us through his writings.

The details of his death, however, are for most people somewhat obscure. We do of course know that a certain Nathuram Godse fired three shots to take his life, but the conspiracy behind it largely remains hidden from greater public scrutiny. This work is a small attempt towards addressing this lack of awareness on the subject. Since the conspiracy was not merely a criminal one but had an ideological dimension as well—something that portends greater danger in the long run—the events need to be understood in detail. I have therefore, along with discussing the facts of the case as we know them from court documents, the Kapur Commission Report and other relevant papers, also tried to show the ideological conflict between the various political forces during India's struggle for freedom.

This book was originally written in Hindi, and since I myself ventured to translate it, the English version contains some additional information which I could only get after the publication of the original.

The hatred spewed these days against the likes of Gandhi, Nehru and other makers of modern India is striking, and my endeavour is to present a narrative based on historical facts and research in this so-called 'post-truth' age. I humbly commit myself to an intellectual satyagraha against the tirade of misinformation corrupting the minds of our young and thus our national life.

I am immensely grateful to Ravi Singh of Speaking Tiger for bringing out the English version of this book. My editor, Nazeef, worked tirelessly to make the book suitable for English readers. I would also like to thank Mr Ashok Maheshwari and Satyanand Nirupam for publishing the Hindi version. I thank my friend Akshat Seth, who helped me in the translation work—almost wholly translating the third part himself. My lovely daughter Ananya deserves a special mention for encouraging and prodding me to bring this book out in English. I cannot of course thank my readers across the country enough, who made this book a success in its Hindi, Punjabi and Marathi versions. Their constant support is an indestructible source of energy for this satyagraha.

ASHOK KUMAR PANDEY
25 November 2021, Delhi

PART ONE

Who Were They?

Neither were they among the heroes who sacrificed everything to fight for the freedom of the motherland, nor among the revolutionary intellectuals of that period working for a better future for the country.

All that sets them apart is the fact that they managed to kill Mohandas Karamchand Gandhi, the man revered as the 'Father of the Nation' by Netaji Subhas Chandra Bose and 'Mahatma' by Rabindranath Tagore. Their only glory was in the murder of a seventy-eight-year-old Gandhi who, when the need arose, refused to shrink from staying in an unsecured house in a remote village of riot-torn Noakhali, roamed hundreds of villages on foot, crossing rickety wooden bridges to rehabilitate Hindus; and soon after, tried to save Muslims in riot affected areas of Delhi when planning to visit Pakistan to save *their* minorities against the goons of the Muslim League. The man who cared little for the very real danger to his person and was not ready to violate the sanctity of his prayer meetings by allowing the screening of visitors, despite a previous attack. The man who led the Congress in the freedom movement but never accepted any position of power, and chose politics as a medium for social service. Their only success was that they managed to kill this man, who had invited them to share their grievances following the abortive assault at his prayer meeting.

They carved out a bleak slot for themselves in history by killing a baresark Gandhi. Had they failed in their final attempt, they would have remained nobodies and Gandhi would have sent another invitation to them to discuss their grievances.

The Guilty Men of Red Fort

Among those who were convicted in the Red Fort trial, except for the Maratha Digambar Badge, his south Indian servant Shankar Kistayya, and the refugee Madanlal Pahwa, all were from that group of Brahmins of Maharashtra who were considered to be followers of Bal Gangadhar Tilak. In truth, they were more anti-Gandhi than pro-Tilak and their roots were in the resistance to British paramountcy in Poona to re-establish *Brahmin* dominance. We shall look closely at these antecedents later. For now, it is crucial to note that all the conspirators were affiliated to the Hindu Mahasabha in one way or another and were disciples of Vinayak Damodar Savarkar. The special court of Honourable Justice Atma Charan gave its ruling[1] on the 10th of February 1949:

1. Nathuram Vinayak Godse is found guilty under section 120-B of the Indian Penal Code read with section 302 of the code, under section 19 (c) of the Indian Penal Code with section 6 of the act and (6) to death under section 302 of the Indian Penal Code. He is to be hanged by the neck till he is dead: the sentences of imprisonment shall run concurrently.

2. Narayan Dattatreya Apte is found guilty under section 120-B of the Indian Penal Code read with section 302 of the code, under section 19 (c) of the Indian Penal Code. Substances Act read with section 6 of the Act and (6) to death under section 109 of the Indian Penal Code read with section 302 of the code. He is to be hanged by the neck till he is dead: the sentences of imprisonment shall run concurrently.

> 3. Vishnu R. Karkare is found guilty under section 120-B of the Indian Penal Code read with section 302 of the code, under section 114 of Indian Penal Code. Act read with section 6 of the Act and (5) to transportation of life under section 109 of the Indian Penal Code read with section 302 of the code: the sentences of imprisonment shall run concurrent with the sentence of transportation of life.
>
> 4. Madanlal Kashmirilal Pahwa is found guilty under section 120-B of the Indian Penal Code read with section 302 of the code, under section 5 of the Explosive act of Indian Penal Code read with section 302 of the code: the sentences of imprisonment shall run concurrent with the sentence of transportation of life.
>
> 5. Gopal Vinayak Godse is found guilty under section 120-B of the Indian Penal Code read with section 302 of the code, under section 5 of the Explosive act of Indian Penal Code read with section 302 of the code: the sentences of imprisonment shall run concurrent with the sentence of transportation of life.
>
> 6. Shankar Kistayya is found guilty under section 120-B of the Indian Penal Code read with section 302 of the code, under section 5 of the Explosive act of Indian Penal Code read with section 302 of the code: the sentences of imprisonment shall run concurrent with the sentence of transportation of life.
>
> 7. Dattatreya Sadashiv Parchure is found guilty under section 120-B of the Indian Penal Code read with section 302 of the Code and under section 109 of the Indian Penal Code read with section 302 of the code, is convicted thereunder and is sentenced to transportation for life under section 109 of the Indian Penal Code read with section 302 of the code. He is found 'not guilty' of the remaining offences as specified in the charge, and is acquitted thereunder.

The motive of killing Gandhi brought together a non-matriculated celibate, an educated debauch, a middle-aged businessman who started life as a humble labourer, a victim of the tragedy of Partition, a middle-class family man, and a medico who was dreaming of someday occupying the premiership of Gwalior. While Shankar Kistayya was a victim of circumstance, others were prisoners of their own politics of hate. The definition of the nation and the objective in life which this politics gave them were products of hate the roots of which were immensely deep. They were in history, philosophy and also in the caste hierarchy which Gandhi was running his anti-untouchability campaign against. Their feeling of *patriotism* thus never allowed them to stand beside those who were fighting British imperialism. They could never align with the forces fighting for an independent India based on the universal principles of democracy, equality and religious tolerance. Theirs was a different dream, which led them to farm an unholy alliance to kill the person who was the greatest advocate of Hindu–Muslim unity, who opposed Partition in every possible way, and who, when it became imminent, tried his best to avoid a population transfer and ensure a dignified life for minorities in both countries. All this was diagonally opposed to the racist sect of nationalism in which they were baptized.

Nathuram Godse

It was a moment of special joy for Vinayak Godse, a Chitpavan Brahmin, petty employee of the postal department in Uksan, a small village ten miles from the Kamshet railway station on the Bombay–Poona railroad, when a son was born in his home on 19 May 1910. Before this, three boys had died soon after birth while the female babies had survived. The importance of a male child in an orthodox Brahmin family needs little emphasis. Sundry rites and ritual services were conducted and voguish vows made that, if a boy were born, he would be brought up like girls. The child was named Ramchandra, but was adorned with a nose-ring (*nath*) and his parents started calling him Nathuram—Ram who wears a *nath*. He was followed by three more male children. One of them, Gopal Godse, became Nathuram's accomplice in the assassination of Gandhi. This family of four boys and two girls continued to struggle with financial problems, among other difficulties caused by Vinayak's frequent transfers.

Whether the sorcery worked or it was just a matter of coincidence is another matter. To understand how a childhood marred by the bullying of peers due to this nose-ring affected Nathuram, one may look to the psychoanalysts.* However, some information on his childhood is available through the writings of Gopal Godse, which do occasionally shed light on his personality. Gopal recalls that Nathuram used to recite *shlokas* before the statue of the family goddess, from scriptures he had never read! He is said to have stopped doing so at the age of sixteen and this memory of Gopal who was hardly six years old then must be based on hearsay. Gopal further informs us that Nathuram later started taking part in sports like wrestling and developed a special interest in swimming. He claims that Nathuram developed as a healthy young man who used to help people and participated actively in social work. He also recounts an incident when his brother saved a Dalit boy from drowning when the family was living in Lonavala and was scolded for this by his father. It's impossible to verify such claims and they might simply be intentional boasts in an attempt to glorify Nathuram.

However, he didn't perform well as a student. While he used to read scriptures in Marathi, he had no interest in his school syllabus and couldn't matriculate due to poor performance in English. His father wanted him to look for a clerical job in some government department after his matriculation and to share household responsibilities. But Godse has no interest in studies and left Poona to join his father at Karjat and learned carpentry for the next year and a half. Before he could master this art though, Vinayak was transferred once again and he had to shift to the remote district of Ratnagiri in 1927.

Coincidently, Vinayak Damodar Savarkar was detained in Ratnagiri at the time after a grant of clemency by the British government and release from the cellular jail in the Andamans.[2]

* For example, one can read Anup Kumar Dhar, 'Survival of Voilence: Violence of Survival', *Identity, Culture and Politics*, vol. 5, no. 1 & 2 (2004), pp. 60–85 (available online: https://www.researchgate.net/publication/272416366_Survival_of_Violence_Violence_of_Survival, last accessed on 8 December 2021). Another aspect of it can be seen in Ashis Nandy's *At the Edge of Psychology* (OUP, 1980) where he comments: 'Perhaps it was given in the situation that Nathuram would try to regain the lost clarity of his sexual role by becoming a model of masculinity.'

He was allotted a bungalow and a monthly pension was fixed, but he was restricted from participating in any kind of political activity. Gandhi too had tried to meet him in Ratnagiri but was not allowed to. Savarkar was quite popular in Maharashtra, and when Godse went to meet him he was mesmerized by his charm.

Within a few months, Savarkar appointed him as his personal secretary and taught him English. Young Nathuram became his protégé. However, he accompanied his father when in 1929 he retired and decided to settle in Sangli. Here he learned to sew and stitch and set up his own tailoring shop; later a fruit shop was also added to this.[3] His parents wanted him to get married but Nathuram was not inclined towards family life and under the spell of his mentor, Savarkar, soon joined the newly established Sangli branch of the Hindu Sanghatan, an organization recently formed in Nagpur. For the next few years he took active part in Sanghatan activities along with running his business.

Savarkar was released from Ratnagiri and shifted to Bombay in 1935. It's quite interesting that his pension continued even after his release! Perhaps he was the only political leader to receive a pension[4] from the British government.

The story of his release is also a savoury one. After elections under the new constitution of 1935 and an overwhelming victory of the Congress, the British government was eager to instal interim ministers in the provinces with a view to pressing the Congress to accept office. In the interim period of the deadlock, Khan Bahadur* Dhanjishah Cooper, with the support of Jamnadas Mehta, a representative of the Tilakist Democratic Swaraj Party, expressed his willingness to form an interim ministry in the province on the condition of the release of Savarkar. Mehta had been running a campaign for his release for long and found the climate suitable to make it happen. Lord Brebourne, the then governor of Bombay, accepted this proposal subject to Savarkar's promise of 'good behaviour' in the future. The condition was readily accepted and Savarkar was released on 10 May 1937.[5] Savarkar would abide by the terms of his release with full devotion and never utter

---

* One of the titles given by the British to their trusted allies.

a word against the British regime after that. His staunch admirer Manohar Malgonkar, who has defended him vehemently in his book *The Men Who Killed Gandhi*, comments, 'British officials were no longer the villains; the real enemies were the Muslims.'[6]

After his release, Savarkar held meetings all over Maharashtra to further his communal agenda. When he came to Sangli, Godse joined him and then accompanied him on the rest of the journey. The Hindu Sanghatan soon joined the Hindu Mahasabha, which had turned into a political party in 1933. It had until then been only a social-religious organization. When the Mahasabha took out a protest march in the Hyderabad State in 1938, Godse was one of those arrested. By the time he was released, after a year in jail, the Second World War had begun. Savarkar, who had sent letters for clemency with a proposal to help the British in the First Word War, was now running a campaign for the recruitment of Indians into the British army, and gave a call to his followers to offer their fullest cooperation to British war efforts. Godse

Cartoon published in *Agrani*.

became a full-time political worker after his release. Congress, on the other hand, started the Quit India movement in 1942 and refused to cooperate with the government. It was obvious that independence was round the corner, and Savarkar tried to fill the void created by the arrest of almost the entire Congress leadership by actively cooperating with the government, on the one hand, and creating an underground armed group called Hindu Rashtra Dal, on the other. Nathuram was an office bearer of the Dal. The main tasks of the *dal* were to promote Savarkar's ideology* and provide armed training. However, the experiment could achieve only marginal success and its membership 'never exceeded 150'.[7]

In 1944, Nathuram started his Marathi newspaper, *Agrani*. Savarkar provided a sum of 15,000 for his venture, which was a big amount in those days. The paper has a picture of Savarkar on its header with a Sanskrit maxim—'*Varam janhitam dhyeyam, kevla n janstuti*' (The aim is to serve public interest and not mere popularity). The real meaning of this 'public interest' can be gauged from a cartoon printed in this newspaper in 1944 in which Savarkar and Syama Prasad Mukherjee, both prominent leaders of the Hindu Mahasabha, bow in hand are pointing arrows at Gandhi, depicted as Ravana with ten heads—in this case, those of Sardar Vallabhbhai Patel, Netaji Subhas Chandra Bose, Jawaharlal Nehru, Maulana Azad and other prominent Congress leaders along with Dr Ambedkar. Despite its fiery communal outlook, *Agrani* could not gain much popularity among readers even in areas where the Hindu Mahasabha was dominant. In 1946, when after the war the Congress swept the elections once again and constituted a government in the Bombay province, advertisements to *Agrani* were suspended due to its communal reportage and it was then ordered to pay Rs 6,000 as security for good behaviour. This was not a small sum, but the communally charged atmosphere of the period had by now won the paper many supporters who contributed generously to save it. Nathuram and his manager, Apte, however, failed to abide by the pledge of good behaviour, and finally, not only was the security forfeit but the paper itself was banned.

---

* See Part 2 for details.

दैनिक अग्रणी

हिंदुराष्ट्र

दैनिक 'अग्रणी'कडून सहा हजार रुपयांचा जामीन

हर्मन विलहेल्म गोअरिंग, रिबेनट्रॉप आदि नाझी पुढाऱ्यांना

न्यूरेम्बर्ग न्यायालयानें फांशीची शिक्षा ठोठावली. हर हेसला जन्मठेप

हिंदुत्वनिष्ठ पत्रावर सरकारचा भयानक प्रहार

पुणें दि. १-१०: 'अग्रणी' च्या दि. २६ च्या अंकांतील 'सेनापति भोसले यांचेवर कर्णावती रक्षणाचें दायित्व सोंपवा' या आशयाच्या लेखावर आज प्रथम रु. तीन हजार जामिनाची नोटीस बजावली गेली; पण आज रात्रीं त्याच लेखासाठी संपादक श्री. न. वि. गोडसे यांचेवर मुद्रक या नात्यानें आणखी तीन हजार रुपये जामिन मागणीची नोटीस बजावली गेली; म्हणजे जामिनाची एकूण रक्कम सहा हजार रुपये झाली आहे.

दिनांक ? ला जिना-वेव्हेल भेट!

मुंबईत संध्याकाळपर्यंत २ ठार, ८ जायबंदी

डाक्का दंगलीनें आतांपर्यंत ९२ बळी घेतले !

कलकत्त्यांतही संध्याकाळपर्यंत तीन जणांना भोसकले

प्लेग वार्ता

छाप—बंद

The first issue of *Hindu Rashtra*.

दैनिक
हिंदुराष्ट्र
शोभेची दारू
पराभूत गांधीवाद समूळ उखडून टाकलातरच देश जिवंत राहील–
भगव्या ध्वजाखालीं अेक होण्याचा आदेश

Front-page article from a 1947 issue of *Hindu Rashtra* arguing that Gandhism must be uprooted for the nation to survive.

The very next day they changed the title to *Hindu Rashtra* and kept up the communal reportage targeted at Gandhi and the Congress. The communal polarization of that period worked to their benefit yet again when the new newspaper was ordered to pay Rs 5,000 as security; many were willing to lend their support and they comfortably managed to collect this sum. The last issue of *Hindu Rashtra* was published on 31 January 1948 with front-page news of the assassination of Gandhi. The paper and its proprietors had achieved their ultimate goal.

Narayan Dattatreya Apte

The second conspirator present with Nathuram Godse, on the evening of 31 January 1948, when he shot three bullets into Gandhi's body with a Beretta pistol, was not from a lower middle class family like him. He was in fact a descendant of a reputed Chitpavan Brahmin family of Poona. His father and grandfather were highly regarded scholars and he too was well educated; his father was a well-known Sanskrit scholar and historian. The esteem the Apte family enjoyed can be gauged from the fact that his grandfather Vaman Shivram Apte was a close associate of Tilak and was the first principal of Fergusson College, established by the Deccan Education Society.[8] Unlike Godse, Narayan was a slap-happy young lad who smoked and drank, wore expensive clothes, and enjoyed flirting with women.

Narayan Apte was born in 1911 in his family home, 'Anandashram', in Poona at Budhwar Peth. He was the eldest of three sisters and four brothers. After earning a BSc degree from Bombay University in 1932 he joined the American Mission High School in Ahmednagar as a teacher. While studying, he was married to a girl named Champa from an eminent Chitpavan Brahmin family of Poona. He was well-liked among both students and teachers at school, and later began a liaison with Manorama Salvi, a high school student. But in 1938, he moved to Ahmednagar to open a rifle club to impart training to young men in arms. His idea of the rifle club was successful and similar clubs soon sprung up in many other places including Poona. In Ahmednagar, he met Vishnu Karkare and, deeply influenced by Savarkar, he soon became a member of the Hindu Mahasabha. However, he did not take much interest in party work and was seriously thinking about resuming his academic career. With this in mind he passed the Bachelor of Teaching exam. In the meantime, he was *blessed* with a male-child whom he called Pappan. The first child, of course, was the apple of his parents' eye. But after two years, it was found that the child was not developing well mentally. Apte was devastated and decided to return to Poona.

In Poona, he met Nathuram and joined the Hindu Rashtra Dal. Both were functionaries of the party and both set up training camps in their respective areas. During the Second World War he joined the Royal Indian Air force as a recruitment officer and earned the rank of Flight Lieutenant. The post was created exclusively during the war and was temporary. However, Dr Pankaj Phadnis, a functionary of Abhinav Bharat, a society formed by Savarkar in 1904, claims that he was not a military officer but a British agent. Phadnis had applied for information to which, in a letter sent in January 2016, the then Defence Minister Manohar Parrikar informed him that there were no records of Apte ever being in the Air Force. Phadnis talks of the 'four-shot theory'—the argument that Gandhi was not killed by the three shots fired by Godse but by a *fourth* shot fired by someone else—on this basis, and believes that Gandhi was in fact murdered by Apte.[9] However, it is certainly possible that the record of his temporary services as a recruiting officer in an emergency like the World War was not kept.

Savarkar (seated, centre) with the staff of *Agrani*.
Seated beside him are Apte (left) and Godse (right).

Malgonkar informs us that Apte was offered a permanent commission which he declined citing family responsibility and continued to work as a recruitment officer, but soon joined Nathuram at *Agrani*. The newspaper was constantly battling difficulties during the war and Apte took on the role of manager. Meanwhile, in July 1944, when Gandhi was in Panchgani, the name of Apte and Godse surfaced in reference to an attack on him. According to a report in the *Times of India* dated 23 July 1944, Apte was arrested and questioned in this regard.*

Visits to Bombay to meet Savarkar and arrange money for the

* See Part 2 for more details.

newspaper remained fairly regular. He had bought a Bullet motorcycle for himself, which he used to travel from Poona to Bombay. At the same time, he began to see his former student Manorama Salvi, who was then at Wilson College and was staying at the Ramabai Hostel in Bombay. Both often stayed in hotels under the name of Mr and Mrs Apte.

Apte lost his job with the end of the war and became fully engaged in the work at *Agrani*. Independence was round the corner and organizations like the Muslim League, Hindu Mahasabha and RSS scaled up their activities for a larger pound of flesh. These were perfect conditions for a newspaper like *Agrani* which thrived on communal ferment,[10] and despite restrictions by the government, its financial status improved with the help of donors.

Money was never a hindrance in their plan to kill Gandhi. Godse and Apte continued to make high-class train and airplane trips, stay in good hotels; Apte would order whiskey and enjoy dance, while Godse had his clothes dry-cleaned and would travel by taxi. Even expensive arms were bought, first in Bombay and then in Gwalior.

Apte was the leader of this gang until Madanlal Pahwa's unsuccessful attempt on 20 January. Godse took over command after that, and Apte's role became secondary.

Vishnu Ramchandra Karkare

Karkare's name has come up earlier in reference to Apte. Born and raised in the Lady Northcote orphanage in Bombay, all Karkare knew about his childhood was that he was born in a Karad Brahmin family. He started his life at a tea shop in Bombay at the age of ten and later ran away to Poona where he survived on odd jobs. After fifteen years of hard work doing *menial* jobs he ran away to Ahmednagar and eventually started a tea shop in an unused cow shed near a motor stand. His 'blood-purifying chutney' along with *puris* became famous, and in stark contrast to his poor childhood he became known as Karkare Seth. He learnt to write Marathi and speak Hindi by himself and established a cheap hotel, Deccan Guest House, and got married. He also started a theatre group and took great interest in politics.

It seems strange that for someone who went through such a difficult life the preferred drug of choice would be religion. Highly influenced by Savarkar, Karkare started the Hindu Mahasabha office in Ahmednagar and became its district secretary. When Savarkar came to Ahmednagar in 1938, he put up a special show of his theatre group for him. Savarkar initially tried to avoid it but finally agreed to attend for only fifteen minutes. When he came, however, he sat for the full three hours and enjoyed it a lot. Karkare's enthusiasm reached new heights and he soon contested the municipal elections and was elected as councillor unopposed.

Malgonkar claims that at the time of the communal violence in Noakhali, he went there with a collected sum of Rs 3,000 and established relief centres. It is difficult, however, to trust the veracity of this claim as it was almost impossible in that charged atmosphere to move from village to village wearing a Hindu turban and caste mark on the forehead, as claimed by him.

He further claims that to get his reports published, he approached Godse and Apte and got one of his companions, B.D. Kher, recruited as an assistant editor to their newspaper. While in Poona, he used to stay with Kher. After Partition, when refugees started pouring into Ahmednagar, Karkare began working with great enthusiasm to help them. He helped organize a camp of some 10,000 refugees in an abandoned prison. At the same time, he started campaigning against Muslims in Ahmednagar. Madanlal Pahwa, a refugee settled in Bombay, became his special ally, and with his help, Madanlal attacked Muslim fruit sellers, occupied their shops and started his own business there.[11]

Karkare shouldered the responsibility of arranging arms and ammunition in the conspiracy to kill Gandhi.

Madanlal Kashmirilal Pahwa

Madanlal Pahwa migrated to India from Pakpattan, a remote village in the Punjab province of Pakistan. During the war, Madanlal served as a wireless operator in the Royal Indian Navy, but his services were terminated in 1946 after the war ended. A few months later, when he had to leave his village in the venomous atmosphere of Partition, he came to Bombay, where he had spent some time when serving in the navy. While living in Chembur Camp, he unsuccessfully tried to secure a remunerative job. In the meantime, he met Dr Jagdish Chandra Jain, who was a professor of Urdu and Ardhamagadhi in Ruia College. Dr Jain has provided details of his meeting with Madanlal in his book *I Could Not Save Bapu.** Dr Jain was impressed with Madanlal's honesty and helped him find work as a salesman for a publisher. Madanlal did good business and must have sold books worth Rs 200. Dr Jain opined, 'He was a simple, intelligent and hardworking boy of an impulsive temperament, ready for any kind of adventure.'[12]

Madanlal soon started selling firecrackers and met Karkare in Ahmednagar, where he had gone in search of cheap suppliers. Dr Jain mentions that while in the beginning he was equally dismayed at the atrocities against women in India as in Pakistan, he became increasingly communal after associating with Karkare.[13] However, it seems that he had said all that only to impress the Gandhian Dr Jain. After all, he had not informed him about selling illegal arms under the cover of firecrackers either. Tushar Gandhi has disclosed that, after Partition, Madanlal came directly to Gwalior and joined the gang that attacked trains taking Muslims to Pakistan and shifted to Bombay only after receiving news about his father's illness.[14] But it is doubtful whether he indeed left Gwalior due to his father's ill-health. In an interview given to Saira Menezes on 20 January 1998, he confessed that his name figured in the police records in Gwalior, so he fled to Bombay to escape the police.[15]

Dr Jain recounts that Madanlal came to meet him in January 1948 with Karkare and had mentioned his meeting with Savarkar in which he had praised Madanlal and asked him to continue his good work. In that meeting, while boasting about an attack on a Congress leader, Raosaheb Patwardhan, during his address on Hindu–Muslim unity, and an attempt to blow up a Muslim man's house with dynamite, he repeatedly said that the police were with them. This becomes

* The original book was published in Hindi, but it was translated into English at the demand of the counsel for Madanlal, and it was published in English from Jagran Sahitya Mandir, Banaras.

noteworthy with reference to the shocking negligence by the police after the first attempt to assassinate Gandhi.[16]

It was through Karkare that Madanlal met Godse and Apte in Poona in December 1947 and became part of the Gandhi assassination conspiracy. He revealed this secret to Dr Jain on his way to Delhi. It's funny that while going to assassinate Gandhi, he had also planned to see a girl for his marriage! Dr Jain did not take it seriously, but when the news of the failed attack on Gandhi and subsequent arrest of Madanlal surfaced, he informed the then chief minister and home minister of Bombay B.G. Kher and Morarji Desai, respectively.

Despite this Dr Jain had to write: I could not save Bapu…

Gopal Vinayak Godse

Gopal was the younger brother of Nathuram, and this is his primary and only introduction. However, he was very different from him—a worldly man who valued his government job so much that he applied for a casual leave for participating in the assassination plot. He was impressed with his brother's fanatic ideology but was never active alongside him.

After passing his matriculation, he joined the military ordnance factory as a civil clerk and was sent to fight in the Second World War in 1941. After the end of the war he was restored as assistant storekeeper at the Kadki ordnance depot near Poona. Living in a rented house with his wife and two daughters, he was a most ordinary man before 14 January 1948, when Nathuram revealed his plan to kill Gandhi to him at a dinner.

It appears that the .38 calibre Webley & Scott revolver that he had received during his stint in the war, which he had buried in the village instead of depositing it, led to his involvement in this conspiracy. However, but for the venom of communalism, it may have been impossible to turn a simple public servant into a blood-thirsty killer. Malgonkar writes that as soon as he learned about Apte and Godse's plan he turned into a blood-thirsty terrorist; Godse only wanted the revolver, but Gopal put forth the condition that he would part with it only if allowed to be part of the conspiracy! Tushar Gandhi in his book

Let's Kill Gandhi says that even after his release Gopal never regretted his act. Tushar Gandhi's grandmother Sushilaben expressed her desire to meet him after his release. The Gandhi family went to Poona and met him. Gopal has presented this as if the Gandhi family supported him! He recounts another incident where he steadied a seventy-year-old Gopal when he faltered at an event,[17] which was also presented as if Tushar respected him a lot. Malgonkar considers him a case of split personality disorder, whose meekness had been a mask, that all his life had been a period of waiting for just an opportunity such as this to show his fangs,[18] and whose meek personality, after the failure of the first attempt, came out of its stupor leading to him leaving the band as if he was never a part of it. He tried his best to save himself during trial, and when eventually convicted, wrote a book after his release to justify the act and glorify Nathuram and himself as patriots.

It was Gopal who revealed in an interview in 1994 that Nathuram was a member of the Rashtriya Swayamsevak Sangh and had in fact never left it. His granddaughter Satyiki Savarkar reiterated in 2016 that all the Godse brothers were members of the RSS and never renounced their membership.[19] However, the RSS has always denied this fact. Since the RSS doesn't keep a record of its membership, it is almost impossible to verify the claim. I leave it to the readers to decide who to believe.

Dattatreya Sadashiv Parchure

Gopal's Webley & Scott failed them and it was Dr Parchure who arranged the Italian Beretta for Nathuram on 28 January 1948 which ultimately killed Gandhi.

You may call it a coincidence that Parchure was also connected to Poona. His father Sadashiv Gopal Parchure was close to M.G. Ranade, R.G. Bhandarkar and B.G. Tilak as a member of a debating society. But unlike them he had no interest in politics and opted for an academic career which took him to Ahmedabad, and ultimately, Gwalior. He was quite popular as a professor at Madhav College and the then ruler of Gwalior, Jivajirao Scindia, appointed him a member in the department of education and municipal affairs.[20]

After passing his FA (or the First Examination of Arts) from Victoria College, Lashkar, Gwalior,[21] Parchure earned his MBBS degree from Bombay and joined the state services in Gwalior. But he was dismissed in 1934[22] and established his private clinic. Despite being a trained doctor of allopathy, he used to practice Ayurveda and homeopathy as well.

However, he was more inclined towards communal politics and his house at Patankar Bazaar was practically used as an office of the Hindu Mahasabha. He organized a Hindu Rashtra Sena of which he was the self-styled dictator. The 'army' of this forty-seven-year-old doctor was used to attack Muslims after Partition. Madanlal Pahwa was associated with this army in Gwalior before fleeing to Bombay. His stature had grown considerably under the patronage of the local ruler and he was dreaming of becoming prime minister of Gwalior. When the ruler of the princely state Jivajirao Scindia gave the opportunity of forming the government to the Congress instead of the Hindu Mahasabha, his frustration only added to his hatred of the Congress.

He met Godse at a secret training camp of the Hindu Mahasabha and the RSS in the erstwhile state of Alwar and at one point the Hindu Rashtra Dal and the army of Parchure were about to merge, but they got stuck on the question of leadership. When Godse and Apte contacted him for a revolver, he saw in it a path for revenge and fully supported them.

Shankar Kistayya

He has no identity of his own. He was a bonded labourer of the court approver Digambar Badge and thus bound to share his sin. A poor boy from Sholapur, he was promised a monthly salary which was never given. He tried to flee but was caught and ensnared in a police case by Badge which left no escape for him. Unable to understand either Marathi or Hindi he was unaware of the conspiracy till the end. He was later released by the Punjab High Court on this basis. Parchure too escaped conviction in the Punjab High Court as he backed out on his statement made before the magistrate in Gwalior and his lawyer succeeded in getting him released on technical grounds. Savarkar was let off in the absence of corroborative evidence; nevertheless, such pieces of evidence were readily available but not presented in court for reasons unknown. The Kapur Commission* did unearth them and conclude that Savarkar shared the responsibility for the conspiracy, but by then he was long dead.

There were other characters in this conspiracy. G.M. Joshi from Bombay, whose house was a home to Karkare, Apte and Godse; the Dixit brothers, who provided the first consignment of arms and financial support; and some unnamed people who were never arrested, as well as the three people associated with the procurement of the revolver that would fire the fatal shots. These characters and many such characters will be revealed in the story ahead. There were many others who were in positions of authority at that point of time and whose conduct raises multiple questions.

Finally, one fact needs to be mentioned. Except for the court approver Badge, none of the conspirators were habitual criminals. Most of them had loose tongues, and going through the details of the conspiracy one can easily be amused at their recklessness. They committed childish mistakes, and the police could have nabbed them with a little alacrity. Nathuram was an idealist in his own way. But these ideals, based on misleading facts, frivolous arguments and inhuman motivations, turned him into a killer.

* See Part 2, Chapter 6.

PART TWO

The Gandhi Murder: A Chronology

> The assassination of Gandhiji was a culmination of decades of systematic brainwashing. Gandhiji had become a thorn in the flesh of the hard-core Hindus and in course of time this resentment turned into a phobia.
>
> —Chunnibhai Vaidya[1]

Be it a staunch Gandhian like Chunnibhai Vaidya, who had been associated with Vinoba Bhave and Jayaprakash Narayan, or the pro-RSS writer Shabu Prasad, who has tried to put Nehru in the dock in his new conspiracy theory, there is consensus that the issue of the payment of fifty-five crore rupees, by the Indian government to Pakistan,* was in no way the reason for the murder of Gandhi. Shabu Prasad analyses the matter based on technicalities and concludes that there can be no doubt about the fact that the murder was planned well before the declaration to issue the amount.[2]

Shabu Prasad indicates that it would have been impossible for Godse and Apte to travel by air and in high-class train coaches, stay in good hotels, spend so much money on firearms and have access to accurate information about the daily routine of an important person

* See Part 3, Chapter 1.

like Gandhi but for the help of people close to him. He claims that such a plan of assassination could not have been made in ten days.

Chunnibhai refers to the rightist agenda of hate, which was directed against the Congress in general and Gandhi in particular. It was injected into young minds that the real enemy was Gandhi and not the British as he was the biggest impediment to their project of an exclusive Hindu Rashtra ('Hindu Nation'). This agenda was effective especially in Poona and the adjoining regions of Maharashtra. When refugees poured into these regions, their plight intensified these feelings. The refugees were victims of the hateful agenda of the Muslim League. They wanted their revenge, and it was easier to harm the Muslims living peacefully in India. They wanted them to vacate their houses so that their own families could occupy them. This happened on both sides of the newly drawn line of partition. Muslims, who lost their houses and property on this side of Punjab, tried to do the same to the Hindus on the other side. An eye for an eye was the rule in those crazy times and communal organizations of both sides added fuel to the fire. Gandhi, who was trying to bring some sanity and save the minorities on both sides, naturally became their foremost enemy.

1. Poona, the Peshwa Capital, Chitpavan Brahmins and the Dream of a Hindu Rashtra

> Those who were dissatisfied with the politics of Mahatma Gandhi for whatsoever reason, all claimed to be the followers of Tilak. Those who do not want to use Khadi, those who do not like (the movement for) eradication of untouchability, those who do not like the efforts of Hindu–Muslim unity, and those who do not want to participate in the campaigns like the peaceful violation of law or non-payment of tax to the British government, all such people can oppose these concepts under the pretext of Tilakism. Such disgruntled Tilakists are many in number in Maharashtra.
>
> —Acharya Javdekar[1]

The roots of the Gandhi murder also lie in the movement that emerged after the fall of Peshwa rule, which, though ostensibly against the British, aimed to re-establish Peshwa rule. This movement was against any kind of social reform and was the loudest advocate of a social system based on the *varna* system. Well-known rightist author, Koenraad Elst, who has written hundreds of pages to justify Godse, has termed Poona the capital of the 'last great Hindu nation'.[2] The fact is, while there were hundreds of Hindu states, Peshwa rule was the only one with Brahmin rulers. It seems that, to him, Brahmin Rule is synonymous with Hindu Rule.

Elst goes on to discuss the history of Chitpavan Brahmins. According to him, these taller and light-bodied Brahmins (who often have blue eyes), migrated from Central Asia or 'Shakdweepa' in the ninth century. According to their own scripture, *Sahyadri Khand*, they were washed ashore as corpses but Vishnu's incarnation Parshurama 'brought the corpses back to life' by a reversal of the cremation process. The pyre (*chita*) merely purified (*pavanam*) them, hence the name 'Chitpavan'. For a long time, they were looked down upon and used for menial services by the native *Deshasth* Brahmins. But they succeeded in securing a place in Shivaji's court and a Chitpavan Brahmin, Balaji Vishwanath Bhat, was appointed as prime minister or *Peshwa* in the court of Shahuji Maharaj. With the decay of the Bhonsles, Peshwas shot to prominence and occupied the Maratha Kingdom in 1713 and grew in social status. Though their defeat at Panipat in 1763 eroded their political power and they had to surrender to the British in 1818, their social stature remained intact.[3] How worried they were after losing power and how shocking they found subsequent attempts at social reform can be gauged by the remark of one of the preeminent Chitpavan Brahmins, Lokhitwadi Gopal Hari Deshmukh, in an article published on 1 April 1849. He writes:

> ... When will the screams of Brahmins be heard by God? Then someone, a very wise (Brahmin) orthodox man says, 'Oh men, how did the Yadvas die in the past? Did Ravana spare anyone from his wrath? All Gods were encaged! Thereafter, did Rama not take over Lanka with the help of *Vanras*? Did the stones not float on the water? Similarly, the British will go down sometime. Religion will be re-established. The Brahmins will be happy.'[4]

It's interesting that *Western-educated* Gopal Hari Deshmukh is considered relatively progressive. He had made propositions against not only child marriage, the dowry system and polygamy, but also against the caste system in his book *Hindu Ashtak*.[5] Thus the aim to re-affirm Brahmin hegemony was at the core of the anti-British nationalist discourse which emerged in Poona under the leadership of Vishnushastri Chiplunkar during the last phase of the nineteenth century. Tilak inherited this movement after the demise of Chiplunkar.

Gandhi's secretary Pyarelal has committed to paper a voluminous record of his last days—*Mahatma Gandhi: The Last Phase*. In its second part he has analysed this movement. He comments:

> Maharashtra has a strong tradition of militant Hindu nationalism. It is the citadel of Brahmin orthodoxy of a most exclusive and rigid type. In self-dedication, patriotism, sacrifice, and renunciation, it has produced exemplars which it would be difficult to excel. But its idealism has very often been mixed with a rugged pragmatism and cynical view of life and politics which was diametrically opposed to that of Gandhiji. Some of the proponents of this outlook had somehow come to feel, quite unwarrantably, that the rise of Gandhiji's philosophy was the cause of the memory of that great leader of Maharashtra, the late Lokamanya Tilak, and the premier position that Maharashtra held in the country's politics during his lifetime, being eclipsed. They regarded Gandhiji's political leadership and movement of non-violence with a strong, concentrated feeling of antipathy and frustration which found expression in a sustained campaign of calumny against Gandhiji for over a quarter of a century. The fact that despite it a growing section in Maharashtra rallied to Gandhiji's movement, further exasperated them and deepened their sense of frustration. It was this section that had tried to bomb Gandhiji in 1934 at Poona while he was engaged in his anti-untouchability campaign. Their plans this time were far more systematic and thorough, and included such refinements as conditioning the minds of the youth for their prospective task by making them wear, as a part of their training, photos of Congress leaders like Pandit Nehru and others besides Gandhiji inside their shoes, and using the same for target practice with fire-arms etc.[6]

Vishnushastri Chiplunkar (1850–1882) was the chief protagonist of this group of orthodox Brahmins in Poona. However, there were also social reformers like Ramakrishna Gopal Bhandarkar (1837–1925) and Mahadev Govind Ranade (1842–1901) who were active in that period, who not only pressed for internal reforms in Brahmin society but raised serious questions on problems like the caste system. Deshmukh, Bhandarkar and Ranade were among those English-educated intellectuals who were deeply moved by similar movements in the West and emphasized the necessity of social reforms before political ones. They played an important role in the social awakening, or the so-called renaissance, in Maharashtra during the nineteenth century through movements like the Brahmo Samaj, Paramhans

Sabha and Prarthana Samaj. Arvind Gunachari terms this period as a rational revivalism, since all its torch bearers attempted religious reforms by quoting extensively from ancient scriptures.[7]

But soon this movement began to weaken, and revivalism started to spread in its irrational form. Vishnu Bhikaji Gokhale (1825–1871), popularly known as Vishnubuva Brahmachari, is considered to be the first important leader of this strand of revivalism, who in his book *Vedokta Dharmaprakash* praised the traditional Hindu religion, its moral precepts and traditions, and while criticizing the tendency to draw inspiration from the West, advocated establishing religion in its purest form. This group of revivalists calling for a return to the Vedas were thus against social reform and were votaries of Manu's rules on the four-varna system. Vishnushastri Chiplunkar became an outspoken champion of it and lashed out at the Brahmo Samaj for questioning traditional practices. In the articles published in his Marathi magazine, *Nibandhamala*, and later, *Kesari*, he vehemently attacked not only Bhandarkar, Deshmukh, Ranade and Jyotiba Phule but also Dayanand Saraswati, who was running a similar movement in Punjab. He called the Prarthana Samajists copycats and lackeys of the West.[8] In this way, he gave his movement the form of an anti-British movement which, on the one hand, earned recognition from anti-British movements going on in other parts of the country, but on the other hand, secured the support of the orthodox Chitpavan Brahmins of Poona, who were perturbed by the reform movements.[9] Bal Gangadhar Tilak (1856–1920) was his follower and emerged as the unquestioned leader after his death. He was a firm believer in the dictum that it is political movements that are important and any special endeavour for social reform, or their enforcement through legislation, is unnecessary.

While Tilak was radical in politics, he was a conservative on social issues. For example, when the Age of Consent Act came in and it was decided to have a minimum age of sixteen years for boys and ten years for girls to enter into a nuptial arrangement, people like Gopal Ganesh Agarkar, Bhandarkar and Ranade openly supported it, but Tilak opposed it by arguing that it would disintegrate the social fabric of Hinduism.[10] Similarly, with respect to widow remarriage, while

Agarkar wrote articles and participated in widow wedding events, Bhandarkar remarried his own widowed daughter, Phule campaigned against the tonsure of the widows, Tilak and his followers strongly opposed it. Not only this, Tilak's view on women's education was also very problematic. He opined that it should be in accordance with the Hindu social system. He believed that a woman's education should not be to change her social status but to aid her in traditional marital and domestic roles. Since she gets married in childhood, according to Tilak, her marital home is her most suitable workshop.[11] When Pandita Rambai started the Sharda Sadan for the education of widows, Tilak led a movement against her through his newspaper *Kesari*.[12]

Two examples from the last leg of his life will suffice to understand his views on caste. While delivering a lecture in Athani on reservations for untouchables in legislative assemblies on 11 November 1917, he said, 'What will farmers do by entering the legislative assembly? Will tailors operate their sewing machine and shopkeepers hold their scales?' (To which the journalist Jagan Phadnis has commented, 'Were Brahmins going to ignite lamps in the assembly?') The next year, Tilak participated in the Conference for the Abolition of Untouchability held in Bombay under the presidency of Sayajirao Gaekwad III, the Maharaja of Baroda. Speaking on the occasion on 24 March 1918, he declared, 'If God were to tolerate Untouchability, I would not recognize Him as God at all… I do not deny that in some old days the autocracy of Brahmins had created that usage. Untouchability is a disease and it must be removed.' It was obviously lauded. Sudheendra Kulkarni has tried to prove him an anti-caste crusader on the basis of this speech in an article published in *The Quint*,[13] but Phadnis narrates rest of the story. Encouraged by this speech of Tilak, when Maharshi Vitthal Ramji Shinde requested him to sign a memorandum regarding the prevention of untouchability, after some dilly-dallying he finally refused and requested him to wait till his return from London.[14]

Prof Nalini Pandit has aptly summarized his politics in these words:

> By giving more importance to the immediate political questions, the radical nationalist side also supported the upper middle class and ignored the feelings and interests of Bahujan society. Opposing

> the demand for equality of the 'Satya Shodhak Society', he hurt the Bahujan society. Tilakji aggravated the resentment of Dalit leaders by not signing a memorandum in support of the removal of untouchability. He lost the sympathy of the farmers by favouring moneylenders... [D]ue to Tilakji's tough personality, fervent patriotism, fearlessness and selfless attitude and incomparable self-sacrifice, everyone respects him infinitely; there is a sense of pride towards him. Nevertheless, the non-Brahmin Bahujan society of Maharashtra did not participate enthusiastically in [his] movement.[15]

There were many among the Chitpavans who never supported Tilak in his regressive agenda on social reform. Gopal Krishna Gokhale, whom Gandhi considered his mentor, was one of them. In this regard, Gandhi has recorded an interesting incident in his book *Satyagraha in South Africa*. When he returned from South Africa and went to Poona in an attempt to mobilize support for the movement there, he found that two groups were active in the city—the Sarvajanik Sabha of Tilak and the Deccan Society of Gokhale. When he met Tilak in this regard and revealed his intention to hold a meeting, Tilak asked him if he had met Gopalrao (Gopal Krishna Gokhale). When Gandhi said he hadn't, he told him that if he were to preside over the meeting, none from the Deccan Society could attend it, and that if Gokhale presides, no one would attend from his side.[16]

Another example is his son, Sridhar Tilak. In sharp contrast to his father's regressive views on social reform, Sridhar continued to write and struggle against casteism. He praised the Satyashodhak Samaj of Jyotiba Phule and had friendly relations with Ambedkar. Dr Ambedkar had once said: 'Sridhar is the real *Lokmanya*'. What is more, he was banned from writing for *Kesari* by the Tilakists. On 8 April 1921, when he established the Samata Sangha, Ambedkar was the chief guest. A *sahbhojan* (common feast for the so-called upper castes and Dalits) was organized during this meeting. Where Tilak organized the Ganesh Festival, his sons organized the 'untouchable fair'. Disruptions were created in it. A fight ensued but he did not bow down. After the death of Tilak, the Tilakists dragged him to court for the rights of *Kesari*. Unable to cope with financial crises, Sridhar committed suicide by jumping in front of a train in Bombay. Before he died, he wrote letters to Prabodhan Thackeray and Ambedkar in which he expressed his desire to continue the struggle and a wish to reincarnate as a Dalit. Suraj Yengde, in his book, *Caste Matters*, records that Ambedkar paid tribute to him at Jalgaon and also wrote an obituary of him. After Tilak, the mentality of those who occupied *Kesari* can be gauged from a letter written by V.N. Gadgil to Sardar Patel on 24 November 1949, where he informs the latter that Gandhi's killers were praised in an article printed in *Kesari* on 15 November 1949.[17]

It is noteworthy that outside Poona and in Bombay, the other important city of Maharashtra, such ideas couldn't get many supporters despite the presence of Brahmins in large numbers. The orthodox Brahmin society of Poona which began to refer to itself as Tilakist after the demise of Tilak was neither staunchly nationalist like Tilak, nor did it have the same fervour towards the national movement. Along with all the above aspects of Tilak, it should also be remembered that he was a strong supporter of Hindu–Muslim unity in the national liberation movement. He wrote in *Kesari*: 'When Hindus and Muslims together demand Swaraj from the same platform, the British government must realize that their days are numbered.' And he followed this in spirit when, as president of the Congress, he signed a pact with the Muslim League in 1916 to counter the British plan of communal division through the Morley–Minto reforms. The pact is known as the Lucknow Pact. When orthodox leaders like Madan Mohan Malaviya and B.S. Moonje from the Hindu Mahasabha criticized it, he countered:

> Some eminent people accuse us of attaching far greater importance to the Mahomedans. I would go to the extent of saying that personally I would have no objection if self-rule were granted to the Muslims alone. If the Rajputs also got a similar right I won't mind. Nor would I object to this right being given to the most backward classes among the Hindus. This statement of mine reflects the national spirit of all India. When you are struggling against the third force, above everything else, all you need is your own unity—communal, religious, political and ideological... The struggle is triangular at the moment.[18]

It's obvious that Tilak was trying to convert the triangular (Hindu, Muslim and British) conflict to a direct and united one against the British. Compare this with Savarkar who was adored by the Tilakists. In his presidential address to the Ahmedabad conference of the Hindu Mahasabha he proposed: 'India cannot be assumed today to be a unitarian and homogeneous nation, but on the contrary, there are two nations in the main: the Hindus and the Muslims in India.'[19]

Savarkar was making the fight easier for the British, by helping sow divisions and weakening Tilak's hand. The Tilakists who stood behind Savarkar accepted the legacy of Tilak in bits and pieces and with antithetical motives. This class was hurt when Gandhi emerged as a prominent leader in the Congress and the country after Tilak, with initiatives like taking the movement to the villages, including non-Brahmins in it, and the struggle for eradicating untouchability. With many important Brahmin leaders joining him and the waning influence of the orthodoxy in national and local politics, this hatred for Gandhi grew further. The orthodoxy saw its dream flourishing in the notion of the Hindu nation, which often kept silent on the question of caste and spoke loudly about Hindutva. This notion maintained silence on social reform and dreamt of a society based on the *Manusmriti* which would restore the past glory of the Brahmins.

Be it the Hindu Mahasabha or the RSS, the leadership was entirely in the hands of orthodox Brahmins at the time. Keshavrao Baliramrao Hedgewar was the chief (*sarsanghchalak*) of the RSS while Madan Mohan Malaviya, B.S. Moonje, Syama Prasad Mukherjee and Vinayak Damodar Savarkar were the leaders of the Hindu Mahasabha. The existence of these organizations gave solace to the orthodox Brahmins of Maharashtra. Any direct struggle for the re-establishment of a Hindu Rashtra could have been counterproductive, so a perception of attaining the lost glory of the Hindu religion was made on an edifice of Muslim hate. They zealously participated in these movements to protect their privileges. They indirectly helped the British in their policy of 'divide and rule' when colonialism was replaced by Muslims as the chief enemy. The Muslim League was playing a similar role for their masters. Tilak's name was being used for a purpose that was contrary to the goal of his life, and was used as a cover for declaring people like Gandhi and Nehru, who were working for Hindu–Muslim unity and the creation of a modern democracy based on the principles of socio-economic equity and secularism, as enemies.

After all, Godse too regretted the growth of the influence of Gandhi after the departure of Tilak.[20] It seems there was an abiding impression in the minds of the Poona orthodoxy that but for the emergence of Gandhi they would have remained at the helm of regional and national politics. The Kapur Commission, set up to investigate the Gandhi assassination in the sixties, mentions this ideological group of 'Poona Savarkarites' in its report.[21]

On the other hand, the Muslim League under the leadership of M.A. Jinnah, was spreading similar venom in the hearts of Muslim youth. Both were setting enough examples to make it easier for the other to incite their youth to adopt the path of violence. Violence was the means for both to attain their unholy goals. Both believed in taking lives instead of sacrificing them. Riots were the weapon for both. When atrocities took place in Noakhali against the minority Hindus, Gandhi went there to extinguish the raging flames. But the supporters of Hindutva avenged the act by killing equally innocent Muslims in Bihar, which gave Jinnah an apt pretension to enhance his game in other parts of the country. Such incidents continued to grow in pre-Partition India and the country had to witness one of the cruellest episodes of communal violence in modern history.

The assassination of Gandhi was a result of this vicious propaganda. It is thus necessary to understand Savarkar's philosophy of Hindutva which was the culmination of this line of thinking.

Savarkar and Hindutva

> *Indian War of Independence* was written by a man proud of his religious and cultural heritage, proud of Maharashtra's past and yet someone who sought to blend regional and religious loyalties together in an over-arching loyalty to the Indian nation.
>
> —A.G. Noorani, *Savarkar and Hindutva*[22]

The early Savarkar of *Indian War of Independence* was a staunch nationalist who was proud of India's communal harmony. It was this Savarkar who earned immense popularity among young revolutionaries across the country for his intellect and valour. He was a bit obsessed with past glory but had an eye for identifying the common bond between different religions and the need of their unity for ousting a foreign force from his motherland. To him the most necessary task was to attain freedom; the enemy were the British. He was a young and firebrand revolutionary who didn't hesitate to resort to armed struggle and chose violent means to terrorize the enemy to attain freedom for India.

But the Savarkar who was released from the Andamans after numerous clemency petitions was a completely different person. This departure is most obvious in his book *Hindutva*, published in 1923. The publisher claims in the preface to the second edition of the book that a part of it was written during confinement in the Cellular Jail, and was completed later during his stay in the Yerawada jail. It is also claimed that since many Congress activists were lodged in the same jail with special facilities like reading and writing material, Savarkar 'in spite of his being treated and confined apart as a revolutionary prisoner under special restrictions, found it feasible to get hold now and then of real papers and pencils'. The publisher, S.S. Savarkar, with an address of 'Savarkar Sadan', goes further to claim that the book was smuggled out from the jail 'all undetected by jail officials'. It was first published by an advocate from Nagpur, V.V. Kelakar, in 1923 under the nom de plume 'A Maratha'.[23]

That a revolutionary prisoner, eventually released from the Cellular Jail after multiple clemency petitions, would write a treatise inside the jail and get it smuggled out 'all undetected' is a claim too big to believe. It is also noteworthy that while *Indian War of Independence* was immediately banned, the British never banned *Hindutva* and its second edition was printed in 1942.

The book starts with a Sanskrit couplet:

> *Asindhu sindhu paryanta yasya bharata bhoomika*
> *Pitribhuh punyabhushchaiva sa vai hinduriti smritah*
> (A Hindu is a person who regards this land of Bharatvarsha from the Indus to the seas as his Father-land as well as the Holy-land that is the cradle of his religion)

The publisher clarifies that this *shloka*, which attempts to define a Hindu, has not been taken from any religious scripture but was written by Savarkar himself, and goes on to claim that 'the couplet has now come to exercise the authority of a quotation from holy scriptures…it is the best possible definition of Hindu *Rashtra*'.[24] While the couplet was on the 103rd page of the first edition, it got prominence in the second edition and featured with the title.

Thus, it was Savarkar who first proposed the theory of a Hindu Nation, way back in 1923, and he is thus the father of the 'two-nation theory'. This racial nationalism was later supported by his counterparts in the Muslim League and stood opposed to the territorial nationalism propounded by the Congress and revolutionaries like Bhagat Singh. While this territorial nationalism was based on the assumption that everybody residing in the territory called India was a part of it and had a claim to its nationality, racial nationalism advocated a theocratic state and claimed that there were two nations within the country—a Hindu India and a Muslim India, which cannot coexist.

Hinduism vs Hindutva and Hindustan vs Hindu-sthan

At the very outset, Savarkar makes it clear that 'Hindutva is different from Hinduism'.[25] He argues that 'Hinduism is only a derivative, a fraction, a part of Hindutva', while 'Hindutva embraces all the department of thought and activity of the whole Being of our Hindu race'.[26] In the process he attempts to define the term 'Hindu' as a race. The first criterion is set on the basis of geography and he concludes it using a couplet from the *Vishnu Purana*, which says that 'the land which is to the north of the sea and to the south of the Himalaya Mountain is named as Bharata inhabited by the descendants of Bharat'.[27] Next, he adds that the other common characteristic is language. It was tricky ground for a nation like India where scores of languages are spoken and written in different parts of the country. Savarkar plays it clever, and without going into details accepts 'one of the eldest daughters of Sanskrit, Hindi or Hindusthani as the common language of the Hindus'. While he discusses at length the different components of this common language, the impact of Persian and Urdu is wittingly left out. Savarkar could not have been ignorant of the contribution of Persian and Urdu to almost all north Indian languages, including his very own Marathi.

But these were still only the necessary conditions and there were a few more sufficient conditions to make Hindutva exclusive and create a binary between *us* and *them*. He argues:

> So although the root-meaning of the word Hindu like the sister epithet Hindi may mean only Indian, yet as it is we would be straining the usage of the words too much—we fear, to the point of breaking—if we call a Mohammedan a Hindu because of his being a resident of India.[28]

Thus, he introduces the concepts of Fatherland and Holy Land in his definition of a loyal and valid subject of the nation. Fatherland denotes a place where one's ancestors had lived, and the Holy Land is the place where one's place of worship exists. Since, for Muslims and Christians, even if they are converted, their holy lands exist in countries other than India, they cease to be legitimate citizens of Savarkar's Nation. Love for the motherland was not enough. Savarkar necessitates the bond of common blood and declares, 'They (Hindus) are not only a Nation but a Race,'[29] and goes on to claim that they have a common culture, laws and rites. This is why this concept of racial nationalism is sometimes termed cultural nationalism. In a multi-cultural country like India, this claim is often established by mainstreaming the cultural practices of the dominant Brahminical class.

So what is to be done with the others? What will be their place in this Nation? Savarkar gives an example:

> An American may become a citizen of India. He would certainly be entitled, if *bona fide* to be treated as Bhartiya or Hindi, a countryman and fellow citizen of ours. But, as long as in addition to our country, he has not adopted our culture and our history, inherited our blood and has come to look upon our land not only as the land of his love but even of his worship, he cannot get himself incorporated in the Hindu fold.[30]

In a democratic setup, one may ask: Why should anyone get incorporated into the fold of any religion? Why can't one adhere to one's own religion and yet be a worthy citizen of the country? In Savarkar's notion of a nation, however, this is a must. Let us ponder over this case a bit. How can the American in this example, or for that matter any other non-Hindu, fulfil his conditions? He/she may adopt the culture and history of the country, but how can one inherit someone else's blood or change his/her place of worship? For a Hindu living in the USA, Banaras will always remain a place of spiritual belonging. For the majority of Muslims in India, there is no other Fatherland. Their ancestors have lived here for centuries. Most of them have never stepped outside India and have their mosques in their villages and cities. But Mecca is still a revered place for them. Under the racial nationalism of Savarkar, this suffices to make them illegitimate citizens of India. Put simply, every non-Hindu Indian was a non-citizen of his Hindu Rashtra.

There is one more interesting fact that we may note. Savarkar, and later Golwalkar, used *Hindusthan* in place of the more popular *Hindustan*. While he accepts its origin from the word Sindhu, he is not ready to give any credit for it to foreigners and tries hard to prove the formulation as being Indian in origin. The suffix 'stan' underlines the non-*Hindu* origin of the name—note country names such as Afghanistan, Kazakhstan, Kyrgyzstan, and so on. So why not Sanskritize it? Which is easily done by turning 'stan' to 'sthan' (place)—a simple insertion of an 'h' at the right place![31] However, he couldn't show its mention in any of the religious texts he quoted from.

In terms of realpolitik, Savarkar was frank enough to make an appeal to the Hindus to 'Hinduize all politics and militarize Hindudom!' in his message on the eve of his fifty-ninth birthday. It is worth mentioning that this declaration was made in 1942 when the Quit India movement was in full swing. And the appeal of militarization was accompanied by an appeal 'to enter the army, the navy and the air force'.[32]

His attitude towards Muslims can be gauged by a statement about Kashmiri Muslims:

> I wish that the Moslems in Kashmir do not forget that they are subjects of a Hindu state and unless and until they cut off all their connection with such disloyal creeds and organisations as the

> Pakistani ones and owe an undivided loyalty to the Hindu state and the unity and in-divisibility of the Central Indian State as well, they cannot claim 'the rights' which are due to the majority of the loyal citizens alone. As soon as the Moslems whether in the Hindu States or in India as a whole fulfil these conditions the Hindu Mahasabha will certainly allow them the benefit of its national formula of democratic representation based on the population proportion.[33]

Without going into further details, I would like to quote M.S. Golwalkar, who was the second *sarsanghchalak* of the RSS from his work *We, or Our Nationhood Defined*, to understand the approach of the right wing towards minorities:

> The foreign races in Hindusthan must either adopt the Hindu culture and language, must learn to respect and hold in reverence Hindu religion, must entertain no idea but those of the glorification of the Hindu race and culture, i.e., of the Hindu nation and must lose their separate existence to merge in the Hindu race, or may stay in the country, wholly subordinated to the Hindu Nation, claiming nothing, deserving no privileges, far less any preferential treatment—not even citizen's rights.[34]

One may well ask why any minority would accept such a pathetic situation for itself. These were serious efforts to break any possibility of communal unity in the country and thus pushed the country into a situation which made Partition inevitable.

2. Non-Violence and a Fearless Life: Attempts on Gandhi Before January 1948

> Gandhi instigated, if he did not initiate, three major revolutions of our time, the revolution against racialism, the revolution against colonialism, and the revolution against violence.
>
> —B.R. Nanda, *Gandhi and His Critics*[1]

While analysing the *Mahabharata*, in an article published in a Hindi literary magazine, *Kathadesh*, Prof Purushottam Agrawal comments: 'Memory is our moral responsibility.' We often fall into oblivion as individuals and as a society. We conveniently forget that Gandhi was not the only victim of religious fundamentalism; it killed many other people, including Ganesh Shankar Vidyarthi, who was a frontline warrior against communalism and imperialism. We have lost millions of lives in communal riots since then. The line of partition was drawn not only on the ground; this sword passed through many an innocent neck. Innumerable women had to bear its brunt for rest of their lives. And it did not end there; its marks can still be clearly identified on both sides. It killed many important leaders including Pakistan's first prime minister Liaquat Ali Khan, and Benazir Bhutto, two of our prime ministers, Indira Gandhi and Rajiv Gandhi, and writers like M.M. Kalburgi, Gauri Lankesh, Narendra Dabholkar and many more innocents in lynchings and riots. We tend to forget all this, and every time this fundamentalism returns in a new guise, with the slogan 'Religion is in danger', and each time it becomes crueller.

It is thus important to remember that the attack of 30 January

1948 on Gandhi was not the first one. He was attacked time and again in India as well as South Africa. On each occasion, the attackers were armed with the weapons of religious/racial fundamentalism, and Gandhi faced them with his non-violent weapons of courage and truth. It is not mere coincidence that all the attacks on him after his arrival in India were carried out by votaries of Hindutva. Godse and Apte tried to kill him more than once. Why was Gandhi such a big danger for *them*? He had disagreements with the communists and Muslim fundamentalists as well. Gandhi never minced words criticizing the violent methods of the revolutionary movement. But they never attacked him physically. There was much ideological opposition in the struggle for independence, but few were out to kill each other. Then why did Hindutva thinkers want to kill him? What was the reason for this hostility, that they never trained their guns on the British but killed Gandhi instead?

The reasons are obvious. The first is that Gandhi was a staunch Hindu and a dedicated adherent of that liberal tradition of Hinduism which holds fast to the maxim '*vasudhaiva kutumbakam*' (the whole world is a family). This shloka says:

> *Ayam nijah paroveti, ganana laghuchetasam*
> *Udar charitanam tu, vasudhaiva kutumbakam*
> (Only narrow-minded people think in terms of me, mine and other; for the broad-minded one, the whole world is like a family, like their own)

This tradition advocates an altruism that treats the whole earth as family. There have always been liberal and orthodox traditions within every religion and a conflict between them. The liberal tradition diversifies the religion, makes friendly relations with other religions, and acquires knowledge from all over the world where the orthodoxy constantly looks for the enemy. First, other religions are made the enemy, then the dissidents within it and everyone else which it perceives as an adversary, and finally it destroys itself. The forces of Hindutva declare communists as enemies after Muslims and Christians, persecute Dalits, try to shackle women within the household, and then start fighting among themselves. Islam persecutes its own minority sects like the Shias, Ahmadiyyas and

Sufis. Once violence becomes a value in life it requires a continuous supply of blood. Gandhi chose non-violence as the supreme value in his personal, social, and political life. He drew from the *Mahabharata* not precedents for violence but rather its fundamental teaching, i.e. the futility of violence. Prof Agrawal, a well-known literary critic, once commented in a Facebook post:

> 'I killed my own brethren and ruined my clan in the greed for a Kingdom. This victory at the price of Arjun's son Abhimanyu and the sons of Draupadi seems like a defeat. Karna was our sibling and was killed only because our mother concealed this fact. Just as dogs, greedy for flesh, become inauspicious, so too have we received evil, this flesh in the form of a state is not our desire… Gods are the fallen from heaven, and sages corrupted by penance… When the smoke stops rising from the houses, even the beggars have returned after begging (indicating a reluctance to even show his face to anyone), then I will go begging at three or four houses… I will spend my life like this…'
>
> —These are a few words from the vivid moaning of the victor Yudhishthir at the end of the *Mahabharata* (*Shanti Parv*).
>
> Before this, the mourning of Gandhari and her dialogue with the Pandavas and Lord Krishna in *Stree Parv* is even more plaintive. It is impossible to read this without tearing up and without being distracted by the horrors of war. It is an insult to the Indian intellect to treat the *Mahabharata* as a legend of victory.
>
> *Mahabharata* is not a legend of Victory but a profoundly moving deliberation on Violence–Non-Violence and Religion–Unrighteousness. That is why the Indian tradition of poetics considers it Poetry as well as *Shastra* (legislation).

Gandhi accepted the proclamation of the *Mahabharata*: '*ahimsa paramo dharmah*' (non-violence is the supreme *dharma*), and stood against alien rule with absolute firmness, courage, and humility. To him non-violence was a symbol of courage. In an article published in *Harijan* on 25 July 1946, Gandhi quoted a Gujarati poem which says, 'The path to the almighty is the path of the brave and not of cowards.'[2] In the religious structure of Gandhi, the practise of non-violence and truth was the path to the almighty. This courageous non-violence is preached in various Hindu religious texts. In the *Srimad Bhagavad Gita*, this is considered one of the characteristics of religion. Every religion has a spiritual aspect and a political one. The former teaches us to be better human beings while the latter uses religion as a weapon for political power and cultural hegemony. The first one wishes, 'Let no one suffer' ('*ma kashchit duhkha bhagbhavet*'*), while the latter jumps into riots with a sword, chanting the age-old slogan: 'Religion is in danger.' One speaks of rightful criticism, and change and reform according to the needs of the new era, and the other opposes every change to maintain the authority of the dominant class. One may question whether the changes and reforms within a religion have any effect on the oppressive structures created by said religion, but it can certainly be said that the liberal reading of any religion teaches co-existence in social and political life, and tends to make it much more tolerant.

James W. Douglass cites an episode from Gandhi's visit to London in 1909 when he had gone to deliver a speech at an invitation from radical students of India House on Dussehra and had shared the dais with Savarkar. India House was founded in 1905 by the freedom fighter Shyamji Krishna Varma and was home to radical Indian students. Savarkar arrived in London on 3 July 1906 and immediately found lodging at India House and soon became a protégé of Shyamji Krishna Varma. Savarkar founded the Free India Society, inspired by the thought of the Italian nationalist Giuseppe Mazzini (Savarkar had written a biography of Mazzini). The Society held regular meetings every Sunday where they celebrated Indian festivals and patriots, discussed Indian political problems and the overthrow of the yoke of the British in India.

Gandhi's comment on this invitation by Savarkarite students was that 'I have accepted the invitation unwillingly so that I can speak among the attendees about the inappropriateness of violence in the process of reform'. While Savarkar drew from the *Ramayana* the inspiration to kill the enemy, Gandhi saw Ram as a person who struggled for his values through self-sacrifice and suffering, and said

---

* *Sarve bhavantu sukhinah / Sarve santu niramayah / Sarve bhadrani pashyantu / Ma kashchit duhkha bhagbhavet // Om Shantih, Shantih, Shantih.*

that only by suffering for the truth could India's independence be won.[3]

The liberal tradition of religion always stands against its narrow interpretation and its petty political experiments. It was this tradition that gave Gandhi the courage to tell the truth by going to a meeting of the opposition. It was this sublime courage that made him eager to interact with even those who attempted to kill him. His killers had courage too, but their courage came of a failure to respond to their adversary, leading them to violent conspiracies and political assassinations. This is a big difference, and one needs the moral virtue proposed by the *Padma Purana* to appreciate it—*shruyatam dharmasarvasvam shrutva chaivavadharyatam, atmanah pratikulani paresham na samacharet* (May all listen to what is said about the correct dharma, or way of life. The sum and substance of dharma is that one should not do to others, or wish for others, what is proved to be not good for the doers themselves). Gandhi says, 'My patriotism is subservient to my religion.' For Louis Fischer, 'He was too religious to serve one land, one race, one caste, one family, one person, or even one religion. His religion was humanity.'[4]

This is the point where one should remember the declaration of the Vedas—*vasudhaiva kutumbakam* (the world is a family)—and its pre-condition—*udar charitanam* (for generous people)—which stands tall against all such parochialism. For generous people, the world is a family; if one's outlook is narrow, even the neighbour is made an enemy.

Prof Nirmal Kumar Bose, who worked as his secretary during his stint in Noakhali, has underlined that the basis of Gandhi's principle of non-violence was courage. Gandhi was unfazed by threats to his life and did not allow Patel to breach the sanctity of his prayer meetings by examining every attendee, even after the failed attempt on his life. Gandhi was inconvenient for the people pursuing their agenda of hate under the garb of Hindutva. As a devoted Hindu, Gandhi was the mirror that reflected the grotesque face of these fanatics. One may recall that even the Muslim League chose a liberal and secular leader, Shafi Ahmed Kidwai, to assassinate. To them, people like Maulana Abul Kalam Azad were 'traitors' because they sided with the Congress in favour of Hindu–Muslim unity.[5]

The other reason was the resolve of the Congress under Gandhi's leadership to build an egalitarian and secular, democratic nation. It is no coincidence that the Congress adopted the goal of democratic *swaraj* based on the principles of secularism, egalitarianism and the One-person One-vote rule by incorporating fundamental rights in the resolution passed at its Karachi Session in 1931[6] and the first attack on Gandhi took place at Poona during his campaign against untouchability in 1934.[7] It is well documented that Gandhi and Nehru played a decisive role[8] in finalizing these proposals.* The constitution finalized by the drafting committee chaired by Dr Ambedkar was based on these proposals. It is natural that all the credit is given to Dr Ambedkar, the chairman of the drafting committee, but it is also a fact that despite substantial differences within the Congress on many issues like the Hindu Code Bill, it was Nehru who got the consent from Parliament. Without his support, the Constitution could not have been passed in its present form.

The conservatives were aware of these realities, and Mahatma Gandhi and Jawaharlal Nehru thus seemed to be the biggest obstacles to their intentions of creating a nation based on the *Manusmriti*, where they could run their dictatorship. They considered themselves spokesmen for the Hindu side and wanted an opportunity to build a Hindu Pakistan, like Jinnah's Muslim one. The Hindu nation proposed by Savarkar was one such model of racial nationalism. They could neither compete through argumentation nor could they gather such support in favour of their policies that their claim to be representatives of Hindus be accepted. Their absence from the freedom struggle did not allow their support base to grow, until just before the riots broke out, beyond a few princely states and among people who wanted to save their privileges under British Raj. The anger and dissatisfaction that had arisen just before and after Partition led many people rapidly into their fold, but their numbers were never enough for them to compete with the mass base of Gandhi and Nehru. Their numbers

---

* These resolutions proposed the right to equality regardless of religion, caste or gender and guaranteed free and manadatory primary education to all. They also promised to protect the cultural identity of minorities and the principle of universal suffrage.

were enough, however, to allow them to arrange weapons and other resources for the assassination of Gandhi. They had successfully divided this nation and were no longer of any use to the British. In this frustration, they chose to kill the Mahatma.

Attempts on Gandhi's Life in South Africa

The incident at Pietermaritzburg, where Gandhi was thrown out of the first-class compartment of a train, is well known, but other attacks on his life during his stint in Africa are seldom discussed. James W. Douglass beautifully contextualizes these incidents in his book *Gandhi and the Unspeakable*. He registers a wonderful poetic statement of Gandhi in the initial pages of his book:

> Just as one must learn the art of killing in the training for violence, so one must learn the art of dying in the training of non-violence.[9]

Ordinary in its structure, this sentence has immense depth. If killing is an art, being mentally prepared to sacrifice fearlessly for your principles is a greater art. While unfathomable hatred is required for the former, the latter requires immeasurable faith in humanity. Non-violence was not only a tactic for Gandhi but a value of life, and thus valour was interwoven into it. He later defines the art of dying: 'The art of dying comes as a natural corollary of the art of living.'[10]

This art of dying is different from being suicidal. Death in itself is not a goal here. Neither is martyrdom romanticized. It's an indifference generated through the course of a meaningful and abounding life. Deep faith in life eradicates the fear of death and both become inseparable.

One can have disagreements with Gandhi. It is not easy to believe that the world can be revolutionized through a 'change of heart'. Gandhi himself couldn't accomplish his mission. But the many failed revolutions and the senseless violence of our time does point to the continuing relevance of Gandhi's belief that any order founded on violence will only lead to greater violence. Making the world better is a question to which the answers have still not been found.

First Attack: Mob Lynching

The first attempt on Gandhi's life took place in January 1897 when a mob of white people tried to lynch him in South Africa.

His campaign against apartheid in Africa had made him many enemies. While in India, he wrote a pamphlet, which was used as a pretext for intense negative propaganda in South African newspapers, and when he was returning, a rumour circulated that he was deliberately bringing a number of Indians along with him to spread the plague and was planning to establish a majority in Africa. A 'European Protection Committee' was formed immediately and it was decided not to allow Indians to set foot on the African shore. The mob was violent. Harry Escombe, who had once argued in favour of Gandhi's membership to the Bar of the Supreme Court of South Africa, was the acting prime minister of Natal at that time, and in view of upcoming elections, sided with the racist mob. The passengers were ordered to quarantine in the ship for twenty-three days on the pretext of containing the plague. People were forced to stay inside the boat in the cold of January with the crowd constantly insisting on sending them back. There were slogans to the effect that if any Indian landed on the beach, he would be killed. Gandhi was constantly trying to boost the courage of his co-passengers. The captain of the ship threw a party in honour of Gandhi on the eve of Christmas. During the celebrations, he asked, 'What will happen to your principle of non-violence if the whites stick to their stubbornness?' Gandhi replied, 'I hope that my God will give me so much strength and wisdom that I can forgive them for this.' The captain had a smile of disbelief on his face.

By the end of the quarantine period, Escombe could assess that the situation was out of control and the danger of genocide was real. Such racial/religious frenzy is like riding a tiger: the moment you decide to get down, you're in danger of being killed by the same beast. The frenzied mob was not ready to obey Escombe. Authorities had to use force to disperse them, but the danger still loomed large over Gandhi. He was advised to sneak into the city but Gandhi refused and decided to go to a friend's house in Durban, walking two miles on foot. The mob followed him. Gandhi had lost all hope of surviving this but when Mrs Zane Alexander, wife of the superintendent of Durban police joined him, the police had to, perforce, be vigilant and Gandhi was saved. But the house of his friend Rustomji Sheth was still surrounded by the mob and violent slogans were raised. The superintendent of police sent a message to Gandhi and Gandhi agreed to leave disguised as a police officer to save the lives of his friend's family.

But the story doesn't end here. When pressure mounted and Escombe invited Gandhi to identify the assailants so they could be sued, Gandhi replied unhesitatingly, 'They were merely misled people. The real responsibility lies in the government of Natal and you as the head of government.' Escombe knew that he was facing a different kind of person. He appealed him to forgive the assailants and Gandhi readily signed the paper. Later, he wrote about this incident in his book *Satyagraha in South Africa*:

> I had a most valuable experience, and whenever I think of that day, I feel that God was preparing me for the practice of Satyagraha.[11]

This story has a corollary. Three years after this incident, Escombe met Gandhi and apologized not only for this incident but also for the anti-Asiatic legislations passed by him. Gandhi smiled and told him that he had already forgiven him and had no malice towards him. Three hours later, Escombe's servant came to Gandhi and informed him that his master had died of a heart attack a while back. Many years later, when the statue of Escombe was erected in Durban, Gandhi remembered the incident while paying tribute.

Second Attempt: 'Gandhi—The Man'

The story of this attack is told by Gandhi's friend Millie Polak, who was the wife of his closest aide in Africa, Henry Polak. Henry, a Jew ten years younger than Gandhi, came to Africa from Britain in 1903. Millie was a Christian and a feminist social reformer who stood for women's suffrage. After a job in his uncle's business, Henry started working at *Transvaal Weekly*, a local paper in Johannesburg, and met Gandhi at a vegetarian restaurant in 1904. Remembering this meeting, he wrote, 'There was nothing in the famous Indian leader that could be called special. I was disappointed.' But after that a friendship developed between the two that went beyond the personal, and Polak not only participated shoulder to shoulder in Gandhi's satyagraha in Africa but continued his mission even after his return to India. Gandhi later wrote about Polak, 'He has the amazing ability to bring anything to life that might appeal to his brain.' Henry wrote *Mahatma Gandhi* a year after his death, while Millie wrote a book of his memoirs in 1931, *Mr. Gandhi: The Man.**

She mentions an incident from 1908 in this book.

One evening when Gandhi was returning with her after delivering a lecture to a packed Masonic Hall audience in Johannesburg she noticed a man standing near the outer gate—

> Mr Gandhi also specially noticed him, it was evident, for he went directly to him and linked his arm in the man's, saying something in a quiet, earnest voice to him. The man hesitated for a moment, then turned and walked away with Mr Gandhi, I meantime keeping my place on the other side of him. We walked the length of the street. I did not understand what the others were talking about, even could I have heard it. But I could not hear, for both men were speaking in a very low voice. At the end of the street the man handled something over to Mr Gandhi and walked away.
>
> I was somewhat puzzled by the whole proceeding and, as soon as the man had gone, I asked Mr Gandhi what was the matter.
>
> 'What did the man want—anything special?' I queried.
>
> 'Yes,' replied Mr Gandhi, 'he wanted to kill me.'
>
> 'To kill you,' I repeated. 'To kill you? How horrible! Is he mad?'
>
> 'No, he thinks that I am acting traitorously towards our people; that I am intriguing with the Government against them, and yet pretending to be their friend and leader.'
>
> 'But that is all wicked and dreadful,' I protested. 'Such a man is not safe; he ought to be arrested. Why did you let him go like that? He must be mad!'

* For details on Gandhi's relation to the Polak family, see Prabha Ravi Shankar, 'Mahatma Gandhi and The Polaks' (https://www.mkgandhi.org/articles/mahatma-gandhi-and-the-polaks.html, last accessed on 8 December 2021).

> 'No,' replied Mr Gandhi, 'he is not mad, only mistaken; and you saw, after I had talked to him, he handed over to me the knife he had intended to use on me.'
>
> 'He would have stabbed you in the dark. I…'
>
> But Mr Gandhi interrupted me—
>
> 'Do not disturb yourself so much about it. He thought he wanted to kill me; but he really had not the courage to do so. If I were as bad as he thought I was, I should deserve to die. Now we will not worry any more about it. It is finished. I do not think that man will attempt to injure me again. Had I had him arrested, I should have made an enemy of him. As it is, he will now be my friend.'[12]

Gandhi was right. Perhaps his long struggles had honed his discernment of people. Many decades later when Madanlal Pahwa threw a bomb in his prayer meeting on 20 January 1948, while most people shrugged it off as an act of a misled refugee youth, Gandhi was once again correct in his apprehension—'Don't you see there is a terrible and widespread conspiracy behind it?'[13]

The Third Attempt and the Saviour With a Naked Dagger

Gandhi's struggle in South Africa was against the policy of apartheid of the Europeans towards Asians. His legal practice was flourishing and he was a patriarch to about forty subordinates working in his farm, law office and household,[14] but the quest for a respectable existence converted him into the leader of Indian people living in South Africa. It was not an easy struggle. Petty Indian workers from agricultural farms, factories and shops, whose own country was under subjugation, were pitted against the almighty colonial power. They were no match for the brutal power of the British. In these adverse conditions, Gandhi developed new tools of resistance. Without going into details, we may quote an incident from Douglass:

> On September 11, 1906, three thousand Indians packed the old Jewish Imperial Theater in Johannesburg, South Africa. The South African Indian had come together to respond to a pending ordinance requiring that they carry registration cards, a critical degrading step

> toward their expulsion from the country. Gandhi had helped draft a resolution that the Indian would not submit to the law and would instead suffer the penalties for their refusal.
>
> When the resolution was proposed and seconded, an old, experienced Muslim leader, Sheth Haji Habib passionately declared to the meeting that, 'in the name of God,' he would never submit to the law. He appealed to everyone present to join him in taking such an oath before God.
>
> ... Gandhi rose to speak to the crowd about the crucial implications of adding Sheth Haji Habib's oath to the resolution. He said: ... We all believe in one and the same God, the differences of nomenclature in Hinduism and Islam notwithstanding. To pledge ourselves or to take oath in the name of that God or with him as witness is not something to be trifled with. If having taken such an oath we violate our pledge we are guilty before God and man.
>
> The pledge must not be taken with a view to produce an effect on outsiders. No one should trouble to consider what impression it might have upon the Local Government, or the Government of India. Everyone must only search his own heart, an if the inner voice assures him that he has the requisite strength to carry him through, then only should he pledge himself and then only will his pledge bear fruit.
>
> ... We may have to go to jail, where we may be insulted. We may have to go hungry and suffer extreme heat or cold. Hard labour may be imposed on us... We may be fined heavily and our property may be confiscated... We may be deported...some of us may fall ill and die... But I can boldly declare, and certainly, that so long as there is even a handful of men true to their pledge, there can only be one end to the struggle, and that is victory.
>
> The crowd had listened to him in silence. Finally, three thousand people stood. With upraised hands, they took an oath: With God as their witness, they would not submit to the law.[15]

This was a new vision for Gandhi. In January 1908, Gandhi offered a small prize in his journal *Indian Opinion*, to the reader who could come up with 'the best designation for our struggle'. His nephew Maganlal came closest with *sadagraha*.[16] But Gandhi corrected it to *satyagraha*: 'Truth (*satya*) implies love, and firmness (*agraha*) engenders and therefore serves as a synonym for force.' Satyagraha means the force which is born of truth, love and non-violence.

And this became his biggest strength: non-violence in the face of tyrannical power, tolerance against suppression, compassion in the face of hatred and faith against distrust. When a South African friend William Hosken suggested that the Indians were having recourse to passive resistance and termed it 'the weapon of the weak', Gandhi indignantly denied that he was practising passive resistance. On the contrary, 'Satyagraha was positive force, a projection of spiritual energy against the enemy.'[17] With this strength, Gandhi fought for freedom and self-respect against British colonial power not only in South Africa but also in India.

In the meantime, the Transvaal Asiatic Registration Act was passed in Transvaal at the end of March 1907. This necessitated all Indians to be registered and fingerprinted, and there could be no exceptions. Gandhi launched satyagraha against it and was arrested on 10 January 1908. This was his first jail term. He was sentenced for two months but was called for a dialogue by General Smuts within two weeks. Smuts promised to repeal the law, if Indians agreed to get registered, and there would be no compulsion to carry the registration card at all times. Gandhi agreed to trust his words. But a section of Indians took it as treachery on the part of Gandhi. He tried to explain that if Smuts were to go back on his promise he would start the movement again. Gandhi remained true to his word when, in time, he compelled Smuts to keep his promise following another long struggle. But people were not ready to understand his stand that 'A *Satyagrahi** is never afraid of trusting his opponents.' The leader of the dissidents, Mir Alam, was a friend and client of Gandhi. He declared that whoever opted for registration would be killed. Gandhi replied, 'Death is the appointed end of all life. To die by the hand of a brother rather than by disease or in some other way cannot be for me a matter of sorrow.'[18]

Both kept their word. On the way to the registration, Gandhi and his companions were attacked with sticks. When Gandhi fell down unconscious, with '*Hey Ram*' on his lips, the assailants, thinking

* One who opts for satyagraha.

Gandhi dead, fled,[19] but when he regained consciousness and was informed that Mir Alam and his companions had been arrested, he said, 'They should be released.' He refused to testify against them, but completed his task by signing the papers of registration. Gandhi's co-worker, Thambi Naidoo and Yusuf Miyan had also received severe blows while trying to save him. But Gandhi insisted that the assailants should not be prosecuted. In a letter to the Attorney General, He wrote, '[Mir Alam and company] had acted in the only way they knew against what they thought to be wrong. Hindus should not retain anger against Muslims due to this incident.' However, since the attack was public, there were many people who readily testified and Mir Alam was served with two months along with one of his accomplices.

To quote Douglass again:

> Stories of Gandhi often do not end without a corollary. On 14 March 1913, Justice Malcom Searle of the Cape division of the Supreme Court ruled that the wives of non-Christian marriages had no right to immigrate to South Africa. This was practically to de-recognize the wives of Asians living in South Africa. Gandhi mobilized women for a satyagraha against this decision. Kasturba and many other women led from the front and were sentenced. Finally, a settlement was reached in the spring of 1914 and the British agreed to recognize one lawful wife for any immigrant male. Muslims took it as an insult to their religious belief of polygamy. A meeting of Muslims was organized in the month of March at Johannesburg. Gandhi was advised to avoid that meeting but he insisted.
>
> Gandhi was trying to pacify the enraged masses but the danger of another attack loomed large. Then, suddenly, a tall, well-built and angry Pathan came forward brandishing a naked dagger and declared, declared, 'Beware, there are some mischief-makers in the meeting ready to attack Gandhibhai. If anyone harms him, he will fall victim to my dagger.' When Gandhi smiled and said, '... Come near me... No one is going to harm me.' He cried out, 'You are a fakir! You do not know but I know everything. The man who steps forward to harm you will be finished at that very instant.'[20]

The man who stayed alert with his dagger till the end of the meeting was Mir Alam!

There is one more interesting story to end this section. Smuts, who tried his best to suppress Gandhi's satyagraha in South Africa, went on to become the prime minister by the 1940s. When he met British Prime Minister Churchill in Cairo in 1942, advising caution against his repressive policies against the Quit India movement, he said, '[Gandhi] is a man of God. You and I are mundane people. Gandhi had appealed to religious motives. You never have. That is where you have failed.'[21] Churchill obviously mocked him but ultimately he was proved right.

After living and experimenting with satyagraha and non-violence for twenty-two years, Gandhi decided to return to India in 1914. Smuts commented in relief, 'The saint has left our country. I sincerely hope forever.'

This was the year when Savarkar started writing mercy petitions for his release from the Andamans.[22]

Gandhi in India: Struggle and Attacks

> There was in existence an organization which was extremely anti-Gandhi and its members persisted in pursuing Mahatma Gandhi by creating disturbances at his meetings and their attitude was not non-violent.
>
> —Kapur Commission's Report, Part I, p. 124

The satyagraha of South Africa had been taken note of by many an eminent individual in India before Gandhi's arrival, and he was received like a hero on his return. On 9 January 1915, the ship carrying him dropped anchor at the Apollo port in Bombay which was usually reserved for kings, viceroys and important Indians. He received an invitation from the Governor of Calcutta, Lord Willingdon, and Gokhale, whom he had met in Africa and whom he considered his political mentor, not only invited him to Poona but also proposed that he lead his organization, Servants of India Society. However, many of its members did not agree to this and, eventually, Gandhi too turned down the offer.[23]

But this India was not familiar to Gandhi. Louis Fischer writes,

'He was not well known in India. Nor did he know India.' He had spent twenty-two years in South Africa and was well acquainted with its socio-political intricacies. But despite personal acquaintances with some prominent leaders in India, the socio-political conditions here were new to him. Gokhale advised him to roam across the country for a year and take stock of the situation by keeping his eyes open and mouth shut.[24] Gandhi kept his eyes wide open but it was not up to him to keep his mouth shut.

It was a challenge for him to continue with his experiments of satyagraha in a vast country under British rule and Gandhi was struggling with it. He was accompanied by his disciples from the Phoenix ashram. They initially stayed at Rabindranath Tagore's Santiniketan. When Gandhi visited Santiniketan, Tagore was not there, but he met his old friend 'Deshbandhu' C.F. Andrews. In those days, the revolutionary movement was very popular in Bengal. Apart from the Anushilan Samiti established in 1902, there were many open and clandestine organizations which believed in fighting British power with the help of bombs and guns. On 31 March, Gandhi, while addressing a group of militant students in Calcutta, praised their courage on the one hand, and on the other hand, described the technique of assassination as a means of freedom completely foreign, and said that he stood against them. He added:

> If the advocates of assassination have a program for the country, they should place it openly before the public. If I am for sedition, I must speak out for sedition. I must think out loud and take the consequences... If you are prepared to die; I am prepared to die with you.[25]

Next year he was in Banaras. The Hindu College, founded in 1892 by Annie Besant, had been upgraded to the Banaras Hindu University with the joint effort of Madan Mohan Malaviya and Mrs Besant. Gandhi was also invited at its inaugural in February 1916, which was attended by kings from various principalities and other eminent people of the country including the Viceroy. The kings were in their royal mantle, clad in gold and silver, and others were in Western suits, while Gandhi wore a white cloak and a short white *dhoti*. When he went to speak, the stage was presided over by Sir Rameshwar Singh, the Maharaja of Darbhanga. Gandhi was uncomfortable in the whole atmosphere, and when he was invited to deliver his speech after the ceremonial functions, said:

> I compare the richly bedecked noblemen with the millions of the poor. And I feel like saying to these noblemen: 'There is no salvation for India unless you strip yourselves of this jewelry and hold it in a trust for your countrymen in India.' Sir, whenever I hear of a great palace rising in any great city of India, be it in British India or be it in India ruled by our great chiefs, I become jealous at once and I say: 'Oh, it is the money that has come from the agriculturists.'

That was a period when even the Congress was not demanding complete independence, and such things were not usually discussed in public. The atmosphere became tense with Gandhi's talk. He did not stop here. He raised the question of language and while attacking the compulsion to speak English there, and in support of education in the mother tongue, he said, 'Our language is a reflection of ourselves and if you tell me that our languages are too poor to express the best thoughts, then I say that the sooner we are wiped out of existence the better for us!' He spoke of the dirt and squalor he had seen while visiting the Vishwanath Temple and asked, 'If a stranger dropped from above on this great temple and he had to consider what we as Hindus were, would he not be justified in condemning us? Is not this great temple a reflection of our own character? I speak feelingly as a Hindu. Is it right that the lanes of our sacred temple should be as dirty as they are?… If even our temples are not models of cleanliness, what can our self-government be? Shall our temples be abodes of holiness, cleanliness and peace as soon as the English have retired from India?' Reflecting similar sentiments as those expressed in Calcutta, he went on to address the anarchist students in the meeting:

> I honour the anarchist for his love for the country. I honour him for his bravery in being willing to die for his country. But I ask him: Is killing honourable? I deny it. There is no warrant for such measures in any scriptures. If I found it necessary for the salvation of India that the English should retire, that they should be driven out, I

> would not hesitate to declare that they would have to go. And I hope I would be prepared to die in defence of that belief. That would, in my opinion be an honourable death.[26] ... If we trust and fear God, we shall have to fear no one, not Maharajas, not Viceroys, not the detectives, not even King George.[27]

The audience was clearly divided. One section was cheering Gandhi while the other was hooting him. Most of the kings were uncomfortable and left the dais in protest. Even Annie Besant, who had raised the cry 'The moment of English difficulty is the moment of India's opportunity' during the First World War, was growing impatient and told Gandhi to stop. Gandhi said: 'I am explaining my object. I simply...' He could not be heard above the din. The Maharaja of Darbhanga allowed him to carry on. But when Gandhi continued on the repressive role of a section of the British, the Maharaja vacated the dais, the commotion mounted, and Gandhi had to stop. Mrs Besant adjourned the meeting.

But this courage left a deep impact on a section of the students. Vinoba Bhave, then a student studying Sanskrit and the Vedic scriptures, remembered that Gandhi had told the Viceroy to go home: 'If for such plain speaking we are sentenced to death, let us go cheerfully to the gallows.' He wrote to Gandhi asking him some philosophical questions and received an invitation to stay in the ashram at Ahmedabad.[28]

Caste-Race Allegiance and Gandhi

This speech of Gandhi describes the ideological turmoil within him at the time. In Africa, he was leading a migrant community in their search for better working conditions and freedom from discrimination. The question of political freedom could not be raised. Thus he adopted a policy of co-operation with the British colonial power while demanding better conditions for Indians. Opposition to British occupation in Africa was not on his agenda. That is why during the Boer War or the Zulu Rebellion, Gandhi chose to side with the British. He even wore the army uniform as a sergeant major during the Zulu rebellion. Questions are asked and questions should be asked as to why Gandhi did not join his liberation struggle with that of the indigenous people there. The debate resurfaced in 2015 with Ashwin Desai and Goolam Vahed's book *The South African Gandhi: Stretcher-Bearer of Empire*, and in April 2015 there were incidents of white paint being thrown at the statue of Gandhi in Johannesburg; and, more recently, during the movement that began after the infamous murder of George Floyd by police officer Derek Chauvin in Minneapolis, protesters in Washington, DC attacked the Mahatma Gandhi statue at the Indian embassy. But this is not a new discovery and Gandhi has himself written in detail on it. He wrote in his autobiography:

> I bore no grudge against the Zulus, they had harmed no Indian. I had doubts about the 'rebellion' itself. But I then believed that the British Empire existed for the welfare of the world. A genuine sense of loyalty prevented me from even wishing ill to the Empire. The rightness or otherwise of the 'rebellion' was therefore not likely to affect my decision. Natal had a Volunteer Defence Force, and it was open to it to recruit more men. I read that this force had already been mobilized to quell the 'rebellion'.

A statue of Gandhi in Johannesburg, South Africa, defaced with white paint in April 2015.

Muriel Lester, who was his host during the Second Round Table Conference in London, has quoted Gandhi's comments on the policy of co-operation with the government during his talks with Pierre Ceresole, who was running an international volunteer organization for world peace in Switzerland. This statement of Gandhi marks his complete journey, a part of which is selectively chosen to prove him 'the stretcher-bearer of Empire'. He says:

> I didn't think like this in 1914. Then I wanted to be a perfect citizen. So I put myself unreservedly at the disposal of the British. I believed that they are protecting my country from tyranny; therefore I felt I had to help them as wholeheartedly as any Briton. I was asked to do Red Cross work. I said to myself, 'That is lovely,' for I did not want to kill, but I did not flatter myself that Red Cross work was less than killing. It has precisely the same effect in war time, in that it releases other men to kill. If they'd given me a rifle, I would have used it when they'd shown me how and trained me to it. I'd have certainly used it, unless I'd been suddenly paralysed, as has sometimes happened to me when about to do something wrong.
>
> I thought serving wholeheartedly in the war was the right way to gain my country's freedom. Before that, while I was in South Africa, the Zulu rebellion broke out. My sympathies were with the Zulus. I would have liked to help them, but had not the power then to do anything for them. I was not strong enough, not disciplined enough, not experienced enough. I saw no way to help. I had no word to give. What could I do? I thought I would identify myself with the British Government system; then I should be able to make my witness through the system, in order to set right what was wrong in it. I put myself at the disposal of the Government there and I was set to stretcher-bearing. That suited me splendidly. I hoped I should have to tend to wounded Zulus. The Chief Medical Officer was a humanitarian, and when I told him I'd rather tend the wounded Zulus than any others, he exclaimed, 'This is an answer to prayer.' You see, the Zulu prisoners had been beaten and their wounds and stripes were festering, and the others did not want to attend to them. So, I nursed them night and day. They were kept behind bars, and the colonial soldiers used to watch us from outside as we worked, jeering at us for lavishing care on 'niggers'. They used to shout through the bars, scoffing and threatening. 'Why don't you

> let them die? Rebels! Niggers!' It was terrible the way that rebellion was quelled. The soldiers would attack unarmed men. That ought to have taught me a lesson, but even after that, you see, I made further attempts to remain a part of the British State system. I tried to work out my ideals within the State, but it was no good. I learnt much from the endeavour, however. After serving the State in South Africa, I was still powerless to influence it on behalf of the Zulus. And after serving the Empire throughout the war, recruiting, which I held to be my duty, and undertaking any sort of duty they put upon me, I found myself still powerless at the end of it all to win my country's freedom. So I couldn't co-operate with the State any longer.[29]

It is not mere coincidence that the leader of the American Black movement, Martin Luther King, and the tallest leader of African liberation, Nelson Mandela, considered Gandhi as their inspiration and led their movements with his policy of non-violence. Gandhi's principles helped Mandela fight his battle even though Gandhi himself could not help Black people during his stay in Africa. I shall like to end this discussion with a quote from his article on Abraham Lincoln, which he wrote in *Indian Opinion* on 26 October 1905:

> It is believed that the greatest and the noblest man of the last century was Abraham Lincoln... Nobody [then] saw anything wrong in openly selling Negroes and keeping them in slavery. The high and the low, the rich and the poor saw nothing strange in owning slaves... Religious minded men, priests and the like, saw nothing amiss and did not protest... Some even encouraged [slavery], and all...thought that slavery...was a divine dispensation and that the Negroes were born to it... [E]ven those [who thought that slavery was wrong]... preferred to remain silent, being unable to assert themselves... Even today our hair stands on end to hear an account of the atrocities inflicted on slaves. They were tied up and beaten; they were forced to work; they were branded and handcuffed... Lincoln alone of all men made, and put into execution, his resolution to change the ideas of men, ideas which [had been] indelibly carved on their minds...[30]

As Rajmohan Gandhi asks, 'Was the writer of these and similar lines a man who "disdained" Blacks?'[31]

But the situation was different in India. This was his country and his own people. In contrast to the just policies of British he was supportive of, he was constantly witnessing moral decline, repression and injustice. Despite this, he was not yet in favour of expelling the British. His allegiance to English rule didn't end at BHU and he went on to support the British in the First World War by campaigning for army recruitment. But his campaign failed miserably. In Bardoli, where he was a hero of the peasant movement led by Sardar Patel, the people paid no heed to his call for recruitment. From Bardoli to Champaran, Gandhi could see that British rule in India was full of injustice. Suppression and exploitation were its weapons. The seeds that were present in the speech at BHU are seen to flourish in later events, and during the Karachi conference of the Congress, the idea of liberation from British colonialism markedly influences the concept of swaraj. The Salt Satyagraha and the Jallianwala Bagh massacre were two such incidents which played an important role in completely demolishing Gandhi's belief in the justice of the British State. White supremacy now stood before everyone in all its nakedness, with terrible racial arrogance and a hatred of others. Perhaps this experience gave him the opportunity to think afresh about the Blacks of Africa and Europe. Gandhi, who kept quiet on the suppression of Blacks during his stay in Africa, is seen raising his voice time and again during the latter phase of his life. For example, when a group of Black Americans sent him a telegram in August 1924, he published his reply in his weekly magazine *Young India*:

> Theirs is perhaps a task more difficult than ours, but they have some very fine workers among them. Many students of history consider that the future is with them. They have fine physique. They have glorious imagination. They are as simple as they are brave. Monsieur Finot has shown by his scientific researches that there is in them no inherent inferiority... All they need is opportunity. I know that if they have caught the spirit of the Indian movement [the spirit of non-violence] their progress must be rapid.[32]

Similarly, he wrote in his weekly magazine *Harijan* on 30 June 1946:

> The real 'White man's burden' is not insolently to dominate coloured or black people under the guise of protection; it is to desist from the hypocrisy which is eating into them. It is time white men learnt to

> treat every human being as their equal. There is no mystery about whiteness of the skin. It has repeatedly been proved that given equal opportunity, a man, be he of any colour or country, is fully equal to any other.[33]

His most unabashed voice is found in a speech delivered in one of his last prayer meetings on 17 November 1947:

> … South Africa has many wise men and women… It will be a tragedy for the world if they do not rise superior to their debilitating surrounding and give a proper lead to their country on this vexed and vexing problem of White supremacy. Is it not by this time a played-out game?[34]

It's obvious that at a later stage of his life he was playing an active role against white supremacy.

One more fact needs to be mentioned here. Gandhi had written *Hind Swaraj* before returning to India. The concept of *swaraj* in this book was not about freedom from British. Gandhi was arguing for getting rid of British culture, or Western culture, and creating a swaraj based on an Indian value system. This was an endeavour to develop an Indian modernism, leaving out Western rationality and science, which was completely different from the views of his contemporaries like Tagore and others. Removal of untouchability and Hindu–Muslim unity were among its core social values; an emphasis on labour-intensive small and cottage industries was its economic base; and non-violence and satyagraha were the means to achieving this goal. It is evident that even as tactics kept evolving throughout his political life, these core elements remained intact. In an interview to American radio during the Round Table Conference he said:

> It is my certain conviction that no man loses his freedom except through his own weakness. I am painfully conscious of our own weakness. We represent in India all the principal religions of the earth, and it is a matter of deep humiliation to confess that we are a house divided against itself; that we Hindus and Mussulmans are flying at one another. It is a matter of still deeper humiliation to me that we Hindus regard several millions of our kith and kin as too degraded for our touch. I refer to the so-called 'untouchables'.

> These are no small weaknesses in a nation struggling to be free. You will find that in this struggle for self-purification we have assigned as a foremost part of our creed the removal of this curse of 'untouchability' and the attainment of unity amongst all the different classes and communities of India representing the different creeds.[35]

He steadfastly opposed the system of untouchability after his return from South Africa. Not only this, Gandhi, who respected religious texts, was critical of *Manusmriti*. When his anti-untouchability drive was criticized by quoting the *Manusmriti*, Gandhi said at Godhra in November 1917 during the Antyaj Sammelan ('Conference of Untouchables'):

> Hinduism is hemmed in by many old customs. Some of them are praiseworthy but the rest are to be condemned. The custom of untouchability is, of course, to be condemned altogether. It is because of it that, now for two thousand years, Hinduism has been burdened with a load of sin in the name of religion. I call such orthodoxy hypocrisy. You will have to free yourself of this hypocrisy; the penance for it you are already undergoing. It is no good quoting verses from Manusmriti and other scriptures in defence of this orthodoxy. A number of verses in these scriptures are apocryphal; a number of them are quite meaningless. Then again, I have not so far come across any Hindu who obeys or wants to obey every injunction contained in Manusmriti. And it is easy to prove that one who does this will, in the end, be himself polluted. The Sanatana Dharma will not be saved by defending every verse printed in the scriptures. It will be saved only by putting into action the principles enunciated in them—principles that are eternal. All the religious leaders with whom I have had occasion to discuss the matter have agreed in this. All the preachers who are counted among the learned and who are revered in society have clearly announced that our treatment of Bhangis, Doms, etc., has no sanction other than the custom to which it conforms.[36]

Gandhi also openly supported the Mahad Satyagraha in 1927. The Bombay Legislative Council had adopted a resolution moved by S.K. Bole on 4 August 1923. The Bole Resolution 'recommend[ed] that the Untouchable Classes be allowed to use all public watering places, wells and dharmashalas which are built and maintained out of public funds or administered by bodies appointed by Government or created by statute, as well as public schools, courts, offices and dispensaries'. The Mahad municipality, which was part of the Bombay Province territory, had reaffirmed this resolution in 1924. However, the resolution remained on paper.

Dr Ambedkar had gone to Mahad for a two-day conference of the Kolaba District Depressed Classes on 19–20 March 1927. He presided over this conference, which was attended by thousands of delegates. The main agenda of the gathering was to raise awareness about the civil rights of Dalits. It was decided that the attendees would march to Chavdar tank and the 'untouchables' would assert their moral and legal right to access a public water body.

On 20 March, Dr Ambedkar and his co-workers led a peaceful procession of 2,500 'untouchables' through the main streets towards the Chavdar tank. Dr Ambedkar took water from the tank and drank it. Others followed suit. This was known as the Mahad Satyagraha. Then everybody returned to the *pandal.* It was a peaceful protest, but quite revolutionary in its implications.

In reaction, caste Hindus spread the rumour that the 'untouchables' were also planning to enter the temple of Veereshwar. A large crowd of caste Hindus armed with bamboo sticks gathered at street corners and attacked them. Ambedkar appealed to his people to not indulge in counter-violence.

Gandhi wrote 'approvingly of the Untouchables' composure in the face of the attacks'. Praising the Dalits' 'exemplary self-restraint', Gandhi wrote that, the 'so-called orthodox party', not having reason on its side, had used 'sheer brute force'. 'Dr Ambedkar,' Gandhi went on in an article in Young India on 28 April 1927, '[was] fully justified in putting to the test the resolution of the Bombay Legislative Council and the Mahad Municipality by advising the so-called Untouchables to go to the tank to quench their thirst.' He also urged 'every Hindu opposed to untouchability' to publicly defend the courageous Dalits of Mahad 'even at the risk of getting his head broken'.[37] One may recall here what he said during the Round Table Conference: 'I would far rather that Hinduism died than that untouchability lived.'[38] He told a British journalist:

> I would bend the knee before the poorest scavenger, the poorest untouchable in India, for having participated in crushing him for centuries; I would even take the dust of his feet. But I would not prostrate myself even before the king, much less before the Prince of Wales.[39]

However, I have always felt that Gandhi's understanding of ancient or contemporary history was based less on academic study and more on imagination and hearsay, which resulted in the perception that everything was great in ancient times and villages were peacefully self-reliant. The point at which Gandhi gets stuck is the refusal to change the authorized work structure of the varna system. He talks about respect for labour and not considering cleaning work as menial, and tries to prove it by his example, but the question remains: Why should the cleaning work be done by Shudras and why should Brahmins not do it? Interestingly, in his article on the Revolt of 1857, Marx was also looking at Indian villages as self-sufficient units. But neither Marx nor Gandhi could see the horrific system of exploitation concealed by the veil of self-sufficiency that came from the varna system. Marx did not have first-hand knowledge, and was dependent on English newspapers, so his lack of familiarity is understandable. Gandhi was scolded during childhood for playing with a so-called untouchable child and had all manner of direct knowledge about the caste system. It is astonishing that he could not see the degradation of workers, the lowest category in the varna-based social system, a large part of whom were declared untouchable. C.F. Andrews has decoded this dichotomous opposition to untouchability and acceptance of the varna system:

> While Mr Gandhi, in his definition of Hinduism, declares that he believes in the ancient Caste system, he entirely refuses to have anything to do with 'Untouchability'. He also refuses to regard any Caste, such as that of the Brahmin, as superior in rank. He regards all men and women equally as his brothers and sisters, treating them in every single act of life as equals. I have seen him day after day living with the 'untouchables' in the closest possible friendliness and fellowship.[40]

The end of discrimination within the caste system may seem an ideal proposal, but experiences confirm that inequality and hierarchy are embedded into it. Gandhi wrote regularly on this issue and, without going into the details, it may be said that this question was uncomfortable for Gandhi too and was ever present before him in India. When he established his first ashram in Kochrab near Ahmedabad in March 1915, no servant was appointed and every inmate had to work. Among the pledges that were compulsory to stay there, the pledge to not practise untouchability was last but not the least. It was put to the test soon enough when in the month of September, Dudabhai, a Dalit teacher from Bombay, came to live in the ashram with his wife Daniben and daughter Lakshmi. A panic spread among the residents and Kasturba threatened to leave if they were to be allowed in the kitchen. Gandhi told her that it would be extremely painful for him if she left, but he would not prevent her. She would either have to follow the rules or leave. So the tempest subsided, but from time to time there would be explosions of temper. And this protest was not confined to the ashram. The textile mill magnates of Ahmedabad, who were helping run the ashram, pulled out. Gandhi was adamant on his decision and there came a time when the coffers were completely exhausted. Suddenly, one day, a car stopped in front of the ashram. A man came out, handed over an envelope and left. The envelope contained thirteen thousand rupees.[41] To date, nobody knows who the man was.

He had stepped up the anti-untouchability movement since the Civil Disobedience movement began with the Dandi March in the 1930s. Gandhi believed that untouchability was against Hinduism's sense of non-violence and said that if it is not abolished, Hinduism would end.* But it is interesting that on this point, if the orthodoxy was angry with him, Dr Ambedkar too had a strong disagreement. The origins of their disagreement lay in the circumstances in which the Poona Pact was arrived at.

On 17 August 1932, the then prime minister of Britain Ramsay MacDonald announced the Communal Award under which Dalit castes

* For a better understanding of Gandhi's view on untouchability, the reader may see his book *The Removal of Untouchability*.

were given the status of a minority community like Sikhs, Muslims, Buddhists, Indian Christians, and the Anglo-Indian community, thus granting them a separate electorate.[42] Ambedkar considered it a major victory which would give an independent identity to Dalits, and with which the Dalits were given the opportunity of choosing their leadership. Gandhi, who was in the Yerawada jail of Poona, opposed it on the ground that Dalits were part and parcel of Hindu society and according them minority status was a conspiracy to divide Hindus. He had already made his stand clear at the Round Table Conference when he had asked, 'Sikhs may remain as such in perpetuity, so may Mohammedans, so may Europeans. Will untouchables remain untouchables in perpetuity?'[43] He wrote to the Prime Minister that if this award was not withdrawn, he would go on a fast unto death beginning the afternoon of 20 September. When no assurance was received in the correspondence with the Prime Minister, Gandhi went on a fast by the due date. Robert Payne writes that Gandhi used this fast to give 'a kind of shock treatment imposed upon the Indian people against their will' to get rid of untouchability.[44]

The day before the fast started, twelve temples in Allahabad were made accessible to Harijans for the first time. On the first day of the fast some of the most sacred temples throughout the country opened their doors to untouchables. Every subsequent day scores of holy places followed suit. Swarup Rani Nehru, Jawaharlal's very orthodox mother, let it be known that she accepted food from the hand of an untouchable. Thousands of prominent Hindu women followed her example. At the strictly Hindu Banaras University, Principal Dhruva, with numerous Brahmins, dined publicly with street cleaners, cobblers and scavengers. Similar meals were arranged in hundreds of other places.[45] It's difficult to ascertain to what extent these gestures were real or cosmetic and how many hearts were actually converted, but a nationwide debate on untouchability was generated by this fast and the support it garnered was enough to annoy the orthodoxy of that time. Fischer concludes:

> This fast could not kill the curse of untouchability, which was more than three thousand years old. Access to temple is not access to a good job. The Harijans remained the dregs of Indian society.

> Nor did segregation end when Gandhi slowly drank his orange juice. But after the fast, untouchability forfeited its public approval. The belief in it was destroyed. A practice full of mystic overtones and undercurrents, deeply imbedded in a complicated religion, was recognized as morally illegitimate. A taboo hallowed by custom, tradition and ritual lost its potency. It had been socially improper to consort with Harijans. In many circles now it became socially improper not to consort with them. To practice untouchability branded one a bigot, a reactionary. Before long, marriages were taking place between Harijans and Hindus; Gandhi made a point of attending some.[46]

Gandhi was sceptical about the response of caste Hindus. In a letter to Andrews on 30 September 1932, he wrote:

> I did expect a mighty response from the orthodox, but I was unprepared for the sudden manifestation that took place. But I shall not be deceived. It remains to be seen whether the temples opened remain open and the various other things done persist.[47]

Constant efforts were made to devise a formula in order to end the fast and many meetings were held in the jail premises. Gandhi was sixty-three and his health was not such that he could have withstood a long fast. Payne writes that Gandhi had offered more compensation than he ever dreamed of but Dr Ambedkar was a hard bargainer and was adamant on nothing less than his original demands.[48] He was perfectly justified in his approach. As a leader of the depressed classes, he wanted to extract as much as he could to compensate for the loss of the Communal Award. The removal of untouchability had symbolic significance but it could not be an alternative to political representation. After the slavery of hundreds of years, the Dalit class could not depend on the magnanimity of anyone for a respectable position in the society and politics of the country. Finally, a pact was reached and both sides agreed to reject the system of separate electorates. The number of reserved seats in state assemblies was increased from 71 to 147 and was fixed at eighteen per cent for the central legislature. The system of joint electorates was accepted and Dalits were to be given proper representation in public services and local institutions, while earmarking a portion of the educational grant for their uplift.

It is worth noting that Gandhi spoke of representation for Dalits according to their population, and that this was more than the seats given in the Award. Shortly after signing the pact, Ambedkar said he had been 'surprised, immensely surprised' to find 'so much in common' between Gandhi and himself. 'If you devoted yourself entirely to the welfare of the Depressed Classes', Ambedkar said to Gandhi, 'you would become our hero.'[49] Even in his book *What Congress and Gandhi have done to the Untouchables*, which was written some twelve years after the pact, Ambedkar claims the pact as a victory. In a scathing attack on Gandhi and Congress he wrote, 'When the fast failed and Mr Gandhi was obliged to sign a pact—called the Poona Pact—which conceded the political demands of the Untouchables, he took his revenge by letting the Congress employ foul electioneering tactics to make their political rights of no avail.' But not once does he criticize or propose to abandon the pact, nor did he ever demand separate electorates either during British rule or after Independence. Prof Uday Balakrishnan writes in an article published in *The Hindu* on 14 April 2020:

> Perry Anderson and Arundhati Roy argued that Gandhi through his fast coerced Ambedkar into the Poona Pact. Ambedkar, however, was hardly the person to bend to someone else's will. As he observed in a talk years later, he was clear he would not 'tolerate anyone on whose will and consent settlement depends, to stand on dignity and play the Grand Moghul.'... As a practical man Ambedkar was not looking for the perfect solution. As he remarked in a 1943 address to mark the 101st birthday celebrations of Mahadev Govind Ranade, all he wanted was 'a settlement of some sort'; that he was not 'prepared to wait for an ideal settlement'.[50]

One should keep in mind that Ambedkar was preparing for an important election while he wrote the book, and having lost the previous elections in 1937, wanted to counter the Congress with more aggression. However, Congress went on to win the reserved seats with an even greater majority. Rajmohan Gandhi sums it all up:

> What was the context for the fierce language of Ambedkar's 1945 text, which he wrote in New Delhi in his official residence on Prithviraj Road? At this time, he was a Member of the Viceroy's Executive Council. The war was about to end. After three years of detention for Quit India, which had stirred much of India, the Congress leadership was about to be released. The British were on the verge of proposing a new political scheme for India, and new elections were imminent across the country. The brilliant thinker and Member (minister in effect) writing the 1945 tract was also someone who wished to influence any new British scheme. In addition, he was a political leader unable to forget the results of the 1937 elections, which—because the war had intervened—were the last to have taken place. He hoped to do better in 1945–46. Through this 1945 tract, an Ambedkar still vexed by the 1937 results presented his case to Britain's leaders and simultaneously to India's voters. However, the elections of 1945–46 confirmed that the INC attracted the bulk of the Indian electorate, including a good deal of Dalit support. Obtaining caste Hindu as well as Dalit votes, the INC won an even larger proportion of Dalit seats than it had in 1937.[51]

Rajmohan Gandhi also points out Gandhi's growing disenchantment with the caste system after 1932. In 1935, he wrote an article in *Harijan* with title 'CASTE HAS TO GO' wherein he says, 'The sooner public opinion abolishes [caste] the better.' He publicly affirmed his acceptance of inter-dining and inter-marriage in 1936, and on 24 April 1947, he said in Patna that for some time he had 'made it a rule not to be present or give his blessings for any wedding unless one of the parties was a Harijan' and proposed that 'a Harijan or a Harijan girl should be made the nation's first President and Jawaharlal should become the Prime Minister… [S]imilar arrangements [can be] made in the provinces too'.[52] Rajmohan Gandhi underlines that if Gandhi had directly attacked the caste system, he would have lost his following and thus he attacked its weakest part, untouchability, in order to weaken it: 'Realizing that he would unite pro-orthodox ranks if he started with an attack on caste, Gandhi chose to zero in on an evil none could defend… His seeming "defence" of caste was his way of sugar-coating the bitter pills he was asking caste Hindus to swallow.'[53]

To understand how Gandhi looked at the question of caste, one of his notes written on 9 June 1946 is very useful. He writes:

> A Brahmin correspondent asks me to publish the fact that he has become a Harijan and wants to eliminate his name as a caste Hindu from the census too. This is a sequence to my having asked all caste Hindus to look upon themselves as Harijans of the so-called lowest stratum. But what is the point in giving publicity to an inner change? The real proof is for the convert to practise the change in his daily life. He will, therefore, mix freely with Bhangis and take an active part in their life. If possible, he will live with them or get a Bhangi to live with him. He will give his children in marriage to Harijans and on being questioned he will say that he has become a Harijan of his own free will and will register his name either as a Harijan or Bhangi in the census when he has to classify himself. But having done so he will on no account arrogate to himself any of the rights of Harijans as, for example, he will not enter his name as a voter on their list. In other words, he will undertake to fulfil all the duties of a Harijan without seeking any of the rights that pertain to them. So long as separate voting lists are maintained he will cease to be a voter.[54]

I found it necessary to discuss this in some detail for two reasons. One is that it is sometimes said that Gandhi actually started this movement to postpone the Communal Award, which is as false as it can be. Secondly, it speaks of a strange tragedy of Gandhi's life. Whether you judge him to be right or wrong may depend on your ideological leanings. But the fact is that even though he prevented Dalits from being segregated from Hinduism he had to face severe opposition from the orthodoxy; and though he was the first one to propose representation of Dalits on the basis of their share in the population, he is equally severely criticized by Dalit leaders and intellectuals.

First Attack in India

After the Karachi session, Gandhi steadily developed the anti-untouchability movement as an important part of swaraj. After the Poona Pact, he started a weekly newspaper, *Harijan*, in February 1933 from prison itself. He chose this vocative for the so-called untouchables. In the same year, he opened several schools in Wardha, in which there was a system of training in handicrafts and other arts while trying to balance academic and physical education. After his release in 1934, he took a break from active politics and set out on a 'Harijan Yatra' from 7 November, visiting every corner of the country for the next nine months and actively campaigning against untouchability.

During this yatra, Gandhi reached Poona on 19 June 1934 and was invited to deliver a lecture by the local municipal authorities on 25 June. There were two identical cars in Gandhi's convoy. The car carrying Gandhi, Kasturba and two other women got stuck at a railway crossing and the second one reached the municipal building. To the people assembled it seemed that Gandhi had arrived, and as they proceeded to welcome him a loud bomb blasted which hit the municipal chief executive, two policemen and seven others. Taking advantage of the stampede, the assailants fled and it seems that there was no serious attempt to catch them later.

Pyarelal, who was a personal secretary to Gandhi, has written about this incident in his work *Mahatma Gandhi: The Last Phase*. He claims it to be a well-planned attack by the orthodox group of Poona which was associated with the Hindu Mahasabha. Jagan Phadnis has quoted Acharya S.D. Javdekar from his book *Jeevan Rahasya*:

> This Bomb was thrown by a person claiming himself as orthodox [sanatani], to express annoyance at the work of Gandhiji for the emancipation of the Harijans, while he was proceeding to accept the honour. The people who claimed to be orthodox Hindus felt that the Hindu religion could be saved only by eliminating Gandhi.

Hindu Mahasabha was the representative organization of the orthodoxy in Poona and Nathuram was an active member of the organization at that time. However, since no further inquiry was conducted, it is impossible to ascertain whether he was involved in this attack.

Phadnis has referred to numerous editorials and news items published in *Sakal*, the leading newspaper supporting the orthodoxy at the time, which indicate persistent and violent views among the orthodoxy against Gandhi. In its editorial titled 'Critics Angry over the Bomb' dated 2 July 1934, *Sakal* had said:

> It is not possible to suppress the sincere opinions and the selfless work of the orthodox people, who are leading movements of their choice, by taking advantage of the bomb blast and wrongly establishing their connection with it. All those who are trying to take the opportunity for revenge against a particular class, and that too of Brahmins, should remember well that it will never tolerate the atrocities.

The newspaper reports that Gandhi was attacked on 16 July 1934 in Karachi, when a Sanatani tried to kill him with an axe. On 19 July 1934, it reported that volunteers were attacked and assaulted by the orthodox elements in Kanpur when they were returning from a meeting in which Gandhi was felicitated. *Sakal* carries a noteworthy report in its edition of 20 July 1934. It says that on 15 July at Kashi, the president of the committee constituted for boycotting Mahatma Gandhi, Kamalnayanacharya, had declared that there ought to be a boycott of Gandhiji in Kashi of such proportions and intensity that would horrify high-profile politicians not only in India but also in England. Phadnis comments, 'The said new item was talking about boycotting Gandhiji. However, it suggested committing an act which would have a tremendous impact in England as well as in India. The suggestion appears to have been aimed not only at a boycott but at something more serious.'[55]

It is evident that this movement against untouchability had seriously disturbed the Hindu orthodoxy and they were hell bent on opposing it, even by violent means. Gandhi was correct in apprehending the caste system as the Achilles heel of the orthodoxy and was trying to abolish it by continuously attacking it. In a letter to Jawaharlal, he wrote:

> The fight against Sanatanists [orthodox Hindus who believe the doctrine of untouchability] is becoming more and more interesting, if also increasingly difficult. The one good thing is that they have been awakened from a long lethargy. The abuses they are hurling at me are wonderfully refreshing. I am all that is bad and corrupt

> on this earth. But the storm will subside. For I apply the sovereign remedy of ahimsa, non-retaliation. The more I ignore the abuses, the fiercer they are becoming. But it is the death dance of the moth round a lamp.[56]

Interestingly, Savarkar was also running a campaign against untouchability in Ratnagiri.[57] But he had to face absolutely no opposition from the orthodoxy! Not only that, they welcomed him when he arrived in Poona on 1 August 1937. He first joined the Tilakist Democratic Swaraj Party and then the Hindu Mahasabha. Neither did the orthodox Brahmins of Poona have any hesitation in accepting an atheist, nor did the anti-untouchability Savarkar scruple to join ranks with the pro-untouchability orthodox Hindu Mahasabha. Dhananjay Keer, who has written a 'devotional' biography of Savarkar, comments:

> The social views of most of them [the Hindu Mahasabha and Democratic Swaraj Party] were not in keeping with the revolutionary social views of Savarkar. They joined Savarkar because Savarkar had pitted himself against Gandhism. On his own part, Savarkar joined them because they were against Gandhi. Besides, the majority in them in Maharashtra were Brahmins who were not prepared to touch Savarkar's social views even with a pair of tongs.[58]

Thus, opposition to Gandhi was the only common thread to this unholy alliance of convenience. The orthodoxy was aware that a fundamental difference of approach towards untouchability existed between Gandhi and Savarkar. While it was a primary concern for Gandhi, to Savarkar it was secondary to his goal of Hindutva. Gandhi maintained that stance till his last breath. Even in Noakhali, while trying to save the lives and property of the Hindu minority, he didn't hesitate to register his disagreement about untouchability on the one hand and the practice of *naqab*-wearing on the other. After his return from Noakhali, he agreed to stay at Birla House only because Patel and others insisted that refugees were staying in the Harijan Colony, and his presence would be inconvenient for them. For Savarkar, the issue of untouchability faded away soon and he can be seen later siding with the orthodoxy on the questions of temple entry and untouchability. In 1939, as president of the Mahasabha, assuring the orthodox elements he said:

> Of course we should on no account molest or disrespect the sentiments of our Sanatani brothers so far as their personal freedom is concerned... In the meanwhile our Sanatani brothers may rest assured that barring the fundamental rights which every citizen is entitled to in public life, the Hindu Mahasabha will always refrain from having any recourse to law to thrust any religious reform on any sect within the Hindu fold even in the case of untouchability.[59]

While Savarkar was changing his views like dresses, to Gandhi these were uncompromising values of life.

Speaking at the public function in Poona after the failed attack, Gandhi said:

> It is unfortunate that this incident should take place when I was engaged in the work of Harijans. I do not wish to become a martyr. But I am ready if the time demands. To kill me is a very easy task. But why kill innocent persons in an attempt of murdering me? My wife and three girls, who are like my daughters, were in my car. What wrong have they committed?[60]

Gandhi's enemies seem to have accepted at least this appeal. Apart from the one on 20 January 1948, all other attempts to assassinate him targeted him alone.

Attacks on Gandhi: Attempts by the Ideological Group of Poona

In the initial stages of the Second World War, Gandhi was not in favour of non-cooperation at this difficult time.[61] But with the way this war was imposed on India, Gandhi strongly opposed it and took the clear stand that the British should leave India. After a meeting with the Viceroy on 5 February 1940, he sent a cable to Karl Heath: 'THANKS. NO SETTLEMENT POSSIBLE. DIVERGENCE [IS] TOO GREAT.'[62] A month later, the Ramgadh Congress declared not to extend any co-operation to the imperial government, whether financial or in terms of recruitment. When Gandhi started the Individual Satyagraha, the first volunteer to be detained was Vinoba Bhave, and then Jawaharlal Nehru was sentenced for four years' rigorous imprisonment. Patel and Maulana Azad were also arrested later.[63] In March 1942, he rejected the Cripps proposal of Dominion Status and demanded a withdrawal of the British in an orderly manner. He sent a proposal of 'Quit India' through Meeraben after the Allahabad Congress, and on the question of an alternative, reverted in an article published in *Harijan* on 24 May 1942: 'Leave India to her fate, to God or in modern parlance to anarchy.'[64] Next he coined the mantra of 'Do or Die' during the Bombay Congress, and on 8 August 1942 began the Quit India movement. The British government termed the Congress a rebel against its authority and arrested all its major leaders including Gandhi, and two days later, Congress was declared illegal.[65]

This was a big change in Gandhi who had supported the British during the First World War. It was the result of his first-hand experience of the suffering of his people and the oppressive policies of the British. Now he was openly calling British rule devilish. The Gandhi who was fond of the democratic vision of the British till the first decade of the twentieth century had now seen their real face, from Champaran to Jallianwala Bagh, and it was clear to him that colonial rule was oppressive to Indian people.

But Savarkar did not change his stand between these two wars. Praying for his release during the First World War, he wrote in 1914:

> Ever since this world shaking war that is now being fought in Europe has started, nothing has sent such a thrill of hope and enthusiasm in the heart of every true Indian patriot as the fact that Indians including the youth of India have been allowed to wear arms to fight against the common foe in defence of this country and the Empire... I most humbly beg to offer myself as a volunteer to do any service in the present war, that the Indian government think fit to demand from me. I know that the Kingdom does not depend on the help of an insignificant individual as I am, but then I know it also that every individual, however insignificant, is duty bound to volunteer his or her best for the defence of that Kingdom.[66]

Reading this entire letter, one wonders how Savarkar, who was so fiercely opposed to the British before his arrest, not only describes himself as a patriotic citizen of the English empire, but also talks about fighting on their side. Based on this letter, it is claimed that Savarkar was appealing not only for *his* release but that of all political prisoners. The authenticity of this claim can be gauged by noting two facts. First, there is no mention of 'others' in his earlier letters of clemency in 1911 and 1913. He was only appealing for his own release in these letters. Secondly, the stated reason behind the demand for the release of the remaining prisoners in this letter is that, were the British government to release them, they would not only be grateful to them but could be used for the British war effort! It is evident that this demand for release smacks of sycophancy when he claims that there were many others like him who were ready to accept British patronage on their release. At the same time, a skilled writer has made a clever attempt to show his dedication to the British government with flattery, asserting that if his release was an obstacle in the release of others who were willing to serve the British, then at least they should be released and given a chance to serve the imperial government. It is obvious that Savarkar was not demanding the release of those patriots who were ready to face all hardships of inhuman prison life but not the slavery of British rule. He was only trying to prove *his* loyalty to earn *his* release from the hardships of the Cellular Jail.

Savarkar was a free man at the time of the Second World War. It is often said that he wrote his apologies for his release so that he could come out and fight for the freedom of the country. But there was no change in his attitude after his release from jail. In his apology he promised to be an obedient servant of the British, and he was seen to be playing that role very sincerely for the rest of his life. He appealed, '... Hindus should come forward and get recruited in thousands into the army, navy, air force, artillery and other factories related with the War.'[67] He organized war councils to assist the Hindu youth interested in recruitment. The Viceroy reciprocated this by nominating his people to the National War Council and Savarkar duly thanked him for this.

Viceroy Linlithgow noted after a meeting with Savarkar on 9 October 1939 in Bombay:

> [Savarkar] said, ... that His Majesty's government must now turn to Hindus and work with their support. After all, though we and the Hindus have had a good deal of difficulty with one another in the past that was equally true of the relations between Great Britain and the French and as recent events had shown of relations between Russia and Germany. Our interests were now the same and we must therefore work together. Even though now the most moderate of

> men he had himself been in the past an adherent of a revolutionary party as possibly I might be aware. (I confirmed that I was.) But now our interests were so closely bound together the essential thing was for Hinduism and Great Britain to be friends and the old antagonism was no longer necessary. The Hindu Mahasabha, he went on to say favoured an unambiguous undertaking of Dominion Status at the end of war.[68]

He was eying an opportunity in exigency. Almost all the major leaders of Congress were either in jail or underground. He was hopeful of getting a good deal in lieu of his co-operation. Just as Jinnah, while co-operating with the British in their war effort, was claiming himself the sole representative of Muslims, and was trying to snatch Pakistan for himself, Savarkar was seeking recognition as the sole representative of the Hindus. Although, the Congress had demolished their claims in all elections held till then. Savarkar and the Hindu Mahasabha could only garner the support of a ridiculously small section of Hindus. Savarkar did not miss the opportunity to join ranks with Jinnah; their aims were identical now. One wanted a Muslim nation and the other wanted a Hindu one, while both were happy to be subordinates of the British under Dominion Status. When the Congress governments were sacked across the country due to the Quit India movement, the Muslim League and Hindu Mahasabha formed coalition governments in Sindh and Bengal in a blatant display of opportunism. It will be apt to remember that the Muslim League was invited to form its government after the then chief minister of Sindh, Allah Bux, was sacked for returning the title of 'Khan Bahadur' in support of the demand for the freedom of India,[69] and the 'nationalist' Hindu Mahasabha not only supported Muslim League but kept mum when the League brought in a resolution for Pakistan in the Assembly. Savarkar justified this tactic in the twenty-fourth session of the Hindu Mahasabha in Kanpur in the following words:

> In practical politics also the Mahasabha knows that we must advance through reasonable compromises. Witness the fact that only recently in Sind, the Sind-Hindu-Sabha on invitation had taken the responsibility of joining hands with the League itself in running [the] Coalition Government. The case of Bengal is well known. Wild Leaguers whom even the Congress with all its submissiveness

> could not placate grew quite reasonably compromising and sociable as soon as they came in contact with the HM and the Coalition Government, under the premiership of Mr Fazlul Huq and the able lead of our esteemed Mahasabha leader Dr Syama Prasad Mookerji, functioned successfully for a year or so to the benefit of both the communities.

While addressing the Madura Conference of the Hindu Mahasabha (twenty-second session) in 1940, Savarkar admitted that his party had been aligning with Muslim groups in different provinces in opposition to Congress. Savarkar unhesitatingly accepted that,

> *In the electoral field* also we have secured this year some notable successes which proved that at least the intelligent part of the Hindu electorate has unmistakably begun to realise that their best interests as Hindus could only be served by voting for the Sanghatanist representatives and that it is suicidal for Hindus to vote for a Congress candidate so long as he is bound to the Congress ideology. As a case in point, we may mention the hotly contested election to the Calcutta Corporation. The Bengal Hindusabha came out with flying colours at several polling stations in spite of the fact that it was the first time when Hindu Mahasabha openly challenged the long and firmly established monopoly of the Congress at the Hindu polls, and the consequence was that the Congress could not form a majority party in the corporation on their own ticket. At some other places, as for example in Sindh, Mahad, etc. we inflicted almost cent per cent defeat on the Congressites and got a clear majority.
>
> Thereupon the Sindh Provincial Hindusabha repudiated openly the pretensions of the Congress party to represent the Hindus and began to contest elections on Hindu tickets to Legislatures and local bodies. At several places they succeeded in inflicting defeats on the Congress candidates and today representatives of the Hindu Sanghatanist party form so influential a minority in the provincial legislatures and some of the local bodies as to be able very often to hold the balance so as to influence the formation of the Moslem Ministries themselves. In addition to that, there are two to three Hindu Ministers in the Ministry itself who are pledged to the Hindu ticket.[70]

The truth is, while the League did not deter from its demand for Pakistan and used this opportunity to strengthen itself, the Mahasabha happily played second fiddle to them. They were only interested in suppressing the Quit India movement. Syama Prasad Mukherjee's enthusiasm clearly shows the intent of the Hindu Mahasabha headed by Savarkar when he, as finance minister of the coalition government of Bengal, wrote to Sir John Herbert on 26 July 1942:

> Let me now refer to the situation that may be created in the province as a result of any widespread movement launched by the Congress. Anybody, who during the war, plans to stir up mass feeling, resulting internal disturbances or insecurity, must be resisted by any Government that may function for the time being.[71]

It is obvious that Savarkar and the Hindu Mahasabha were co-operating with the British in suppressing the Quit India movement. Savarkar, who was offering to fight for the British in the First World War was co-operating with them in the hope of getting a share of power in the Dominion state. The young Savarkar who termed 1857 as a common struggle of Hindus and Muslims, knew that after crushing this struggle, the then Governor of Bombay, Lord Elphinstone had noted in a meeting on 14 May 1859: '*Divide et Impeta* was the old Roman motto, and it should be ours.'[72] But the old Savarkar willingly participated in this imperial policy. Between the two world wars, his was an unprincipled self-seeking journey.

But this time he could not succeed. Despite the leadership being in jail, the Quit India movement gained unprecedented momentum. Gandhi's mantra 'Do or Die' caught the imagination of people across the length and breadth of the nation. The victory in the Second World War cost Britain dearly, and it was clear that their rule would not last long. As Gandhi commented, 'So much bloodshed for such a hollow victory!' Gandhi had also lost his health along with Kasturba and his secretary Mahadev Desai, whom he used to refer to as his fifth son. Poona's Agha Khan Palace seems like a magnificent building, but this old palace was the perfect place for malarial infections due to its marshy surroundings. Stanley Wolpert terms it worse than the most dreaded of Indian jails.[73] The whole nation protested for him to be released, which he was, finally, on 6 May 1944. He was infected with malaria and after staying for a few days in Bombay, was shifted to

Panchgani for rest on the advice of doctors. Freedom was at the door and so was the threat of partition. Gandhi had termed partition as anti-Islamic and profane. While in Panchgani, he continued to make contact with Jinnah and everyone else who could prevent partition.

It was here that Gandhi was attacked next. About twenty young men from Poona reached Panchgani by a chartered bus, and after roaming around the city chanting anti-Gandhi slogans, tried to attack Gandhi during his prayer meeting. Manishankar Purohit and Bhilare Guruji caught hold of the assailant and the attempt was averted. Purohit was the owner of the Surti Lodge of Poona and Guruji was a Congress worker who went on to become an elected member of the legislative assembly from Mahabaleshwar. Tushar Gandhi quotes Bhilare Guruji:

> Nathuram was brandishing a jambhiya, dagger. I grappled him with Manishankar Purohit and wrestled him to the ground. Gandhiji hailed us and instructed not to be rough with attackers. He wanted them to bring Nathuram to him so they could talk. Vishnu Karkare, Thatte, Badge and Gopal Godse were also present in the group which had arrived from Poona to hold anti-Gandhi demonstrations.[74]

Phadnis says that when Gandhi was in Panchgani, Godse had boasted to Joglekar, a reporter at his newspaper *Agrani*, that some important news would be received from Panchgani. The news was published in the 23 July 1944 edition of *The Times of India*, titled 'The people of RSS created havoc in the meeting of Gandhiji'. Mr M.A. David, editor of *Poona Herald*, filed an affidavit before the Justice Kapur Commission that Nathuram Godse had 'rushed towards Gandhiji carrying a knife with the intention of killing him on that day in Panchgani'.[75] However, Dr Sushila Nayyar, while disposing before the Commission, said that she did not remember anything and on the basis of her disposition the Commission did not confirm Godse's role in this attack. But in its concluding remark to this incident the Commission said:

> Although on this evidence the alleged incident of the attack and its alleged details cannot be held to be proved, the important fact which emerges is that there was in existence an organisation which was extremely anti-Gandhi and its members persisted in pursuing

> Mahatma Gandhi by creating disturbances at his meetings and their attitude was not non-violent. At Panchgani in 1944 the persons who disturbed the meeting were Poona people led by N.D. Apte who was later sentenced to death for the murder of the Mahatma. The factum of disturbance led by N.D. Apte is also supported by Ex. 34 dated August 1, 1944 which also shows that it was organised by the *Hindu Rashtra Dal*, which is a militant Hindu organisation in Poona.[76]

These incidents never perturbed Gandhi. Partition was the most important issue for him and he wanted to avert it through talks with Jinnah. He was still hopeful about dialogue, and after a reply from Jinnah in the affirmative, decided to proceed for Bombay on 9 September 1944. Pyarelal notes that Nathuram Godse and L.G. Thatte had declared that they would not allow these talks to happen. Thatte and Godse threatened that they would not let Gandhi move out of his ashram and would break the car that was to take him. Gandhi proposed to go all alone in their midst and proceed to Wardha (railway station) on foot, unless they themselves changed their mind and asked him to get into the car. The police had information that the assailants could cause some serious harm, so they first tried to persuade and then arrested them. A large-sized knife was confiscated from their leader. Pyarelal records:

> When the police officer who arrested him banteringly remarked that at any rate he…had had the satisfaction of becoming a martyr, quick came the reply, 'No, that will be when someone assassinates Gandhiji.' 'Why not leave it to the leaders to settle it among themselves? For instance, Savarkar…might come and do the job,' jocularly remarked the police officer in question. The reply was, 'That will be too great an honour for Gandhiji. The *jamadar* will be quite enough for the purpose.'
>
> The person referred to as *jamadar* was his fellow picketer—Nathuram Vinayak Godse. Three and a half years later the tragic prophecy was fulfilled.[77]

While Thatte was kept in detention, others were let go after this incident.[78] Concluding its assessment of this incident, the Kapur Commission wrote:

> This incident was only a pointer to the existence of the class of people and is corroborative of what was stated by Mr Munshi* about this school of thought in Poona which was extremely anti-Gandhi, and which did not hesitate to resort to political assassination.[79]

Gandhi may have been felled by a man's gun, but his killer was this ideological group. This ideological group continued to engage in violent acts. On 26 June 1947, there was a bomb blast in Poona. In this regard, one N.R. Athawale was caught, who revealed that Narayan Apte of *Agrani* had planned it. Apte was also arrested in this connection on 4 July 1947, but he was not monitored thereafter.[80] A bomb was thrown in Ahmednagar at the meeting of socialist leader Raosaheb Patwardhan. Karkare and Madanlal were found guilty in this connection. Despite the arrest order for both, the police remained idle. The report of the Kapur Commission indicates the involvement of a considerable number of people from the administration and police with this ideological group who shielded them.

The report refers to a meeting of the Provincial Hindu Mahasabha in Delhi on 18 January 1948, in which one Kesho Ram made a speech and characterized the Mahatma as a dictator, and said that he might meet the fate of Hitler soon.[81]

Gandhi had written an empathetic letter to Hitler on 24 December 1941:

> You are leaving no legacy to your people of which they will feel proud. They cannot take pride in a recital of cruel deeds, however skilfully planned. I therefore appeal you in the name of humanity to stop the war…[82]

Neither did Hitler have time to listen to him, nor did his Indian heirs who were trying to create a violent model based on the theories of racial supremacists of the West in response to the Gandhian model based on a distinctive Indian modernism. Nor did Gandhi know that his assassins would someday find such heirs who would be proud of the legacy of these conspirators and apologists of the British.

---

* Kanaiyalal Maneklal Munshi was a Congress leader at the time. He later joined the Swatantra Party and Jana Sangh. He was also a founding member of the Vishwa Hindu Parishad.

3. Last Days: Delhi, Noakhali, Delhi

> I have not convinced India. There is violence all around us. I am a spent bullet.
>
> —Gandhi to his biographer Louis Fischer, on 26 June 1946[1]

The last days of Gandhi were ones of disquietude and loneliness. He repeatedly tried to lead an apolitical life. Attempting to provide equal facilities to the poor at a naturopathy centre in Poona, or migrating to an unknown village, he was constantly trying to adopt social work as an alternative to politics. He resigned from the primary membership of the Congress in 1934, but after being in politics all his life, politics was not ready to leave him in this period of turmoil.

Independence was round the corner and every political group was eager to snatch its pound of flesh. The transfer of power was almost certain after the Second World War, but the British were not going to relinquish their prized possession without securing their international interests in the post-colonial world. The growing communal animosity was bliss for them. Muriel Lester has quoted Gandhi in her memoir where he admits that the policy of divide and rule was only successful because communal and caste divisions are deep-rooted in Indian society. The British only widened those cracks and communal organizations like the RSS, Hindu Mahasabha and Muslim League aided their effort. Churchill never wanted the existence of an undivided India and in Pakistan he was eying a future ally. History proved him right.[2] Jinnah was adamant for Pakistan at any cost. Gandhi's efforts to pacify him through friendly dialogue proved futile. Gandhi tried to establish nationalist leaders like Khan Abdul Ghaffar Khan, but amidst the communal frenzy of that time, the appeals of leaders like Khan Abdul Ghaffar Khan or Maulana Azad could not produce the desired effect, and Jinnah's clout only grew with time. Gandhi enjoyed massive support from Muslims during his Khilafat Movement. The Ali brothers were his close comrades in that movement. But the surviving Ali brother, Shaukat Ali, who was hailing Gandhi as 'my chief' in his absence during the First Round Table Conference, had changed his allegiance by the second conference.[3]

Gandhi does not talk much about the Khilafat movement in the later part of his life. But it's ironical that Jinnah, who condemned the movement for being communal, was openly practising communal politics in the later part of his life. Gandhi could not create an antidote for his politics. After the elections of 1937, Jinnah wanted to join provincial governments with the Congress. While Patel was willing to accept this proposal, Nehru was not ready to give any space to communal forces. Gandhi replied helplessly, 'I wish I could do something, but I am utterly helpless. My faith in unity is as bright as ever; only I see no daylight out of the impenetrable darkness.' It was to be the last time Jinnah would appeal politely for Gandhi's help in winning the support of his more radical young Congress friends for any multi-party provincial cooperation.[4]

The talks of 1944 have been discussed above. Gandhi participated in them as an individual, but Jinnah came as the undisputed leader of the Muslim League. Gandhi commented after that failed dialogue that Jinnah wanted a treaty, but did not know what he wanted. But the fact is that Jinnah clearly wanted a separate nation for the Muslims under his command and was ready to go to any lengths for that.[5] Talks were bound to fail because Gandhi was not ready to accept partition and Jinnah was not ready to accept anything less than partition. While Gandhi unequivocally refuted this theory during the talks—'I am unable to accept the proposition that the Muslims of India are a nation, distinct from the rest of the inhabitants of India. Mere assertion is no proof. The consequences of accepting such a proposition are dangerous in the extreme. Once the principle is admitted there would be no limit to claims for cutting up India…which would spell India's ruin'[6]—Savarkar and the Hindu Mahasabha were echoing Jinnah on the issue of the two-nation theory. Savarkar made it clear during a press conference in 1945:

> I have no quarrel with Mr Jinnah's two nation theory. We, the Hindus are a nation by ourselves, and it is a historical fact that the Hindus and the Muslims are two nations.[7]

It is ironical that Godse and his admirers blame Gandhi for Partition! Gandhi was perhaps the only political personality at the time who could see the catastrophe that would result from the partition. His comment after the failed talks of 1944 could be revisited in this regard:

> [I am] convinced that Mr Jinnah is a good man [but] he is suffering from hallucination when he imagines that an unnatural division of India could bring either happiness or prosperity to the people concerned.[8]

The devastation at the time of Partition and the subsequent tensions caused by communal hatred in both countries have justified Gandhi's fears. Jinnah knew that the only obstacle in his way was Gandhi. In a letter to Yahya Bakhtiyar in 1945, he says, 'What I am afraid of is… Gandhi. He has brains and always tried to put me in the wrong. I have to be on guard and alert all the time.'[9]

Imminent Independence and the Divided House

Gandhi returned a dejected man from Simla. The proposal offered by Churchill, keeping the forthcoming elections in England in view, was nothing but a farce. Lord Wavell had accepted before the British parliament that virtually nothing was being conceded.[10] Jinnah was adamant that the League should be recognized the sole representative of Muslims, and the then president of Congress, Maulana Azad was naturally not ready to endorse this claim. Without going into the details, it will suffice to quote Prof Sucheta Mahajan:

> A study of the Simla Conference is a revelation of the 'communal' roots of British policy—roots which penetrated the terms of the

> offer, the actual proceedings of the Conference, its breakdown and the subsequent post-mortem. A communal conception of politics underlay the offer itself. 'Caste Hindus' and Muslims were put on par, as were the Congress and the League, by being recognized as the main representative parties of the two communities. Even the Government's denial of the legitimacy of Jinnah's claim to be the sole spokesman of the Muslims did not constitute, as would seem at first sight, a digression beyond the communal parameters of the British policy. For the ground for rejection was not the necessity of including a Congress-nominated Muslim but the need to reward the loyalism of the Punjab Muslims. Wavell's counter-proposal of four nominations from the League and one selection from the Unionists was a balance between the claims of the communalists and those of the loyalists, the other bulwark of British rule. The '4 plus 1' formula was 'virtual refusal to regard the Congress as a non-Hindu, secular organization, and acceptance of Jinnah's contention that it was as much a communal party as the League'.[11]

However, when Attlee replaced Churchill the next year, a delegation of three cabinet ministers was sent to reach some agreement before power transfer. Sir Stafford Cripps, Lord Pethick-Lawrence and A.V. Alexander reached Delhi in March 1946. The mission is referred to as the Cabinet Mission. While the minority was given a veto power in the Simla proposals, Attlee declared in the House of Commons on 15 March 1946 that a 'minority will not be allowed to place a veto on the progress of the majority'. Since this speech was made on the eve of the departure of the Cabinet Mission to India, it was taken to be an expression of the Mission's likely stand.[12] Cripps and Pethick-Lawrence were old friends of Gandhi. When Gandhi came to Delhi to meet them, he stayed in the Bhangi Colony as always. The prisoners of war from the Indian National Army (INA) were on trial at the time, and an INA defence committee with lawyers like Bhulabhai Desai and Asaf Ali was constituted under the chairmanship of Jawaharlal Nehru.[13] Gandhi had met them at Red Fort, and when the soldiers of the INA came to meet him at Bhangi Colony after their release, the evening turned musical with anthems dear to Subhas Chandra Bose.

Jawaharlal Nehru, outside the office of the INA Defence Committee.

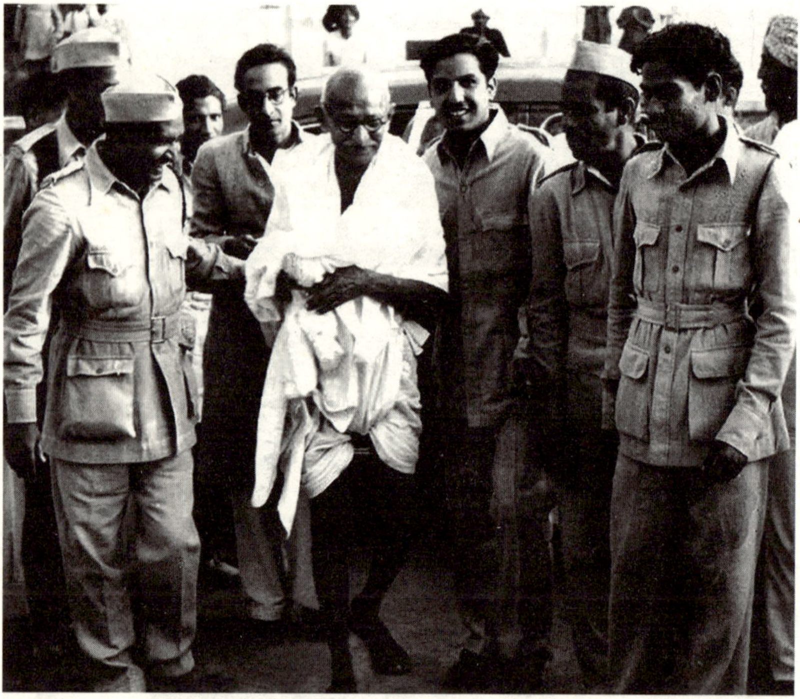

Gandhi with the fighters of the Indian National Army.

This was also the time when communal tensions were rising to an alarming level. A *shakha*—branch—was started by the RSS at the same ground where Gandhi used to organize his prayer meeting in the evening.[14] Prayer meetings were frequently interrupted. Prayer messages from all religions were read in Gandhi's prayer meetings, but one evening in the last week of March—

> ... [W]hen Manu began to recite the Muslim credo, an angry young Hindu rushed up to her, shouting, 'You go away from here. This is a Hindu temple!' Gandhi told the intruder he was free to leave, and that the others wanted to pray. The young fanatic refused to be silenced... At another prayer meeting that week, two well-dressed sturdy young Hindus rose to tell Gandhi to leave their temple. 'This temple belongs to Bhangis,' Gandhi replied. 'I too am a Bhangi.' The arrogant toughs remained standing, however, shouting at him. Now the others shouted that he should continue to pray. Gandhi tried to

> pray softly. 'Go to the Punjab,' someone shouted. Those standing near the man tried to force him out, but Gandhi urged patience, his Ahimsa now tried to its passionate limits. Then, wisely, he opted to leave the platform, sensing perhaps that his life was in danger. Still, Delhi's police took no notice, arrested none of the disrupters.[15]

Digambar Badge had stated during defence lawyer V.V. Oak's cross-examination in the Gandhi murder case on 27 July that both Apte and Godse were among the protesters at Gandhi's prayer meetings in the Bhangi Colony.

The Mission held talks with every stakeholder for the next two and a half weeks, but the deadlock continued. There were only two options for power transfer. One was to accept Jinnah's contention and divide India along religious lines and the other was to accept Congress's claim that it represented the whole country. Interestingly, most of the British administrators were against partition and wanted to keep India within the Commonwealth so that British influence could be maintained even after the transfer of power. Congress was against such a proposal. Except for that of Bengal, every governor was against partition at that point of time.[16]

A consensus was arrived at, to some extent, on a second proposal under which a federal government was proposed where the states were to be divided into three groups on the basis of their religious demography. Hindu-majority states, i.e. Madras, Bombay, Central Provinces, Bihar and Orissa were to be clubbed in Group A, while the Muslim-dominated states of the West (Punjab, Sindh and North-West Frontier Province) and East (Bengal and Assam) were to be Group B and C, respectively. All the groups were to be autonomous and the centre was proposed to have control over security, foreign affairs and communication. Both the League and Congress agreed on this, but differences emerged on the question of the right of states to exit from their respective groups. While Congress wanted states to have a right to exit, the League opposed it. The reason was simple: there were Congress governments in Assam in the east and in the North-West Frontier Province in the west and they were not ready to work under the patronage of the League. The Cabinet Mission intentionally left the right to join a group unclear. The Congress and the League interpreted this in their own way, accepting the long-term proposals of the Cabinet Mission Plan on 6 June and 24 June, respectively. Jinnah was informed by the British authorities on 25 June they were satisfied with the answers and that both parties were entitled to join the interim government. If the Congress refused to join the government on the question of the right to exit and the right to join a group, then the Viceroy would form the interim government and try to include the maximum members of the parties agreeing to the proposal.

Gandhi understood the fact that it would not be possible to run a joint interim government, and repeatedly asked the Viceroy to call either one of them to form the government. He was sceptical about the success of the long-term plan of the Constituent Assembly without a short-term plan to establish an interim government. On 24 June he advised his fellow Congressman:

> Whatever the Cabinet Mission may say or write it will remain in their mouths or on the printed paper. They have opened here a Reform Office. Whatever they do and the interpretation they put will be final. The Government office not being in your hands you cannot have control over it. You should consider all this. You should do nothing in haste.[17]

But his colleagues were thinking otherwise and were keen to form a government. His advice to the Congress Working Committee to reject the long-term proposition without its being linked to the short-term plan of the interim government had few takers. He conceded his defeat in the Working Committee on 2 June 1946, 'I admit defeat. You are not bound to act upon my unsupported suspicion. You should follow my intuition only if it appeals to your reason. Otherwise you should take an independent course. I shall now leave with your permission. You should follow the dictates of your reason.' A hush fell over the gathering. Nobody spoke for some time. Abul Kalam Azad then asked, 'What do you desire? Is there any need to detain Bapu any further?' Gandhiji returned to his residence.[18] Finally, the Cabinet Mission issued a statement that, after the elections to the Constituent Assembly, there would be a new attempt to form the government.

The most prominent fact amid all these technical matters is the lack of any kind of trust between the Congress and the League.

Jinnah constantly disagreed and was demanding that the elections to the Constituent Assembly be postponed as the case of the interim government had been postponed. He was not ready to recognize the Congress or nationalist Muslims as Muslim voices. The Congress wanted to include Maulana Azad in the cabinet, but Jinnah insisted that the Congress should only propose upper-caste Hindus. Gandhi had written to Pethick-Lawrence on 12 June 1946:

> It will be wrong on my part if I advise the Congress to wait indefinitely until the Viceroy has formed the Interim Government or throws up the sponge in despair. Despair he must, if he expects to bring into being a coalition Government between two incompatibles. The safest, bravest and the straightest course is to invite that party to form a government which, in the Viceroy's estimation, inspires greater confidence. Then there is a possibility within 24 hours of forming a National Government. If, however, no party inspires confidence such a declaration should be made and the Viceroy should run the Government in the best way he knows.[19]

This incompatibility between the Congress and League was growing with each new day. In the previous elections for the state legislative held in the winter of 1946, the Muslim League had won 428 out of 492 Muslim seats while the Congress won 930 out of 968 general seats.[20] Gandhi's repugnance for these elections could be gauged by his letter to Maheshdutta Mishra written on 1 March 1946:

> What you wrote about the election is all right. It was unnecessary for me, but not for you, since you wanted to make a clean breast of everything. I have not shown your letter to anyone nor do I intend to. Many things happened in the election in which I took no interest, nor did I do anything about them. You already know about Rajaji. The outcome is that Rajaji has withdrawn from it.[21]

Gandhi was not interested in this tug of war for power, but both the Congress and the League were buoyant after the results. However, these results were a clear validation of the claim of Jinnah that the League was the sole representative of Muslims. In fact, he took these elections as a referendum for Pakistan and used the election campaign to build consensus for it.[22]

The Congress agreed to the proposals of the Cabinet Mission for a continuous strengthening of the centre, while for Jinnah there was a roadmap for Pakistan in the two Muslim-dominated state groupings. As Bipan Chandra has noted, 'Patel maintained that the Mission's plan was against Pakistan, that the League's veto was gone and that one Constituent Assembly was envisaged. The League announced its acceptance of the plan on 6 June in so far as the basis of Pakistan was implied in the Mission's plan by virtue of the compulsory grouping.'[23] Gandhi was also hopeful that the partition could be avoided through this plan. He wrote in *Harijan* on 12 March: '[T]he answer [whether India will be divided or not] will be known within a few months, if not weeks. And I am not the only optimist this time.'[24]

It is obvious that the agreement on the surface was marred with disagreements. Members of the Cabinet Mission returned on 29 June 1944 dejected,[25] and by July their plan was in tatters. Nehru was maintaining that the matter will be finalized in the Constituent Assembly where the Congress had a decisive majority, but Jinnah had no faith in the Congress and was not ready for anything less than Pakistan. Stanley Wolpert records that:

> At his first press conference after resuming his presidency of the Congress in early July 1946, Nehru insisted that Congress would enter the forthcoming Constituent Assembly 'completely unfettered by agreements and free to meet all situations as they arise'. This was a blatant repudiation of the Cabinet Mission's plan, especially the virtual autonomy promised to the groups of provinces, without which Jinnah's League would have rejected, instead of having accepted, the plan. When Jinnah read the press reports of Nehru's statement, he was outraged, calling on the Muslim League to prepare for 'direct action', bidding 'good-bye to constitutions and constitutional methods'. Gandhi was almost equally surprised at his...impulsive behavior. 'If it is correctly reported, some explanation is needed,' he wrote to Jawaharlal. 'It must be admitted that we have to work within the limits of the State Paper... If we do not admit even this much...Jinnah Saheb's accusation will prove true.' But Nehru refused to retract a single word he said, not fearing Jinnah's threats and not caring for Bapu's anxiety.[26]

On 19 July 1946, Jinnah declared the commencement of Direct Action from the 16th of August. Gandhi's scepticism proved well-founded. He wrote in a letter to Vallabhbhai Patel in late July:

> A great many things seem to be slipping out of the hands of the Congress. The postmen* do not listen to it, nor does Ahmedabad, nor do Harijans, nor Muslims. This is a strange situation indeed.[27]

Cities of the Dead and A Restless Gandhi

> My technique of non-violence was on trial.
>
> —Gandhi, on 1 November 1946[28]

To Gandhi, Congress was not only a means to attain power but an institution to realize the dream of swaraj which was more than mere political freedom. A transfer of power from the British to Indians was not enough to attain swaraj. In an article published in *Harijan* on 28 July 1946, he said:

> Independence must begin at the bottom. Thus, every village will be a republic or panchayat having full powers. It follows, therefore, that every village has to be self-sustained and capable of managing its affairs even to the extent of defending itself against the whole world. It will be trained and prepared to perish in the attempt to defend itself against any onslaught from without. Thus, ultimately, it is the individual who is the unit. This does not exclude dependence on and willing help from neighbours or from the world. It will be free and voluntary play of mutual forces. Such a society is necessarily highly cultured in which every man and woman knows what he or she wants and, what is more, knows that no one should want anything that others cannot have with equal labour.[29]

One may recall a famous quote by Bhagat Singh where he asserts that mere replacement of the British by Indians was not enough to revolutionize India. He was appealing to the youth to go to the farms and factories, to unite the proletarians in order to make an

---

* The reference is to the postal strike in Bombay and communal riots in Ahmedabad.

egalitarian society, in his last letters. Both were visionaries in search of a better future for their people. There is no doubt that their ideological positions were different and so were their dreams of the future of India, but both were undeterred revolutionaries ready to die for their faith. Bhagat Singh had departed after his supreme sacrifice but Gandhi was restlessly witnessing the withering of his dreams.

As the days of transfer of power approached, an all-engrossing discord was clearly visible. The moral degradation of a section of the Congress was more than obvious and violence had replaced the technique of non-violence almost all over country. Gandhi's desperation can be seen in his writings of that period,[30] but he had not lost all hope yet. He wrote on 10 March 1946: 'I want to live for 125 years and, if God fulfils my wish, I want to create a new world in India.'[31] His determination to create this 'new world' was so profound that amidst all this political turmoil, he was consulting on matters ranging from naturopathy to untouchability in his replies to the letters of common people, who remained his strength all through his life. He was co-operating with the Cabinet Mission but knew well that only an understanding between Hindus and Muslims could prevent partition, and that it was vain to expect the British to help in establishing solidarity between the two communities.[32] He was apprehensive about something, and wrote on 12 June, 'A nameless fear has seized me that all is not well. As a result, I feel paralysed.'[33]

'Direct action' was a catastrophic assault on Gandhi's dreams. Despite their differences with the League, none from Congress ever expected that the League would go to this extent. The atmosphere was already tense. There were riots in Aligarh in March 1946,[34] a postal strike in Bombay and communal riots in Ahmedabad. These incidents in Congress-ruled states were naturally disturbing for Gandhi. The nationalist Muslims of the Congress were on target. Sir Shafaat Ahmed Khan was killed in Simla while Shafi Ahmed Kidwai was killed in Mussoorie.[35] National Guards, the military organization of the League, had earlier attacked leaders like Maulana Hussain Ahmad Madani, Maulana Abdul Razzaq, Maulana Muhammad Qasim Shahjahanpuri, Maulana Hifzur Rehman, Maulana Syed Mohammad Nasir and Saifuddin Kitchlew, who were staunch opponents of the

League and votaries of Hindu–Muslim unity. A cousin of Khan Abdul Ghaffar Khan, Ataullah Khan was killed in NWFP by militants of the National Guards along with his wife and numerous followers.[36] Fundamentalism was gaining ground under the leadership of the League, on one hand, and organizations like the RSS and Hindu Mahasabha, on the other.[37] Gandhi's anxiety and his disagreement over the methods applied in prevention are obvious in a letter written to Morarji Desai, the then home minister of Bombay, after the Ahmedabad riots.[38] But his comment on religious intoxication in the 28 July issue of *Harijan* is even more significant:

> In my childhood a cousin of mine and I took *bhang* and laughed and laughed at each other like two mad men. When morning came and we were sober, we were both ashamed of ourselves and could not face each other. That intoxication was comparatively harmless but this is frightful.[39]

The religiosity of Gandhi could not blind him to religious bigotry. He was clearly differentiating between being religious and being a fanatic, and was equating that to *bhang*, an intoxicating substance. The ideologues of Hindutva want to replace religion with this intoxication. One may note that even Marx had compared religion to opium. But he also described it as 'the sigh of the oppressed creature, the heart of a heartless world, and the soul of soulless conditions'. To him, every organized religion creates an illusion of happiness and thus 'the abolition of religion as the illusory happiness of the people is the demand for their real happiness. To call on them to give up their illusions about their condition is to call on them to give up a condition that requires illusions'.[40] In the example given by Gandhi, the incident of intoxication is an aberration to normal behaviour, but to an addict it is the rule. While Gandhi considers intoxication an occasional disorientation of people, to Marx it is interwoven in the concept of organized religion. Thus, Gandhi tends to fight within religion, while Marx wanted to abolish it altogether for establishing a peaceful society. The difference is obvious, but what is common to both is the quest for real happiness of mankind. Since their ideological base is different, it is natural that the concept of happiness is different for the two. But this helps understand why the religious Gandhi and the atheist Marx are equally disliked by fundamentalist forces.

Jinnah launched Direct Action to attain Pakistan by igniting this fanaticism to bypass constitutional means. He had repeatedly threatened this but neither Nehru nor Patel or anyone else in the Congress took it seriously. During a meeting with the Cripps Mission, Patel had said, '[I]f driven to it the Congress could create more trouble than Jinnah's 100 mullahs could and that if left to control the situation, the Congress Government was quite willing and capable of managing and controlling the situation which Jinnah could create', while Nehru mocked it 'as a party of landlords unable to indulge in any form of direct action'.[41] But Gandhi saw it differently. He wrote to Patel on 24 July 1946:

> There are other strikes on top of the postal strike. All this looks pretty significant. It is necessary that you and others should think about it very seriously. The Congress position may seem strong on the surface but it appears to have lost its hold on the people.[42]

But even Gandhi could not have foreseen violence of such magnitude. The very concept of Direct Action was against all those values which Gandhi had propagated and experimented with for the last five decades. Pakistan was first demanded during the Lahore conference of the League in 1940. Jinnah fought for it for six years and was now adamant, and declared in the Delhi conference during 6–9 April 1946 that 'this time Muslim India is not going to remain passive or neutral', and most of the other leaders openly threatened to resort to violent means.[43] Violence started in Calcutta on 16 August. A quote from Yasmin Khan's book *The Great Partition* helps understand this macabre incident. In a chapter titled 'Trust Collapsed', she writes:

> The streets of Calcutta were eerily empty on the morning of 16 August 1946. The Muslim League provincial government had called a public holiday to mark Direct Action day. Three days later at least 4,000 of Calcutta residents lay dead and over 10,000 were injured. The streets were deserted once again. Now the scene was one of carnage, buildings reduced to rubble, rubbish uncollected from the street, telephone and power lines severed. Schools, courts mills and

> shops stay closed… In the intervening days, the worst riots between Hindus and Muslims ever remembered in India, broke out.[44]

Sucheta Mahajan gives the number of dead at over five thousand.[45] Nirmal Kumar Bose records:

> The offensive began from the side of Muslim mobs; but, within a few hours, the Hindus, who rightly or wrongly felt that the government was entirely apathetic or had abdicated in favour of the rowdy elements, also struck back. The resistance stiffened in the course of the next three days; and, in the meanwhile, Calcutta saw the murder of several thousand men, women and children. The worst part of it was that people did not engage in open combat, it was the defenceless minority within each quarter of the town which was actually done brutally to death. Sensitive people lost their sensitiveness and became brutalized in the atmosphere of insecurity which prevailed on account of the virtual collapse of civilized government.
>
> The mutual slaughter continued for some weeks, the virulence abated, but the distrust and repugnance which had come into being in course of the brutalities, poisoned the roots of human relationships. And men began to air the view openly that Hindus and Muslims were so different from one another that it was not possible for them to live side by side.[46]

The riots broke out all over the country. Gandhi was shocked. This was a catastrophe for all his efforts till now. He wrote on 19 August from Sevagram:

> If newspaper reports are to be believe [*sic*], responsible ministers in Sindh and other equally responsible Leaguers almost all over, are preaching violence in naked language. Nakedness is itself a virtue as distinguished from hypocrisy. But when it is a hymn of obscenity, it is a vice to be shunned, whether it resides in a Leaguer or any other person. Any Muslim who is not in the League is a traitor, says one. The Hindu is a *kafir* deserving the fate of such, says another.
>
> Calcutta had given an ocular demonstration of what direct action is and how it is to be done.
>
> Who is the gainer? Certainly not the Muslim masses nor the sober followers of Islam which itself means sobriety and peace. The very salute *salaam alaikum* means 'peace be unto you'.

> Violence may have its place in life but not that which we have witnessed in Calcutta, assuming of course that newspaper accounts are to be trusted. Pakistan of whatever hue does not lie through senseless violence. When I write of senseless violence, I naturally assume the possibility of sensible violence, whatever the latter may be. The Calcutta demonstration was not an illustration of sensible violence.
>
> ... Calcutta has earned a bad repute of late. It has seen too many wild demonstrations during the past few months. If the evil reputation is sustained for some time longer, it will cease to be the City of Palaces, it will become the city of the dead.[47]

But Jinnah was moving fast towards his aim through Direct Action. Wavell met Gandhi and Nehru in the end of August and opined that only a joint government could prevent communal violence. He requested resumption of talks with Jinnah. But both Gandhi and Nehru held Wavell responsible for the trouble and communicated this to London through his emissary Sudhir Ghose. As a result, a joint government was installed, on one hand, and Wavell was replaced by Mountbatten, on the other.

Alone...Towards Noakhali

> It is no kindness; and if it is, it is kindness to myself. My own doctrine was failing. I don't want to die a failure but as a successful man. But it may be that I may die a failure.
>
> —Gandhi, in Noakhali[48]

While answering a question by a student in London during the Second Round Table Conference, Gandhi had asserted that the 'bugbear of communalism is confined largely to the cities, which are not India'.[49] To him the real India resided in its villages and they were not yet infected by the 'bugbear of communalism'. But Direct Action shattered this belief and shook the very base of his ideological position.

The goons of the League had played havoc in the rural belt of East Bengal. Robert Payne writes:

> Their task was to kill Hindus, to humiliate, dispossess and torture any survivors. Men were murdered in cold blood and their houses set on fire, their women raped or mutilated or thrown into wells, their children hacked to pieces. This was deliberate massacre, carefully planned and well executed by men who knew what they are doing. The massacre began on October 10, 1946, and continued uninterruptedly for about a week. During all that time no news of the events in Noakhali reached the outside world. By October 20 some survivors fled to Calcutta, and the news spread all over India. The Hindus now realized that the civil war, begun tentatively with the four days of 'Direct Action' had been resumed.[50]

What happened in the districts of Noakhali and Tippera was an antecedent to the bloodcurdling events during Partition. The hatred spread by communal forces was an indelible blot on our glorious struggle for independence; it was a test for the ideals of Gandhi. He told senior Congress leader Satish Chandra Dasgupta to visit Noakhali with other workers and report as soon as possible[51] and then sent Acharya Kriplani and his wife Sucheta Kriplani to take stock of the situation in the affected areas.[52] After going through the frightening reports, he declared on 23 October, after his meeting with Nehru and the Congress Working Committee: 'The fact that I go there will satisfy the soul and may be of some use.' Gandhi was apprehensive about the support of Muslims in those areas. When the journalist Preston Grover asked him whether Muslims will listen to him, he said, 'I don't know. I don't go with any expectation, but I have the right to expect it. A man who goes to do his duty only expects to be given strength by God to do his duty.'[53] Unlike Champaran or Bardoli, Gandhi chose to tread this path alone, except for Nirmal Kumar Bose, who readily accepted his offer to help him as an interpreter. His memoir *My Days With Gandhi* is a first-hand document of this mission.

Bose informs us:

> Noakhali is a district in Bengal in which the population is 18% Hindu and 82% Muslim. The landed proprietors are mostly Hindu and collectively they own about three fourths of the land. Noakhali is also a renowned centre of orthodox Islam. It is the district which sends out most of the Muslim divines and priests to the

> rest of Bengal; and these divines had consistently propagated the political ideas of the League. All through the League Government in Bengal, for about ten years, Noakhali had also been the seat of peasant discontent. The revision of Tenancy Laws as well as the new arrangements made for the repayment of peasants' debts initiated by the League Government had considerably weakened the economic strength of the propertied classes of Bengal; and many of the landholders had been compelled to migrate to the towns, where they now invested their capital in banking, insurance or trade instead of investing it any further in land or unprotected usury.
>
> This was the economic position of the district. Geographically, it is one of the estuarine districts, where communication for a large part of the year is by means of waterways. And in October 1946, when most of the land was still under water, enthusiastic Muslim leaders of the district struck a heavy blow upon local Hindu inhabitants. The actual onslaught began on the night of the 10th, during the celebration of the Lakshmi Puja, when the Goddess of Prosperity is worshipped by the Hindu people. The outside world was however kept completely in the dark about the events for over a week, for the Government succeeded in blacking out all news.[54]

When Gandhi reached Sodpur on 29 October 1946, Calcutta was already reeling under anarchy. Gandhi heard everyone in detail; he wanted to gather the actual facts before committing himself to any particular line of action. During the prayer meeting organized on the same day he said, 'I had come to Calcutta with a blank mind to do His will. What I could do here and how long I would stay in Bengal, I did not know. All I could say was that I had not come to stay in Calcutta... My proper place is Noakhali.'[55]

The next day he met the Governor Sir Frederick Burrows on his personal invitation. He asked him what he could do in order to restore peace in Bengal. Gandhi was straightforward—the British governor could do nothing. He could only quit in terms of the British government's proposal as early as possible. Gandhi repeatedly said that violence would only help the British postpone the transfer of power. The communal game of the imperial power was laid bare before him. Major General Roy Bucher, the then chief of the Eastern Command of the army in India, also met Gandhi at Government

House. To his offer of military aid, Gandhi's reply had been that if the Chief Minister needed such service he would undoubtedly call for it; but then the military would have to function completely under the civil administration. There could be no question of the abdication of a popular government in favour of the military.

While he was returning past one of the predominantly Muslim quarters of Calcutta an iron ring was hurled at his car, which fortunately did not hurt anybody but flew past between the passengers seated within. Bose opined, however, that it was not directed, in any case, against Gandhiji's person.

The Chief Minister of Bengal and other Leaguers did not want him to visit Noakhali and requested him to postpone it for some time. But Gandhi was adamant about going there at the earliest. While in Calcutta he heard the news of communal violence in Bihar where the Congress was in power and where the victims were Muslims. Seven thousand people were killed in communal clashes across Bihar.[56] When he was asked why he was not visiting Ahmedabad, Bombay or Chhapra, he replied:

> I would certainly have gone to any of the places… If anything approaching what had happened at Noakhali had happened there and if I had felt that I could do nothing without being on the spot. It was the cry of outraged womanhood that had peremptorily called me to Noakhali.[57]

Nehru and Patel reached Bihar and appealed for peace. Gandhi wrote in an open letter to Bihar on 6 November:

> A bad act of one party is no justification for a similar act by the opposing party, more especially when it is rightly proud of its longest and largest political record. I must confess, too, that although I have been in Calcutta for over a week I do not yet know the magnitude of the Bengal tragedy. Though Bihar calls me, I must not interrupt my programme for Noakhali. And is counter-communalism any answer to the communalism of which Congressmen have accused the Muslim League? Is it Nationalism to seek barbarously to crush the fourteen per cent of the Muslims in Bihar?[58]

He reduced his intake of food to undertake some measure of penance for the happenings in Bihar[59] and proceeded for Noakhali the same day. The Government of Bengal had provided a special train fitted with a microphone for Gandhiji and his party. The train left Sodpur station at about eleven in the morning.

People gathered in large numbers on the stations en route and Gandhi, while addressing them, said that he was merely a servant of God, that 'Bengal had touched his heart deeply, and his duty was to wipe away the tears of his suffering sisters'. He had come to Bengal not for one day or one week but for as long as his services were needed in the province. He warned the audience against believing that he had come to set one community against another:

> His object in coming to Noakhali was to ask the Hindus never to run away from their homes even if they happened to be in a microscopic minority. They should try to live with the Muslims where they were. Both had been nourished by the same corn which grew in the fields and both had quenched their thirst with water from the same river. Even if their brother came to slay them, they should refuse to run away, but make every effort to live with him in peace, without sacrificing honour.[60]

For the next three months, he tried to spread the message of courage, non-violence and respect. But he was very clear that the responsibility for establishing peace and providing relief lay with the government. Mere criticism was not enough and posting Hindu officers in place of Muslim officers would not suffice. The people in power must do their duty. He met the responsible officers and representatives of Bengal and pressed them to take action. Bose has narrated an interesting incident:

> Rumour had it that when the riots started in Noakhali the Muslim Superintendent of Police played some part in encouraging the rowdies by his complete inactivity. Some even went so far as to say that his co-operation was not always passive but active at times. Shortly before Gandhiji left for the prayer meeting on the 7th, E.F. McInerny, the District Magistrate, came to pay him a visit. As both emerged from the room, they found Abdullah Sahib, the Superintendent of Police, seated upon a bench nearby. Abdullah Sahib stood up and the Magistrate introduced him to Gandhiji,

> who said with a laugh, 'Aha, so you are the Superintendent of Police. People say that you are a wicked person. Is that really so?' Abdullah Sahib naturally felt very embarrassed at the question; but Gandhiji said to him, 'Now come along with me.' And all of them proceeded to the prayer ground which was about a hundred yards away.[61]

McInerny had earlier issued an official notice which said that unless proved to the contrary, he would assume 'that everyone who accepted Islam after the disturbances was forcibly converted and in fact remained a Hindu'. This was to nullify forced conversions and Gandhi welcomed it.[62]

Gandhi stayed in Choumuhani for the next two days and began visiting the affected villages in company with government officials for evidence of the wanton destruction of life and property to which the country had been subjected. Sucheta Kriplani reported the bloodcurdling details of the situation. Bose quotes a journalist who had been in Singapore during the Second World War, whose opinion was that the damage to property which had resulted from man's hands here was more frightful in appearance and certainly more extensive than anything he had witnessed in Singapore. Gandhi finally decided to stay at Srirampur, where he reached on 20 November. He directed his comrades to proceed to other places and chose to remain there for the next two and half months with his stenographer Dashrath and Prof Bose, cutting himself from the outside world; he even stopped writing for *Harijan*.

One interesting fact needs to be mentioned here. Bose was not among those people who had come under the spell of Gandhi. He was obviously impressed by his ideals but as a scientist he was chiefly interested in the study of the mechanics of non-violent actions. As an atheist he was worried about the arrangements of prayer meetings. He wrote a letter to Gandhi explaining his dilemma. Gandhi said to him, in Hindustani, 'that he found nothing objectionable in it; for people like me had previously lived with him. In community prayers, there would naturally be people who held such views'. Later, he asked Bose, '"Don't you believe in anything?" [Bose replied], "Yes, as a scientist, I do believe in truth. For, in the laboratory or in our scientific investigation, we undoubtedly try to discover the truth by observation and experiment. Unless we believe that there is something worth striving for, why should we engage in the chase at all? Truth may be like a carrot dangling before a donkey's nose, but it is there all the same." Gandhi said, "That will do"; and from that day onwards, never for once did he ask any further question on the subject, nor try to interfere with my belief in any way whatsoever.'

Gandhi used to walk early in the morning to the affected villages. Most of the villages were connected with narrow bamboo bridges called shanko. At the age of seventy-seven, he initially needed help to negotiate the dangerously slippery bridges. But he practised four times a day and mastered the art soon. He also started to learn Bangla with the help of Prof Bose, which he practised till his last day.

Gandhi walked 116 miles on foot and visited forty-seven villages in these seven weeks. Tagore's '*Ekla Chalo Re*' (Go your way alone) became his mantra. He went to terrorized villages with a message of courage; told the weeping women folk to wipe their tears and start working afresh with courage, the freighted men to rebuild their houses and vow to stay at their places. He went to refugee camps and appealed to the dwellers to return to their place, and appealed to the Muslim masses to accept their sin with courage and mend it. He requested the government to relinquish their attitude of religious animosity and take necessary steps for establishing peace and provide proper relief to the victims, while appealing to the Hindu Mahasabha to co-operate in the return of refugees. He himself presented an example of extreme valour by walking alone in hostile terrain for establishing peace. Bose writes, 'Gandhi's advice to the Hindus uniformly was that they should purify their own hearts of fear and prejudice, and also set right their social and economic relations with others; for only could this internal purification give them adequate courage, as well as the moral right, to live amidst a people who now considered them to be their exploiters and enemies… To the refugees, he said again that it did not matter if their homes had been burnt or property looted, so long as they had the will to face the calamity with courage and determination. They should build up their lives anew on the foundation of their own labour. The refugees should bravely face the reality and learn some craft by which they could earn their bread and maintain their families.' He advised

Hindus to relinquish the practice of untouchability, and in the same manner, he advised Muslim women to get rid of the *purdah*.[63]

It was with this courage that he faced the opposition. When human excrement and pieces of glass were left on his path, he decided to walk on foot. The road was cleared the next day. There were constant threats of assassination but he kept to his work, undeterred. A person spat on his face, but he smiled. A person tried to strangulate him so hard that his face turned blue. But he kept on smiling. The guy returned the next day and apologized. None of these obstacles were enough to stop him. His presence attracted people from all over the world and relief reached in large quantities. A group of ex-members of the INA under the leadership of Sardar Niranjan Singh Gill reached there to help the victims. All this instilled courage and confidence in the masses and the mistrust between the two communities decreased. People started to return to their houses. The peace was not imposed from above but born from within. Nehru reached there in the end of December and asked Gandhi jokingly: 'So, is this your long sojourn?'

'You forget I am Mahatma, too!' replied Gandhi with a hearty laugh.

Gandhi left Srirampur on 1 January 1947 for Chandipur, and after staying there for five days, visited many other villages in the districts of Noakhali and Tippera for the next two months.[64]

It is difficult to say whether he returned a successful man when, on 2 March, he left for Patna at the call of Congress minister and his friend Syed Mahmood* of the Bihar government. In a survey of pre-Partition violence, Justice G.D. Khosla describes Gandhi's non-violent counterforce in Noakhali: '[Gandhi] brought the light of reason and sanity to mad Noakhali. [A large] number of Muslims came forward and pledged to protect the Hindu minorities. Confidence once again returned, the Hindus cast away their fears and began to go back to their homes.'[65] However, Sucheta Mahajan establishes through many examples that the Noakhali mission was not that successful, and Hindus continued to feel insecure and Muslims to be hostile.[66]

---

* Mahmood was a Minister of Development and Transport in the Bihar government during 1946-52 and became Minister of External Affairs in the Central government in 1954.

But before jumping to any conclusions, two facts should be kept in mind. First, the time when Gandhi was trying to establish peace in Bengal and Bihar was not a normal time. Independence was round the corner and the country was in the grip of a politics of hatred which ultimately resulted in the Partition and another round of violence. Secondly, Gandhi himself knew that the work had not been completed but had to leave since almost every major leader of the Congress, including Patel, Nehru and Rajagopalachari, wanted him to stay in Delhi at that time because, to them, the decisions of Delhi were to determine the future of areas like Noakhali. But to Gandhi, the future of Delhi was to be decided by rural areas like Noakhali. So when he left for Bihar, it was clear in his mind that as soon as the situation became normal, he would have to return to Noakhali and complete the remaining work.[67]

How could he know in advance that the whole country would soon turn into Noakhali, and that he would have to sacrifice his life to save the country from mindless bloodshed?

4. And He Was Killed...

> I see now how splendid I shall look when I am dead. I have already known how I shall look before my death. Such is this lucky age!
>
> —Gandhi, on 30 June 1947[1]

While Gandhi was running pillar to post extinguishing the fires of communal violence, the decision to partition the country had been taken and communal forces were enthusiastically engaged in spreading religious hysteria across the nation. It was evident that one part would go into the hands of the Muslim League, which claimed to be the sole representative of Muslims, while the other, and bigger, part would be ruled by the Congress, which claimed to be a secular party representing every caste and creed. This was a clear defeat of people like Savarkar who considered themselves the representatives of the majority. Our forefathers never accepted them as their representatives, but the communal frenzy of those days left only a few unaffected. Amidst this religious frenzy, Gandhi, often alone but steadfast in his values, was an inconvenience to all such people. It was Gandhi under whose leadership the Congress emerged as the largest party in the country, following its principles of secularism, and was able to gain support from every quarter. It was Gandhi who was not only trying to establish peace from Noakhali to Delhi but was also expressing his intention to go to Punjab, on the other side of the border, constantly condemning the atrocities being committed against minority Hindus in Pakistan. The ideological group of 'Poona Savarkarites' found this time opportune to eliminate Gandhi, when he was left almost alone amidst the fire of violence.

The murder of an unguarded Gandhi was never a difficult task. He never allowed security around himself. Prayer meetings were open to all and were disturbed repeatedly during this period. He was defenceless, like any other common man as he roamed around the villages in Noakhali singing '*Ekla Chalo Re*'. The conspiracy to kill Gandhi, however, wasn't just a conspiracy against an individual, but an attempt to overturn a lost gamble. This didn't go well for the conspirators though. Let us delve into some detail about this conspiracy to understand its intricacies and repercussions thereafter.

Restless Gandhi and Intrigues

Apte, who was the manager of *Agrani*, began making plans to do something big during this period. In the summer of 1947, he first planned to blow up the Pakistan Assembly. Braggart as he was, the plan soon became public. Dada Maharaj, who was a leader of a religious sect and greatly involved in communal violence, was so impressed with the plan that he came to meet him in July 1947. He had deep pockets and had already procured arms and ammunition from Badge. Karkare was also present in this meeting. Dada Maharaj immediately provided Rs 5,000 to Apte for buying two mortars.

In reality, this 'plan' was only an excogitation. Neither did Apte know anything about mortars nor was it possible to blow up the assembly with them. He had informed Dada Maharaj that he would buy the mortars from Goa but bought a Sten gun from Badge instead. However, neither he nor Godse were acquainted with even a Sten gun! The 'plan' remained elusive, and when Jinnah, with all the other Muslim League leaders shifted to Pakistan on 10 August, the new assembly was established in Karachi, putting a final end to the grand 'plan' of Apte.[2]

On 15 August 1947, when Jawaharlal Nehru unfurled the tricolour at the stroke of midnight, Gandhi was in the Beliaghata area of Calcutta, trying to control the riots which had broken out on 10 August. While spinning his charkha, he dictated a letter to pro-Independence British friend Agatha Harrison, 'You know, my way of celebrating great events, such as today's, is to thank God for it and, therefore, to pray. This prayer must be accompanied by a fast, if the taking of fruit juices may be so described. And then, as a mark of identification with the poor and dedication there must be spinning. Hence, I must not be satisfied with the spinning I do every day, but I must do as much as is possible in consistence with my other appointments.' Advising the ministers of Bengal, he wrote:

> From today you have to wear the crown of thorns. Strive ceaselessly to cultivate truth and non-violence. Be humble. Be forbearing. The British rule no doubt put you on your mettle. But now you will be tested through and through. Beware of power; power corrupts. Do not let yourselves be entrapped by its pomp and pageantry. Remember, you are in office to serve the poor in India's villages. May God help you.

And when C. Rajagopalachari, the new governor of the province came to congratulate him, he said that he could not be satisfied until Hindus and Muslims felt safe in one another's company and returned to their own homes to live as before. Without that change of heart, there was a likelihood of future deterioration in spite of the present enthusiasm.[3] When an officer of the Information and Broadcasting Department of the Government of India came for a message, Gandhi replied that 'he had run dry'. When told again that if he did not give any message, it would not be good, Gandhi replied: 'There is no message at all. If it is bad let it be so.' Again, when a representative of the BBC approached him for a message, which would be broadcast all over the world, he replied: 'I must not yield to the temptation. You must forget that I know English.'[4]

While everyone else was immersed in celebration, Gandhi could hear the silent footsteps of the catastrophe approaching the nation consequent to the communal division. Wolpert demonstrates how the government ignored his repeated warnings:

> On the train to Calcutta, he wrote to Mountbatten, continuing to warn him that 'it would be a blunder of the first magnitude for the British to be a party in any way whatsoever to the division of India'. He felt particularly 'sure the partition of the Punjab and Bengal'

> would prove to be 'a needless irritant'. He was quite prescient, almost clairvoyant in seeing the horror and tragedy bound to ensue from the partitioning of Punjab and Bengal. But Mountbatten's mind was made up. His marching orders in London had been to wrap up Britain's withdrawal from India by no later than June of 1948. Soon after landing in Delhi he had resolved to finish the job ten months earlier.[5]

Once again, Gandhi was proved correct, and the country bled in one of the most frightening incidences in the history of mankind. Neither the 'experienced' Lord Mountbatten, nor Nehru, Patel or Jinnah could control the mindless violence by insane mobs.

Jawaharlal wrote to him that he was being missed in Delhi, but when Gandhi was leaving Calcutta for Delhi in September, his original plan was to visit Punjab after a short stay in Delhi.[6] He broke his fast after both parties took an oath of peace and deposited their arms at his feet, and left for Delhi on 7 September 1947.[7] But when he landed at Shahadara the next morning, the melancholic faces of Patel and Amrit Kaur spoke of the situation in Delhi. Patel had always had a cordial relation with Gandhi and humour was a natural ingredient of his otherwise serious personality. Gandhi missed that. In a letter to Pyarelal, Gandhi wrote on 13 September, 'The Sardar always used to walk with his head high, but I tell you today he walks with his head bent.'[8]

Riots had started in Delhi on the day when Gandhi broke his fast in Calcutta. The city was put under curfew. Roads were empty and Delhi was looking like a city of the dead. Patel requested him to stay at Birla House, because his usual place of stay, the Bhangi Colony, was occupied by the refugees. When Nehru came to meet him at Birla House, he was upset. When Gandhi asked, 'What will you get by annoyance?' Nehru replied, 'I am angry with myself. We go with security arrangements. I feel ashamed of it. Ration shops were looted. Access to fruits, vegetables and groceries have become difficult for people. Dr Joshi, who did not differentiate between Hindu and Muslim, was killed in an attack launched from a Muslim house while he was going to see a patient.'[9] Gandhi began visiting riot-affected areas and refugee camps from the next day and told himself, 'I can't leave this place until peace is established.'[10] He had to pay the supreme price for peace and could never leave Delhi.

The gang under the leadership of Apte and Godse was busy hatching new conspiracies. When Dada Maharaj inquired about his money, Apte put forward two new plans, one of a dacoity on the octroi toll at Hyderabad border, and the other about another dacoity in the trains carrying arms and ammunition for Pakistan. He demanded a car for the first plan and Rs 10,000 to buy flame-throwers for the execution of the second one. Dada Maharaj agreed to provide his Chevrolet station wagon car but refused to give any money. Apte took the car, drove to his girlfriend Manorama Salvi and the next two months were spent in amusement. When the priest came to Poona and asked about his car and the plan, a new story was on hand. An attempt was made to please him by offering to let him inaugurate the new building of *Agrani*. Apte was still talking about the attack on the train, but Dada Maharaj was not ready to dispense with a single penny without inspecting the flame-throwers and returned to Bombay with his car. He had recently got the news of Manorama's pregnancy. Added to the worry of the mental illness of his only child, losing Dada Maharaj's trust came as a massive blow to an already distraught Apte.

On the other hand, Karkare started relief work for refugees in Ahmednagar and instigated them to take revenge for the atrocities of the Razakars in Hyderabad* by hurting the Muslims of Ahmednagar. When the Ahmednagar administration banned the possession of arms, Karkare approached Digambar Badge. Meanwhile, Karkare met Madanlal Pahwa, who had already met Dada Maharaj and his younger brother Dixit Maharaj while trading in illegal weapons under the cover of selling books in Bombay. With the help of Karkare, he occupied a Muslim fruit seller's shop in Ahmednagar. In the month of December, Karkare took him to Poona where he was introduced to Apte and Godse. Gandhi's assassination was planned in this meeting.[11]

* For more details see Mike Thomson, 'Hyderabad 1948: India's hidden massacre', BBC, 24 September 2013 (https://www.bbc.com/news/magazine-24159594, last accessed on 8 December 2021).

After their return from Poona, both carried out several violent attacks in Ahmednagar. On 1 January 1948, in connection with a murder investigation, the police raided the house of S.V. Ketkar, the manager of Karkare. They found a steel trunk with a huge haul of hand grenades, a revolver, bullets, daggers and other weapons. These grenades were the same as were used in many incidents including the attack on a Muharram procession in Ahmednagar. Ketkar admitted that these weapons were kept by his master Karkare. On 9 January, warrants were issued for the arrest of Pahwa and Karkare, but the news was leaked by their sympathizers within the police, and both escaped. After the 20 January attack on Gandhi, a police inspector of Ahmednagar, J.N. Joshi reported that he had gone to 'meet' Madanlal at Ahmednagar railway station on 9 or 10 January where the latter told him that he was going to Delhi for marriage!

Actually, Madanlal was not lying. His family members had chosen a bride for him in Delhi. But instead of going straight to Delhi, he first stopped at Bombay, from where he wrote letters to his girlfriend Shewanta, and met Dr Jain, as we have seen earlier. You may call it negligence on the part of police or take it to be a result of their communal inclination that an inspector who met a wanted criminal at a railway station didn't arrest him; and even after his escape, his acquaintances were not tracked, or the letters sent to his girlfriend could have been discovered and he could have been prevented from reaching Delhi. However, the police were to make even bigger blunders in future.

Gandhi, while trying to establish peace in Delhi, was very disturbed by the news coming from Pakistan. On 10 January, when Madanlal Pahwa was leaving Ahmednagar with the intention of killing him, Gandhi commented on the communal violence in Ajmer in his prayer meeting:

> Not that there were no quarrels between the two communities but today the rioting has been much more serious. It seems from what little has appeared in the newspapers that a large number of Muslims have been killed. There was first a scare among the Muslims and those who could ran away leaving a few behind. Then followed

> the riots. I understand that is what is happening in the villages all around. I shall talk to you again after I have full particulars. All I say is that it is a shameful affair. Let us pray to God to give us the wisdom not to destroy Hinduism by our conduct. It cannot do any good to destroy Hinduism in the process of killing Muslims. If we wish to live we must let live. Man was not made by God to live through killing others. It must not be allowed to happen that the Hindus and Sikhs in Pakistan and Muslims in India are killed and the rest become slaves. We are inviting our own destruction. There is a saying in Sanskrit: 'A man loses his reason when he is to be destroyed.' Our minds have become perverse.[12]

He was equally critical of the narrowness of both sides. When one of his comrades praised the work, discipline, courage and ability of RSS in a refugee camp he replied, 'Don't forget that all these virtues also existed in the Nazi and fascist followers of Hitler and Mussolini. RSS is a dictatorial communal organization.' When he visited an RSS camp on their invitation and was greeted as a 'Great Hindu' he said that he had an obvious pride in being Hindu but his religion was neither intolerant nor exclusive. The beauty of Hinduism is its ability to assimilate the most beautiful virtues of every other religion.[13] He was witnessing the double-edged sword of violence at work and was aware of its futility. He wrote on 9 January:

> Today this capital city is under a kind of siege. Although India is free the capital of India is protected by the army and the police, and I can do nothing but sit here and watch. Votaries of non-violence today have had to put their trust in the weapons of violence. What a severe test it is going to be for us. If this is God's will, what strange design does it hide? But I have to do or die. Those who believe that arms can save Delhi are greatly mistaken. Whether it be Delhi or the world only one thing can save us and that is heart amity.[14]

The arrangement of arms and ammunition was the biggest challenge before Apte and Godse. Karkare and Pahwa were also restless after the seizure of their consignment in Ahmednagar. They reached Poona to meet Badge on 10 January and then proceeded to the office of *Hindu Rashtra* to meet Apte and Godse and suggested that cheaper arms could be arranged from Bombay where Pahwa had some contacts. But his earlier acquaintance had left this business and they could not find a cheaper source in Bombay. Meanwhile, Pahwa went to meet Dr Jain and boasted to him about his adventures in the presence of one of his friends, Angad Singh.

On 12 January, Gandhi woke up at three in the morning as usual. Monday was the day of his *maun vrat* (silence). He wrote an article for *Harijan*; then Sardar Patel came and gave some information on Kashmir. More people kept coming. Gandhi listened quietly, preparing a speech in English for the evening which he gave to Dr Sushila Nayyar for translating into Hindi. Sushila suddenly exclaimed while translating, 'Hey Manu! Bapu is going on hunger strike from tomorrow!'[15]

20 January was decided as the last day of Gandhi by the conspirators. Godse did not want to involve Gopal in the scheme but only to take from him the revolver which Gopal had buried in his village instead of returning it after the Second World War. But when Gopal came to know about the Gandhi assassination plan, the demon within him woke up and he put forth the condition of including himself.

On 13 January, the deal was finalized with Badge, and he promised to deliver the arms at the office of the Hindu Mahasabha, Bombay. On the same day, Godse wrote to the insurance company to nominate Gopal's wife Sindhu Godse and Apte's wife Champa Apte as beneficiaries of his insurance policies of Rs 3,000 and Rs 2,000, respectively.[16]

This is an interesting fact on two counts. These policies were purchased during 1945, when the newspaper was in dire financial straits. Neither did Godse have enough resources to invest in insurance nor was there any reason which compelled an unmarried Godse to buy insurance policies. It is obvious that this was a part of long-term planning. At the same time, the nomination of Gopal's wife makes it a clear indication that he must have known about his participation by the morning of 13 January. Malgonkar and others point out that the plan to assassinate Gandhi emerges after his declaration of a fast unto death on the evening of 12 January. Now, if this plan was made after the evening of 12 January, when was the matter of the firearm with Gopal discussed? It is obvious that the conspiracy to assassinate Gandhi was not planned after the declaration of his fast, but that the opportunity they were looking for was provided by it, whatever the excuses one might make to justify their criminal activities. Though Justice Khosla mentions the date of nomination as 14 January,[17] it doesn't make much difference as Godse met Gopal only on the evening of the 14th.

Badge and Shankar Kistayya boarded the third class of the Deccan Express in the evening, while Apte and Godse boarded the second class. An expert of illegal activities, Badge disguised himself as an ascetic; Shankar carried a brown bag which contained five hand grenades, two gun-cottons, six detonators and fuse wire. When Apte saw the famous Marathi cinema artist Shanta Modak alias Bimba in his coach, he offered her a seat near the window and started talking. When he told her that he was going to Savarkar Sadan in Shivaji Park, Bimba said that her house was very close to the Sadan; her brother was coming to pick her up and she offered them a lift. Both accepted the offer and Bimba dropped them at Savarkar Sadan which was indeed next to her house. Badge and Kistayya reached the office of the Hindu Mahasabha on foot from Dadar station.

Malgonkar says that Godse and Apte reached the office of Hindu Mahasabha half an hour after Badge arrived. This calls into question his claim that Godse and Apte may have got down at Savarkar Sadan that night because Bimba's house was nearby, but that they went straight to the Mahasabha office instead of Savarkar's house.[18] If this had indeed been the case, Godse and Apte, who had come to Savarkar's house by car, should have reached before them since the Mahasabha office was barely 800 metres from Savarkar's house. Bimba made it clear in her statement that her house was adjacent to Savarkar's house, and she saw them enter Savarkar's house while her brother was turning the car back.[19] Later, it also became clear from the testimony of Savarkar's bodyguard that the two did indeed meet Savarkar that night. But Malgonkar, in his attempt to shield Savarkar, omits many such facts.

Apte wanted Dadaji Maharaj to pay for the arms and thus the four of them went to his ashram at Bhuleshwar. But he had slept by then, so they left the arms at his ashram and returned. Apte handed fifty rupees to Badge and told him to stay at the Hindu Mahasabha office while he himself checked in at the Sea Green (South) Hotel at Marine Drive with Godse. It is interesting that Godse and Apte always made better arrangements for themselves while other members of the gang including Gopal Godse were made to stay at cheaper places. They made it a point to use aliases and entered the hotel as S. Marathe and D.N. Karmakar, respectively.

Madanlal was also staying at the office of Hindu Mahasabha and met Badge at night. Here's another important fact that needs to be analysed. Malgonkar tells us that Madanlal was informed about the Gandhi assassination plan on 15 January, and he readily agreed to it.[20] Since he hasn't given a source anywhere in his book, it's difficult to assess the basis of this theory. He claims in the same vein that Madanlal went to meet Dr Jain that very evening before catching a train to Delhi and told him about the plan to kill Gandhi.[21] But the details given by Dr Jain are totally different. He claims that he met Jayaprakash Narayan during an event on 13 January and tried to indicate to him that some conspiracy was being hatched in Delhi. It is evident Madanlal had met him sometime before that. Not only that, according to Dr Jain, while he did come before catching the train to Delhi, he had by then already told him about the plan. The day he gave this information, he came in the evening and stayed till late in the night. He was in a hurry when he came to meet him the other day since he was to catch a train for Delhi.[22] Malgonkar has mixed up two separate incidents. This fact also indicates that the Gandhi assassination had already been planned and that is why Madanlal and Karkare stayed in Bombay waiting for Godse and Apte.

Gopal Godse applied for a leave for a week on the same day. He was sure that the plan was so foolproof that all of them would return safely, and life would go on as usual. This is in fact what happened after the first attack of 20 January, except Gandhi was left unscathed and Madanlal was caught.

On 15 January, Apte booked two air tickets for Delhi under the same aliases which were used at the hotel. They then reached the

Mahasabha office at 8.30 in the morning where they met Madanlal. They booked a taxi and first went to the house of G.M. Joshi to pick up Karkare and then to Bhuleshwar. Troubled by herpes, Dixit Maharaj invited them to meet him in his bedroom and put Badge down for keeping arms in his ashram without permission. But when he found out that none of them knew anything about grenades, he readily started to train them. He himself had no experience but had seen it in movies!

The first meeting of the killers took place in the same bedroom after Dixit went to take bath. It was decided to meet in the Delhi office of the Hindu Mahasabha on 18 January. Karkare and Pahwa set out for the railway station. Till now, Badge's role was limited to the supply of arms only.

Apte and Badge waited for Dixit Maharaj. Apte disclosed a new plan of attacks in Kashmir and demanded two revolvers, but Dixit Maharaj bluntly refused any help. Apte tried to extract some money from him unsuccessfully and had to leave his place dejected. Later, Dixit Maharaj claimed in court that a soothsayer had predicted physical harm on 17 January, which proved correct as he fell from the staircase, and which is why the date remained in his memory.[23]

Apte asked Badge whether he would come to Delhi. When Badge inquired about the purpose, he informed him that Tatyarao (elder brother, a respectful term for Savarkar) had given him the responsibility of killing Gandhi, Nehru and Huseyn Suhrawardy, the prime minister of Bengal. He readily agreed but had some engagements in Poona and decided to visit Poona before leaving for Delhi. Nathuram too wanted to visit Poona to meet Gopal.

That night, Karkare and Madanlal boarded the Peshawar Express for Delhi while Nathuram, Badge and Kistayya left for Poona. Apte decided to stay in Bombay and spend some time with Manorama before leaving on the mission which could make his return impossible.

Gandhi's fast created a furore in Delhi. His age and physical condition were not ideal for enduring a long one. But if there was one thing which had grown with age, it was his self-will. And he was not ready to give up his fast without definite assurances. The day he decided to go on a fast unto death, his youngest son Devdas Gandhi had asked, 'This fast is against Pakistan?' Gandhi replied, 'No, it is against everyone.'[24] While talking to a Sikh friend on 13 January, he said:

> My fast is against no one party, group or individual exclusively and yet it excludes nobody. It is addressed to the conscience of all, even the majority community in the other Dominion. If all or any one of the groups responds fully, I know the miracle will be achieved. For instance, if the Sikhs respond to my appeal as one man, I shall be wholly satisfied. I shall go and live in their midst in the Punjab, for they are a brave people and I know they can set an example in non-violence of the brave which will serve as an object lesson to all the rest.[25]

Devdas, Gandhiji's youngest son, tried to dissuade him from the grave decision. Pyarelal recounts:

> Like everybody else, he had no inkling of what was coming. He learnt of the fast only after the decision had been announced. The next morning, he sent his father a note which he had drafted late at night. The note ran: 'My chief concern and my argument against your fast is that you have surrendered to impatience, whereas your mission by its very nature calls for infinite patience. You do not seem to have realised what a tremendous success your patient labour has achieved. It has saved...thousands of lives and may still save many more... By your death you will not be able to accomplish what you can by living. I would, therefore, beseech you to pay heed to my entreaty and give up your decision to fast.'
>
> This evoked from Gandhiji a reply that will live as an epic of faith. He did not agree that his decision to fast was hasty. 'It was quick no doubt, so far as the drafting of the statement was concerned. Behind this lightning quickness was my four days' heart-churning and prayer. It cannot therefore be called "hasty" according to my definition, or for that matter the definition of anybody who knows. In a statement like this, there is always room for improving the language. It took me, therefore, no time to accept the verbal changes you had suggested. As for the propriety of the decision itself I did not feel called upon to consult you or anybody else. The fact that I did listen to you all only bespeaks my patience and humility... Your worries as well as your pleading are equally vain... You are of course

> a friend and a friend of a very high order at that. But you cannot get over the son in you. Your concern is natural, and I respect it. But your argument betrays impatience and superficial thinking... I regard this step of mine as the acme of patience. Is patience which kills its very object patience or folly? I cannot accept the credit for what has been achieved since my arrival in Delhi...
>
> 'It was only when in terms of human effort, I had exhausted all resources and realised my utter helplessness that I laid my head on God's lap. That is the inner meaning and significance of my fast. You would do well to read and ponder over Gajendra Moksha—the greatest of devotional poems as I have called it. Then alone, perhaps, you will be able to appreciate the step I have taken. Your last sentence is a charming token of your affection. But your affection is rooted in attachment or delusion. Attachment does not become enlightenment because it relates to a public cause. So long as one has not shed all attachment and learnt to regard both life and death as same, it would be idle to pretend that he wants to live only because his life is indispensable for a certain cause. "Strive while you live" is a beautiful saying, but there is a hiatus in it. Striving has to be in the spirit of detachment.'[26]

Later, during his prayer meeting, he commented on the allegations being levelled against Sardar:

> Then the name of the Sardar is being mentioned. The Muslims say that I am good, but the Sardar is not and he must be removed. They say that Jawaharlal too is good. They say if I join the Government it will be a good thing. They object only to the Sardar. I must tell the Muslims that their argument serves no purpose, because the Government is the whole Cabinet, neither the Sardar nor Jawahar by himself...
>
> The Sardar is blunt of speech. What he says sometimes sounds bitter. The fault is in his tongue. I can testify that his heart is not like his tongue. He has said in Lucknow and in Calcutta that all Muslims should live here and can live here. He also told me that he could not trust those Muslims who till the other day followed the League and considered themselves enemies of Hindus and Sikhs and who could not have changed overnight and suddenly become friends. If the League is still there who will they obey, Pakistan or

> our Government? The League's persistence in its old attitude makes him suspect it, and rightly so. He says that he no longer has faith in the bona fides of the League Muslims, and he cannot trust them. Let them prove that they can be trusted. Then I have the right to tell the Hindus and Sikhs what they should do.[27]

He repeated on 14 January:

> But what is needed is action, not mere words. If the Muslims of Pakistan become thus transformed, it is bound to have an effect in India. I have never tried to hide my view that Pakistan has committed crimes against Hindus.[28]

The cabinet met at Birla House that night. When the meeting ended and members came outside, a few refugees from Punjab were sloganeering—'*Gandhi Murdabad*' (Death to Gandhi). Gandhi had heard such slogans while visiting refugee camps, in camps like Kurukshetra, where Hindu and Sikh refugees from Pakistan were living in pathetic conditions, and even in the Old Fort, where Muslims were sheltered due to violent attacks on their houses in Delhi and other parts of the country.[29] Everyone had a grudge against him because everybody had expectations from him. The sloganeering got intense—'*Death to Gandhi. Blood for blood. Let Gandhi Die.*' Nehru was just getting into his car when the Sikhs came up the road. He ran out into the street and shouted: 'Who dares to say such things? Let him come out and face me! He will have to kill me first.' They ran away, and the street was quiet again.

Inside the house, Gandhi heard the confused clamour and said: 'What are they shouting?'

'They are shouting, "Gandhi Murdabad."'

'How many are they?'

'Not many.'

Gandhi sighed and began chanting the name of Ram.[30]

Badge reached Poona at 2 p.m. on 16 January and lodged his illegal arms and ammunition at the house of Congress MLA Ganpat Kharat. Kharat later claimed in court that he was going to the toilet and had no conversation with Badge, although, the very next day he had had the box shifted somewhere else. Nathuram returned to Poona on 15 January and went to meet Gopal. Gopal told him that he would go to the village the following day to fetch the revolver and reach Delhi by 18 January. They had dinner together. Nathuram bought a .22 calibre revolver on the 16th and told Badge to get it exchanged for a better one. Then he went to meet his parents and thereafter board a train to Bombay at 11 p.m. Badge exchanged that revolver for a .32 calibre with one S.D. Sharma and left for Bombay late that night.

Badge met Godse and Apte at Victoria Terminal in the morning of 17 January. Shankar was sent to the office of Hindu Mahasabha from Dadar. They took a taxi and dropped Manorama at her house, and then proceeded to arrange money from a few sympathizers. They succeeded in extracting a considerable amount from old sympathizers like the industrialist Chandradas Meghji, Ganpatrao Afzalpurkar, and M.G. Kale under different pretexts, but could not convince Dadaji Maharaj. He was ready to provide a revolver but not for free. They returned to the office of the Hindu Mahasabha in dejection and went to meet Savarkar. Shankar accompanied them but was left in the taxi when they entered his house. Badge waited in the hall and Savarkar's bodyguard took Godse and Apte to the office of Savarkar on the first floor of the building. When they returned after ten minutes, Apte was beaming with confidence. He told Badge that Tatyarao had blessed them for the success of their mission—'*Yashasvi houn ya*' (Return with glory).

On the way to the airport, Apte said to Badge, 'Tatyarao has said that Gandhi's dream of living for 100 years will not be fulfilled. We will be successful in our mission for sure.'

Gandhi's health was deteriorating. Doctors feared that his kidneys might be permanently damaged due to the fast. People felt the decision to release Pakistan's outstanding fifty-five crores would have an impact on his fast. But even after this decision on 16 January he did not end his fast. He had only one condition: all parties should agree to stop violence in Delhi. He was so adamant that he refused to even mix a little juice with water.

The next day, Nehru went to him with Hindu and Sikh refugees to convince him. Gandhi asserted that whatever the solution, it ought to be something reliable and long-lasting. Ten thousand refugees submitted a letter to him assuring him that there would be no violence against Muslims. The administration promised to arrange houses for Sikh and Hindu refugees within a week. The Maharaja of Patiala informed him that he had instructed the Sikhs to keep away from violent activities and that he himself would be responsible if any such incident were to take place in his state. The Nawab of Malerkotla declared that if any Sikh or Hindu was killed in his state, he would shoot ten Muslims in return. Pyarelal narrates the responses from the Pakistani side:

> The first indication of it was a wire from the indefatigable Mridula Sarabhai. She had been engaging in God's good work of the rescue and recovery of abducted women. Her wire to Gandhiji from Lahore ran: 'Everybody here wants to know what they can do to save Gandhiji's life.' Prayers were offered both in India and Pakistan—prayers in public, prayers in private, prayers by Muslim women in the seclusion of their purda—that God might spare him.
>
> Raja Ghazanfar Ali Khan, the Minister for Relief and Rehabilitation in the Pakistan government, and a noted protagonist of the Muslim League's Direct Action, in a press interview declared: 'The appalling degradation of...morale which has manifested itself in both India and Pakistan during recent months called for a drastic remedy and Mahatma Gandhi has lodged his protest against these conditions in the extreme form... If the present state of affairs lasts, our hard-won freedom is bound to come to an inglorious end.'
>
> 'No country in the world has produced a greater man, religious founders apart, than Mahatma Gandhi,' remarked Malik Feroz Khan Noon of 'outdoing Chengiz Khan and Halaku' fame. Mian Mumtaz Khan Daulatana, the Finance Minister, said that it was their foremost duty to appreciate 'the feelings which Mahatma Gandhi's fast reveals towards the Muslims. This shows that there is at least one man in India who is ready to sacrifice even his life for Hindu–Muslim unity... I assure Mahatma Gandhi from the floor of this House that his feelings for the protection of minorities are fully shared by us.' The Chief Minister, the Khan of Mamdot, speaking on his own and his colleagues' behalf expressed 'deep admiration

> and sincere appreciation with great feeling of concern for Mahatma Gandhi's great gesture for the furtherance of a noble cause', and added that 'no efforts will be spared in this Province to help in saving his precious life'.[31]

The atmosphere was improving rapidly, and a large number of people raised slogans of communal unity and Hindu–Muslim brotherhood near Birla House in the evening. However, amidst the slogans of '*Mahatma Gandhi ki Jai*', some were still shouting slogans of '*Gandhi Murdabad*'. While Nehru and Maulana Azad were holding peace meetings everywhere in Delhi, Dr Rajendra Prasad was in contact with all organizations and was trying to form a consensus.

Patel was busy performing his duties as home minister and was a bit disturbed by the criticisms against him. While leaving for Saurashtra on 16 January for an important engagement, he wrote to Gandhi:

> I have to leave for Kathiawad at seven this morning. It is agonising beyond endurance to have to go away when you are fasting. But stern duty leaves no other course.
>
> The sight of your anguish yesterday has made me disconsolate. It has set me furiously thinking. The burden of work has become so heavy that I feel crushed under it. I now see that it would do no good to the country or to myself to carry on like this anymore. It might even do harm.
>
> Jawahar is even more burdened than I. His heart is heavy with grief. Maybe I have deteriorated with age and am no more any good as a comrade to stand by him, and lighten his burden. The Maulana (Azad) too is displeased with what I am doing and you have again and again to take up cudgels on my behalf. This also is intolerable to me.
>
> In the circumstances, it will perhaps be good for me and for the country if you now let me go. I cannot do otherwise than I am doing. And if thereby I become burdensome to my lifelong colleagues and a source of distress to you and still I stick to office, it would mean—at least that is how I would feel—that I let the lust of power blind my eyes and so was unwilling to quit. You should quickly deliver me from this intolerable situation.[32]

This letter is often presented by writers like Wolpert as evidence of the rivalry between Nehru and Patel and the resultant controversy between Gandhi and Patel. There is no denying the fact that there were disagreements between these great leaders. But these differences of opinion were driven by their different outlooks and not by personal animosity. Such writers seem to ignore Patel's public lecture delivered upon reaching Bombay that same day. He said:

> Our prestige went up when we achieved independence but subsequent events have brought it down. If in spite of having achieved independence, Gandhiji has to fast in order to achieve real Hindu–Muslim unity, it is a standing shame to us. You have just now heard people shouting that Muslims should be removed from India. Those who do so have gone mad with anger. Even a lunatic is better than a person who is mad with rage. He can be treated and perhaps cured, but the other? They do not realise that they stand to gain nothing by driving out a handful of Muslims. I am a frank man. I say bitter things to Hindus and Muslims alike... Some of them (Muslims) went to Gandhiji and complained about my Lucknow speech in which I had criticised them for not condemning Pakistan's attitude on Kashmir... Gandhiji felt compelled to defend me. That pained me. For...I am not a weak person who should be defended by others.

In response, Gandhi said that 'if they would carefully read the Sardar's speech at Bombay, they would realise that there was "no difference of outlook" between the Sardar, Pandit Nehru and himself. They were all working for the same end. None of them was the enemy of the Muslims'.[33]

Apte got a bit confused. When the taxi reached Santa Cruz, he realized that the flight was to depart from the Kalina aerodrome. He panicked and requested the driver to move fast towards Kalina. While reaching Kalina he instructed Badge to pay the bill and ran towards the aerodrome in haste, with Godse. Badge retained the same taxi, went Kurla to collect 400 rupees from a sympathizer, then went to pick Shankar from the Hindu Mahasabha office and returned to Kurla railway station. Aitappa Kotian, the taxi driver, could not forget these strange customers who engaged him from 7 in the morning to 3 p.m. and recognized them in court. If that was not enough, Badge demanded a receipt of this journey which Kotian gladly provided and thus created additional evidence.[34]

Gandhi's health had begun to worsen by the fifth day of the fast. The doctors were very worried about the continued urinary incontinence. He had been asking in delirium to be removed to his bed when he was in it already. A Central Peace Committee, consisting of 130 members representing all communities, was formed under the chairmanship of Dr Rajendra Prasad, the Congress president. The Committee met at Dr Prasad's residence on the evening of 17 January and adopted a resolution assuring Gandhiji that they would do all that lay in their power 'to create, establish and maintain the spirit of peace, harmony and brotherhood between all communities'. The representatives of some Hindu organizations, noted for their extreme communal bias, were not present in this meeting. In their absence, their friends gave a guarantee on their behalf. Some members thought that in view of the fact that the sands were running out fast, an attempt should be made to persuade Gandhiji to end his fast on the basis of the Committee's resolution, without waiting for the absentees' signatures. But Gandhi was not ready to end his fast until the signatures were obtained.[35]

Godse and Apte reached Delhi almost at the same time when the meeting of the peace committee was going on and stayed in room number 40 of Hotel Marina at Connaught Place. They entered their names as M. Deshpande and S. Deshpande in the hotel register. However, they had left another piece evidence while on their way to Delhi. The flight from Bombay to Delhi was via Ahmedabad. In transit, they happened to meet Dada Maharaj who didn't miss a chance to taunt Apte— 'You always talk big, but never perform.' Apte replied, 'When we will do something, the whole world will come to know.' Later, Maharaj narrated the story in court.

Badge decided to stay at a friend's hotel at Dadar and took an early morning train to reach Delhi on the 19th while Madanlal and Karkare travelled in the third class of the Peshawar Express to reach Delhi by 17th. En route, they met Shantaram Angchekar, who was a government servant in Karachi travelling to Delhi for his transfer. He didn't know anyone in Delhi and had no place to stay. Karkare boasted of his alliance with the Hindu Mahasabha and invited him to stay at its office. However, they couldn't find a place in the office, and after unsuccessfully trying to find a room at Birla temple, decided to stay at a cheap hotel in Chandni Chowk.

The next day, Gandhi decided to end his fast after everyone concerned had signed the peace resolution. Karkare went to attend his prayer meeting with Godse and Apte, while Madanlal, accompanied by Angchekar, went to have a look at marriageable girls at the former's relative's place. On their way back, he saw Jawaharlal Nehru at a peace meeting in the old sabzi mandi area and started sloganeering. He was detained by the police when he tried to grab hold of Indira Gandhi's hand but was let go without any interrogation.[36]

Karkare had met Godse and Apte at the office of the Hindu Mahasabha on the 17th. Godse had written a letter of introduction for Karkare to the secretary of the Mahasabha, Ashutosh Lahiri, and he was allotted a room. The three conspirators had gone out together to the prayer meeting of Gandhi on the 18th. While Gandhi couldn't attend the meeting due to his depleted health, he sent a written message to be read out. The conspirators roamed around, scanning the area to finalize their course of action.

Nathuram was waiting for Gopal and Badge at the office of the Hindu Mahasabha late in the morning of the 19th. Apte booked a trunk call for Savarkar Sadan from the Mahasabha's office. Those were the days when long-distance calls were a luxury and a system of trunk calls was in place. However, the call was not received, and once Gopal arrived, the trio returned to Birla House after making arrangements for him. Karkare then went to his hotel and took Madanlal with him, while Angchekar was dumped unceremoniously only to narrate the story later in court.

Badge and Shankar were last to reach Delhi. They arrived by the evening of the 19th and stayed in the hall of the Mahasabha's office itself. Madanlal and Gopal stayed in the room allotted to Karkare, while Karkare stayed with Apte and Godse in their hotel room. Badge carried a .32 revolver and hand grenades, and Gopal had his service revolver with him. The rendezvous was fixed for the morning of the 20th at the office of Hindu Mahasabha, but Nathuram developed and migraine and stayed at the hotel. The rest proceeded for Birla House and roamed around finalizing their plan. The final plan clearly indicates that Apte didn't want any risk to himself and the Godse brothers. As per this plan, Madanlal was to hide, accompanied by Gopal, in one of the servants' quarters which were behind the stage where Gandhi used to sit during his prayer meetings. He was to blast a grenade and Badge and Shankar were to shoot Gandhi, taking advantage of the resulting stampede. As per the plan, Apte, Karkare and Nathuram were not to even carry any arms. Their responsibility was only to guide the others and then flee in the stampede. It is obvious that the 'plan' was to entrap Badge and Shankar. Badge was smart enough to sniff out these intentions.

A drill was due, and they chose the jungles behind Birla House for that. Gopal tried to fire his service revolver, but it didn't work. Badge discovered that he had the wrong cartridges, and it was thus not possible to fire from a long range. A group of policemen passed through when they were trying to fix the Webley & Scott. Gopal talked to them and assured them that they were travellers having some fun in the jungle. They returned to Marina Hotel, where Gopal finally succeeded in fixing his revolver. Zero hour was close, and a new plan was hatched, according to which Madanlal Pahwa was to blast the first hand grenade from the servants' quarters behind the stage, Shankar and Badge were to shoot Gandhi from a close distance, and Madanlal, Gopal, Karkare and Badge were to blast more grenades to create a stampede, so that everyone could flee safely. Apte and Godse did not take any responsibility and they were only to stand among the crowd and give instructions; the dirty work was to be performed by *others* in the gang. Apte, Badge, Gopal and Shankar took a taxi from Regal Cinema while others reached Birla House by tonga.[37]

19 January was a Monday, a day when Gandhi used to practise *maun vrat*. In his written answers to the visitors, he expressed his desire to visit Pakistan so that he could save Hindus and Sikhs. After breaking his *vrat*, he said, 'People say that Jinnah's heart has changed. What is the proof of this? They are still speaking bad things for

Sardar.' He said to Dinshaw Mehta and Jehangirjee, 'I have no faith left for Jinnah. There can be no settlement through him. There is no need for anyone to visit Pakistan… If Liaquat comes here, I can't say whether I will meet him or not. I am tired.'[38]

20 January was business as usual for Gandhi. He woke up at 3 a.m. and prayed. Despite weakness he was feeling good and decided to attend the prayer meeting. He was carried in a chair and since the mic was not working and his voice was very weak, Sushila Nayyar was repeating his lecture in a louder voice. The prayer meeting had just begun when a loud explosion was heard. Everyone panicked but Gandhi remained unruffled and went on with his address as though nothing had happened. During his address, he said:

> I told you it was possible I might go to Pakistan. But I shall go to Pakistan only when the Government invites me as a friend of the Muslims as well as Hindus and the Sikhs. Of course the doctors insist that I must first recoup from the effects of the fast which may take another 15 days and that during the next 15 days I cannot go anywhere or eat anything solid. I can only take liquid diet which may be milk or fruit juice. Milk can of course sustain a man all his life.[39]

Women and children used to sit in the front row, and had so many grenades been blasted, they would have been the biggest casualty. But Badge had decided to abandon the plan, sensing the intentions of Godse and Apte. On the pretext of explaining the changed plan to Shankar, Badge took him to the waiting taxi where he rolled up his own and Shankar's revolver in a towel and placed the bundle on the back seat. Thus, after the blast by Madanlal, when Apte instructed him to fire, Badge simply avoided his look and ran away with Shankar. Madanlal was caught trying to flee and the plan failed.

Gopal later claimed that he made a last-ditch attempt and entered the servants' quarters to shoot Gandhi but found that the grill was set too high in the wall to provide a view of the prayer ground. He let go and ran back to the door to find that he had locked himself in. Then he put down his bag, and applying both hands, prised the chain off its hook. The door opened with a startling bang and he ran away to the taxi where Apte, Godse and Karkare were waiting for him.[40] However, his claim seems to be mere boasting. There were many people including policemen around the place after blast, and it is impossible that he could have fled so easily after the bang.

Surjeet Singh, the driver, said in court that they had instructed him to hurry up and he drove them back to Connaught Place.

Later, when someone commented that the whole matter might turn out to be a harmless prank of an irresponsible youth, Gandhiji laughed and exclaimed, 'The fool! Don't you see there is a terrible and widespread conspiracy behind it?'[41] At another place he exclaimed, 'They are like children. They don't understand. After I am gone they will realise what the old man used to say was right.'[42]

While Gandhi was correct in his assessment of the conspiracy, he was wrong in his understanding of the 'misguided' youth. Years later, when an *Outlook* correspondent spoke to an old and ailing Madanlal Pahwa on 2 February 1998, he had only one regret: 'I wish I had killed Gandhi.'[43]

And the Conspirators Succeed in Failing the Nation...

The news spread like wildfire throughout Delhi and good wishes began to pour in from every quarter on Gandhiji's narrow escape. As soon as Lady Mountbatten received the news she hastened to Bapu. She expressed relief on his escape. But even now he simply said, 'On this occasion I have shown no bravery. If somebody fired at me point blank and I faced his bullet with a smile, repeating the name of Rama in my heart, I should indeed be deserving of congratulations.'[44]

If Gandhi considered it part of a larger conspiracy, there were enough grounds for that. The Communist paper *People's Age* had been saying since August 1947 that the Mahatma was going to be murdered, that the Delhi Police had been infiltrated with RSS people and that the Deputy Commissioner of Delhi was behind the movement and they were not keen on protecting the life of the Mahatma.[45] Kanji Dwarkadas, in his submission to the Kapur Commission deposed that a doctor friend of his went to Mahatma Gandhi in the middle of December 1947 and told him that a conspiracy was being hatched in

Alwar and Bharatpur States to assassinate him. Acharya Jugal Kishore had also warned Gandhiji about it. The doctor mentioned above had sent a leaflet to Acharya Jugal Kishore which called for Gandhiji's murder, and the Acharya wrote back to the doctor that he would place the leaflet before Gandhiji and Panditji.[46]

A hand grenade was recovered from Madanlal and he was detained at the Tughlak Road police station. A servant of Birla House, Chhoturam (whose room was to be used by the conspirators) and a woman named Sulochna had seen him trying to flee after the blast with several others and a young boy had seen a few suspicious people riding in a taxi. This clearly indicated that this was not the handiwork of Madanlal alone and he was most probably only a small pawn in the conspiracy. Madanlal kept claiming that he was alone, but a little sternness was enough to make him reveal certain things. He named 'Karkara Seth' (as he used to pronounce the name in his Punjabi accent) as a financer of this conspiracy and the editor of *Hindu Rashtra* and *Agrani* as the leader. He also informed them about the younger brother of the editor and a bearded supplier of arms.[47] However, by making distorted statements and pretending to not understand any Marathi, he was able to camouflage the identities of his colleagues.[48]

This information, however, ought to have been enough for a police force to track down the conspirators. But the kind of investigation they carried out, despite repeated warnings—'*Wah fir aayega*' (He will come again)—is a truly shameful example of laxity and carelessness in the history of the Indian police.

Whether Tired or Not / O Man Do Not Take Rest

Gandhi was unperturbed by this attack. The conspirators were still bent on killing him.

Badge hired a tonga to reach the office of Hindu Mahasabha where he met Nathuram, Apte and Gopal. Apte was angry and a heated argument broke out between the two. Badge directed Shankar to dump the arms in the nearby forest and reached the Old Delhi railway station to catch a train to Poona. Godse had already checked out of the hotel and decided to proceed to Kanpur with Apte. Karkare wanted to stay in Delhi for some time to arrange legal help for Madanlal. He stayed at Frontier Hotel in the Old Delhi area with Gopal.

Madanlal had also revealed that the chief conspirators were staying at Hotel Marina. The police took him to the hotel. He led them to room number 40. In the drawer of a table they found a typewritten sheet. It was a press note issued by Ashutosh Lahiri, the general secretary of the Hindu Mahasabha. They also found clothing which Godse had given for dry cleaning. It had NGV written on it with black ink. It is strange that neither was Lahiri interrogated nor did the police bother to conduct an inquiry at the office of the Hindu Mahasabha.[49] This could not only have established the identities of the other conspirators but could possibly have led them to Karkare, who was still in Delhi. The note sent to the members of the Constituent Assembly on 16 July 1949 mentions that the police went to the office of the Hindu Mahasabha, but Karkare had left by then.[50] The next morning, police took Madanlal to the Old Delhi railway station. Gopal was there to catch the Frontier Mail and Karkare had come to see him off. Gopal had hidden the unused grenade and his revolver in his handbag. He later admitted that he saw Madanlal with a police party while he was taking his breakfast in the tea room. Manohar Malgonkar claims that Madanlal also got a glimpse of the two but to save them pretended not to have.[51] Whatever be the case, Gopal succeeded in fleeing from Delhi. There was also an incident where a policeman searched his bedding at Dadar but left his handbag unchecked! He was lucky enough to reach home and placed his arms with a family friend named Pandurang Godbole, who lived in the Sadashiv Peth area of Poona.

For the next two days, Karkare tried hard to arrange legal aid for Madanlal but couldn't get any support from his Mahasabha fellows. Finally, he found Advocate Mehta Pooran Chand with the help of Madanlal's relatives and left Delhi on 23 January for Mathura. After staying for a night at Hotel Mohan Gujarat in Mathura under the alias V.M. Vyas, he booked a bus for Agra and changed trains at Itarsi and Kalyan to reach his friend Mr Joshi's house in Thane by the early morning of 25 January. Joshi informed him that Apte and Nathuram had come looking for him two days earlier. Karkare sent Joshi's eighteen-year-old son Vasant to the Central Telegraph Office in Bombay, which was twenty miles from Thane, to send an express telegram to Apte's house at Poona. This was done to not reveal his location. The telegram was coded: Both come immediately—Vyas. Apte's wife sent this message to Gopal and he reached Bombay at once, contacted Manorama Salvi, and arranged a meeting.

Dr J.C. Jain read about the Birla House incidents in the newspaper. He realized that Madanlal's boasts were serious, and his silence could prove dangerous for the life of the Mahatma, and decided to inform the responsible people. First, he tried to contact Sardar Patel, who was in Bombay at the time. But he could only meet his son, Dahyabhai Patel, as Sardar had left for the airport when he reached his house. He went straight to the then chief minister of Bombay state, Mr Bal Gangadhar Kher. He narrated the whole story in the presence of the then home minister of the state, Mr Morarji Desai.[52] It is a bit strange that Jain went to political leaders instead of the Bombay Police and even Desai never bothered to direct him to the police. As a result, no statement was recorded. Later, Jain claimed that he had mentioned all the names, while Morarji couldn't remember what exactly Dr Jain had said to him! However, Desai narrated the story to the then DCP of Bombay Police, Mr Jamshed Nagarvala, and he decided to put guards around Savarkar Sadan.[53]

The journey from Delhi to Kanpur changed a lot of things. Travelling in the first-class compartment, Godse's heart was filled with despair and frustration. He had failed his master. He had talked big in Poona, and he could not go back there now as a failure. While Apte had a sound sleep, Godse was awake all night and decided to take the command in his own hands. He booked a retiring room in Kanpur and informed Apte that he would now kill Gandhi alone. The next day, he boarded the Lucknow–Jhansi Mail to reach Jhansi and then took the Punjab Mail to reach Bombay by the afternoon of the 23rd. They went to Pathikashram at Sandhurst Road. Apte knew people who ran the place but they could only get two beds in the dormitory. Next they contacted Joshi who couldn't tell them anything about the location of Karkare. Nathuram informed Gopal through a friend that he may contact Manorama Salvi for any information about them. On the 24th they booked a room in Hotel Elphinstone Annexe at Karnak Road. Manorama came here in the afternoon and she and Apte stayed there for the next one and half day.

Gandhi was feeling better by 23 January. He remembered Subhas Chandra Bose in the prayer meeting:

> Today is Subhas Babu's birthday. I have told you I cannot remember anyone's birthday or death anniversary. Someone reminded me of Subhas Babu's birthday. Subhas Babu was a votary of violence while I am a devotee of ahimsa. But what does it matter? I know that the most important thing is that we should learn from other people's virtues.
>
> Subhas was a great patriot. He laid down his life for the country. He was not by nature a fighter but he became commander of an army and took up arms against a great empire. The soldiers of that army included Hindus, Muslims, Parsis and Christians. He never considered himself only a Bengali. He had no use for parochialism or caste distinctions. In his eyes all were Indians and servants of India. He treated all alike. It never occurred to him that since he was the commander he deserved more and others less. Let us therefore in remembering Subhas think of his great virtues and purge our hearts of malice.
>
> Once a friend, who was an eminent advocate asked me to define Hinduism. I told him I was neither a lawyer like him nor a religious leader and was really unable to define Hinduism, but I would suggest that a Hindu was one who had equal respect for all religions. Subhas had equal respect for all religions and he easily won every heart. It is good to remember such things on this occasion. [54]

Sardar Patel returned the same day from Ahmedabad, by which time he had been informed by the Delhi and Bombay Police of a conspiracy to kill the Mahatma, and that all conspirators were at large except Madanlal Pahwa, who was also the primary source of their information. He immediately bulked up the armed police presence at Birla House, including nineteen uniformed and seven plainclothes personnel, directed to blend in with the crowd at prayer meetings.

Ghanshyamdas Birla wasn't happy to find police 'in every nook and corner of my house'. He complained to Patel, reminding him how Gandhi never favoured the excessive security arrangements of some of the Viceroys. To which Patel responded:

> Why are you worried? This is not your business. The responsibility is mine. Left to myself I should like to search every man entering Birla House, but Bapu will not let me.

And he knew Mahatma more than anyone else. Gandhi refused his proposal for screening everybody at the Birla House gate when they met in the evening.

Gandhi was never comfortable with the security. He wrote to Birla in a letter on 21 January:

> I do not find this as shocking as you do. Because, if I say no, the Sardar and Jawaharlal, who are hemmed in by so many worries, will be haunted by the added worry concerning my safety. These friends are shouldering a great responsibility today. I personally believe that I am in the keeping of Rama. If He wants to take me away, even a hundred thousand men cannot save me.[55]

He was more interested in solving other issues and told Patel that neither he nor Nehru should leave the cabinet. Mountbatten had been emphatic on this score, and he himself now felt the same. The remark lightened Patel's heart but he said that it was essential to talk things over: much had happened that needed airing. Since Vallabhbhai was leaving for Agra and Patna on the 25th and not returning until the 27th, the two agreed to meet an hour before Gandhi's prayer meeting on 30 January.[56]

The police was investigating by its own methods. A team consisting of two officers, DSP Jaswant Singh, and Inspector Balkishan was sent to Bombay. They were to report to Nagarvala in Bombay and then proceed to Poona to meet DGP CID Rao Saheb Gurtu. They carried a copy of Madanlal's statement with them and they were supposed to help Bombay Police in their inquiry. But the statement was in Urdu and there was hardly anyone in the Bombay Police who could read the script. Later, the officers informed the court that they had also submitted a small note in English which had the mention of the editor of *Agrani* and *Hindu Rashtra*. But Nagarvala insisted that he was not informed about anyone else but Karkare. In fact, Nagarvala was too preoccupied with his conspiracy theory to give much importance to anything else. He was fully assured that a large organization was planning to kidnap Gandhi and he worked on it with full devotion till Gandhi was killed. The lack of co-ordination between the Delhi and Bombay Police is further highlighted by the fact that the two officers of Delhi Police were confined to their hotel room, and when they sought permission to proceed to Poona they were ordered to return to Delhi![57]

It's difficult to believe that they could not find the editor of a newspaper which was twice banned by the Home Department for spreading communal venom! A telephone call to Poona or a mere screening of newspapers originating from Poona would have been enough to find the names of Godse and Apte. However, when the two officers returned empty-handed, the then director of the Intelligence Bureau, DIG T.G. Sanjeevi Pillai requested the DIG of Bombay CID, U.G. Rana to contact Bombay Police with a copy of Madanlal's statement in English and Urdu and help with the investigation. Instead of flying, Mr Rana decided to catch a train! If this was not enough, he chose a train to Bombay via Allahabad where he took a holy dip in the Ganges. He took thirty-six hours to reach Bombay on the 27th. Nagarvala was in no mood to entertain any lead which did not fit his own theory of conspiracy. Sanjeevi requested him to send a report, which reached Delhi a day after the murder of Gandhi![58] Justice Kapur commented in his report:

> [T]he quality of investigation by the field officers was not of that high order which one would have expected. It was a colourless investigation and little effort seems to have been directed to tracing the associates of Madanlal and there was little direction from the top.[59]

On the other side, the conspirators were more focused and attentive this time. Godse and Apte went to Bhuleshwar once again to try their luck. They had done 'something' and were expecting a favour against it, but Dada Maharaj was not impressed and refused to help. However, they were successful in impressing a businessman, Paranjpe, who helped with 10,000 rupees. They booked an air ticket for the 27th of January under aliases, D. Vinayak Rao and S. Vinayak Rao. Apte instructed Manorama to send a telegram at the address of the Hindu Mahasabha in Delhi in his own name if something were to happen to Godse. The telegram was to confuse the investigators into deducing that Apte was in Bombay at the time of the assassination of Gandhi. Manorama dutifully followed the instruction, but the duo had left enough incriminating evidence for this to work.

Gopal and Karkare met them at a desolate yard in Thane during the late hours of the 26th. Nathuram informed them that, from Delhi, he would go straight to Gwalior to arrange a revolver and shall return by early morning of the 29th. Karkare was given Rs 300 for his expenditures and was instructed to wait for them in the garden opposite Old Delhi railway station on the morning of the 29th. Gopal didn't offer any help this time and returned to his secure abode; his valour had failed him.

En route to Delhi, Apte tried to flirt with an air hostess named Lorna Woodbridge and she identified him easily in the courtroom. As per the plan they next boarded a train from Old Delhi railway station and reached Gwalior by midnight. Parchure was a well-known person in the erstwhile princely state and a tongawallah, Gariba, took them to Parchure's house in Lashkar. Parchure had just gone to sleep, but when his eldest son Nilkant told him about the guests, he immediately came down. They were welcomed accordingly and when Godse shared the reason for his visit, he readily agreed to help. The next morning, Parchure sent his son Nilkant and his 'bodyguard' Roopa to fetch a man called Gangadhar Sakharam Dandavate, who arranged an Italian automatic 9 mm Beretta by the evening. The revolver was used in the Second World War and reached India through a war veteran of the Gwalior Infantry. It had changed many hands before reaching a man called Jagdish Prasad Goel, who had sold it to Dandavate. Since no effort was made to unearth the chain of ownership, many unsubstantiated stories are popular in Gwalior and elsewhere.

Godse had found the means to accomplish his goal. Gandhi, discussing means with an American journalist Vincent Sheean—who wanted to know whether his 'objection to the use of force was not [merely] that force could as well be used to support unrighteous wars [but rather] it was fundamental'—remarked, 'I do not know what is intrinsically good. Hence, I do not go by results. It is enough if I take care of the means.'[60] Sacredness of means was fundamental to his value system and the means he chose for establishing peace were non-violence and satyagraha. Not that peace had been completely established; there was news of violent incidents from places like Mysore and he was particularly worried about the news coming from NWFP where he had worked hard with Khan Abdul Ghaffar Khan. Known as Frontier Gandhi, Khan Sahib was one of the few leaders who opposed Partition till the end and fought vehemently against the communal propaganda of the League. There was fresh tension in the atmosphere of Delhi in response to the news of violence in Pakistan. In a meeting organized by the Hindu Mahasabha on 27 January, slogans were raised in support of Madanlal.[61] Two people with grenades were detained in a meeting with Nehru in attendance in Amritsar on 28 January[62] and the Gandhi murder trial papers mention that they might have been a part of the larger conspiracy, but the case was never investigated. However, undeterred by all this, Gandhi was determined to find peace with his sacred means and kept moving towards that.

Gandhi visited the annual *urs* of Khwaja Qutubuddin Bakhtiyar at Mehrauli on 26 January. The tomb had been vandalized in communal violence. While talking to his visitors in the afternoon, Gandhi said:

> When I saw the magnificent tomb of the Auliya in ruins, the thought whether we had degraded ourselves to that extent flashed through my mind. Suppose for a while that more frightful and barbarous atrocities were committed in Pakistan; but need we compete in doing evil deeds? Besides this, I have received a report that in the Frontier Province and Pakistan 130 Hindus and Sikhs were murdered at a certain place in one day and there was wholesale looting in the bargain. I would ask who killed them after all. Nobody can say whether those who were killed were guilty of some crime. But if you take revenge for this horrible massacre here in India, it will most certainly be an act of barbarism. Therefore, we should see to it that we do not commit any such insensible act in the peaceful

> atmosphere prevailing today. Our Government is fully alive to the work of destruction that is going on in Pakistan.[63]

This was the fundamental difference between Gandhi and his detractors. While Gandhi wanted to eradicate 'evils', his detractors were instigating people to indulge in a *competition of evils deeds.* Gandhi's remedy was simple and straightforward: the majority should save the minority. In Noakhali, the majority were Muslim, and Gandhi stood with the minority Hindus. In Delhi, the minority were the Muslims and Gandhi appealed for their protection. His religion did not turn him into an enemy of the other by default. His idea of India was one of an inclusive culture and co-existence. Savarkar and his disciples, on the other hand, wanted to create a Hindu Pakistan. They wanted to compete in evil deeds and hate was their driving force. Their definition of Hindutva converts religion into a potent weapon to destroy others. Thus, they never hesitated before choosing immoral means to achieve their barbaric goals under the garb of false pride in their religion. Gandhi was the mirror which reflected their evil designs. They fixed 30 January for the destruction of that unblemished mirror.

The reduced band of conspirators met in Delhi in the evening of the 29th. While Karkare had reached in time, the other two could reach Delhi only a little before noon. Nathuram chose to stay at the retiring room of Old Delhi railway station and registered himself as N. Venaik Rao. After a brief meeting at the retiring room, they walked towards Chandni Chowk. In another effort to save his partners, Godse had his photograph taken from a cheap roadside studio and sent a copy of it along with a letter explaining the reason behind his act to the office and home address of Apte and the Ahmednagar address of Karkare. These three letters and the copies of the photographs were an attempt to prove that he was alone in killing Gandhi. However, they had already left behind enough evidence. After dinner at a vegetarian hotel, Godse returned to the retiring room while Karkare and Apte went out to watch a movie. Karkare returned by midnight and spent the night on the railway platform, while Apte returned only in the morning.

Margaret Bourke-White interviewed Gandhi on 29 January.

Margaret had spent a long time in India and had shot many remarkable photographs depicting the tragedy of Partition; her book *Halfway to Freedom* is an important document of that period. She asked him if he 'still cherish[ed] the wish and hope to live the full span of life':

> He had lost that wish, Gandhiji said, in view of the prevailing darkness. He was, however, groping for light. If things took a turn for the better and the people responded to his call and co-operated to usher in a new era of peace and amity, he would again wish—indeed, he would be 'commanded' to wish to live the full span.[64]

This reminds one of the *Pavamana Mantra* of the *Brihadaranyaka Upanishad*: *Tamaso ma jyotir gamaya* ('lead us from darkness to light') is interdependently associated with the wish of *asato ma sadgamaya* ('lead us from ignorance to truth') and *mrityor ma amritam gamaya* ('lead us from death to deathlessness'). Gandhi's wish to live 125 years was borne of a desire to lead humanity from ignorance to truth and darkness to light, but when this goal seemed unrealizable, his will for deathlessness was also dying.

The trio met on 30 January 1948 once again in the retiring room and went to a non-vegetarian restaurant for breakfast. As they were about to order, the waiter gave Nathuram and Apte a sweeping *salaam* and a friendly grin. The waiter, in fact, belonged to Poona and had just been transferred to the Delhi railway restaurant. After breakfast they discussed their plan to get close enough to Gandhi during the prayer meeting. The main concern was that there could be a few plainclothes police personnel from Poona among the security who might easily recognize them. But this didn't occur to those in charge of Gandhi's security. Then a suggestion was made that Godse should pretend to be an old-fashioned photographer and enter the grounds with a camera and tripod and with a black cloth draped over this head. But Nathuram turned it down and asked, 'What about a *burqa*?' Women used to sit right in the first circle in the prayer meetings and a *burqa*-clad Godse could reach the closest possible. The trio was excited by this idea and Apte bought one from Chandni Chowk for fifty rupees. But when Nathuram tried it, he could not walk properly, and the idea was dropped. Instead of discussing more ideas to disguise themselves, they now decided to try the weapon once. Godse fired a few shots aiming at a circle on the trunk of a tree in the wooded area at the back of the Birla temple and, satisfied with the performance, decided to return to the retiring room.

By now it was nearing 1 p.m., which was the hour at which they had to vacate the retiring room. Nathuram and Apte went down to the counter and asked the booking clerk whether he could extend their reservation for another day. The booking clerk, Sundarilal, bristled with authority and not only told Nathuram to vacate the room, but also went upstairs and stood around to see that they did in fact vacate the room at the proper time. This made sure that Sundarilal would remember the trio well.

Gandhi was restless. This independence was too different from his dream of swaraj. He wrote a new constitution for the Congress on the 29th. This is frequently used for the propaganda that Gandhi was for abandoning the Congress. The fact is that he was proposing to restructure the Congress as the *Lok Sewak Sangh*, which would follow the ideals of secularism and selflessness. This was still a proposal and had Nathuram not killed him, he would have discussed it with his comrades in the party. One should also remember that he instructed Patel and Nehru to run the government jointly. He was anguished by the news pouring in from different parts of the country about the misdeeds of people in Congress governments and wanted to rebuild the party. Manuben quotes a couplet he recited that night—'*Hai Bahar-e-bagh dunia chand roz / dekh lo jiska tamasha chand roz*' (The bloom in the world's garden is short-lived / enjoy it so long as it lasts).[65] To digress a little, today when some critics of his talk about the lack of art and music in his life, one wonders how they could not see the rich presence of Sanskrit, Urdu, Gujarati and English literature in Gandhi's life. How do they forget that he demanded that Mozart's symphony be played during his only meeting with Romain Rolland!

Gandhi asked Manuben to chant a Gujarati hymn during the morning of 30 January. The hymn was: '*Thake n thake chhatay ho / manvi n lejo visamo*' (Whether tired or not, O man! Do not take rest). This hymn has an echo of a shloka from the *Kathopanishada*—'*Uttishthata jagrata prapya varannibodhata*' (Arise, awake, approach the great ones and learn). The other part of this shloka is: '*Nishita kshurasya dhara duratyaya durgam tat pathah (iti) kavayah vadanti*' (For sharp as a razor's edge, hard to traverse, difficult of going is that path, say the sages). The life of Gandhi exemplified that tireless journey on this sharp edge for the salvation of humanity.

Today was destined for another sharp-edged journey. Patel was to come this afternoon on some special business. News about differences of opinion between Patel and Nehru had started appearing in international media. Gandhi wanted to solve this once and for all. Sardar came at four with his daughter Manuben. Patel spoke. Gandhi spun and listened. Rajmohan Gandhi records this incident in his biography of Patel:

> At 4.30 p.m., Manu...brought milk, vegetables and slices of orange, Gandhi's evening meal. Vallabhbhai's talk with him continued while he had his dinner. Gandhi repeated what he had said on the 23rd. Patel's presence in the Cabinet was indispensable, and so was Nehru's. He had already said the same thing, Gandhi added, to Jawaharlal. Any breach between Vallabhbhai and Nehru would be disastrous, and he would underline this opinion in his post-prayer speech that evening. It was decided that all three (Gandhi, Patel, and Nehru) would meet the next day... At 5 p.m., Gandhi's prayer time, Abha Gandhi presented herself and held up a watch but neither Gandhi nor Patel paid any attention. After some minutes Manuben said, 'It is five ten,' whereupon the two rose, Vallabhbhai to go home and Gandhi to walk to his prayers on the lawn of the house where he was staying.[66]

Nathuram finally selected a khaki dress for that evening. At quarter past four he got ready to leave his third-class waiting room. Apte asked, 'Do you want us to be there?' Godse replied, 'After coming so far, why not?' Godse was first to leave. After ten minutes, Apte left with Karkare in a tonga and mixed with the people at Birla House.

Manuben later entered in her diary:

> Bapu climbed up four stairs and looked up. Then, lifting his hand off our shoulders, he folded them to greet the assembled people and walked on. I was walking on his right. From the same direction a stout young man in khaki dress, with his hand folded, pushed his way through the crowd and came near us. I thought he wanted to touch Bapu's feet; this happened every day…therefore I pushed aside the intruder and said to him, 'Bapu is already 10 minutes late; why do you embarrass him?' But he pushed me so forcibly that the rosary, spittoon and notebook dropped from my hands.
>
> So long as the other things dropped, I scuffled with the man; but when the rosary dropped to the ground, I bent down to pick it up. At the same time three shots were fired, one after another. Darkness prevailed. The atmosphere was charged with the smoke and the sky resounded with the boom. Bapu still seemed walking on, chest bare and '*Hei Ra…ma! Hei Ra…*' on his lips. His hands were folded, and in a moment he fell on the ground. Some men tried to hold him up. Abhaben also fell down. She at once placed Bapu's head in her lap…
>
> The first bullet from the assassin's seven bore automatic hit the belly 3.5 inches to the right of the middle and 2.5 inches above the navel. The second hit the belly 1 inch away from the middle and the third 4 inches away to the right… Profuse flow of blood turned the face wan in about 10 minutes.[67]

Two days back, he had told the American journalist Vincent Sheean, 'It might be that it would be more valuable to humanity for me to die.'[68]

Once again, he was accurate with his prophecy.

The Light Has Gone Out of Our Lives[69]

> Each one of us, who has raised his hands against the innocent, is a collaborator in the murder of Gandhi.
>
> —Mian Iftikharuddin[70]

Mian Iftikharuddin had been among the most progressive leaders in the Congress since the early forties. He was the one who arranged a meeting between Nehru and Sheikh Abdullah during his tenure as the president of the Punjab Congress Committee. But later he chose to support Partition and joined the League. As Minister of Relief and Rehabilitation in Punjab state, he had witnessed the plight of refugees. It will not be irrelevant to remember that Mian Sahib soon lost his position in the Muslim League due to his progressive stand on the question of land reforms. He started a newspaper with Faiz Ahmad Faiz. However, it was confiscated under the regime of Ayub Khan. His statement seems to originate from his own repentance at that moment. Such repentance played an important role in controlling the violence on both sides of the newly drawn border. James Douglass quotes political scientist Dennis Dalton:

> Gandhi's assassination, more than any other single event, served to stop the communal violence surrounding partition. It achieved this in the same way as his fasts, by causing people to pause and reflect in the midst of fear, anger and enmity: to ask themselves if the cost was worth it. A mixture of motives was probably at work, merciful and rational as well as grief-stricken or guilt-ridden. But somehow a determination came to stop killing... There was no higher tribute to his life than the impact of his death, his final statement for Swaraj.[71]

Condolences poured in from every corner of the globe. Newspapers across the world had Gandhi on their first page on 31 January 1948. Except the Hindu Mahasabha and RSS, everyone else expressed their grief publicly in India. Amidst all this, a letter written by Dr Ambedkar to his would-be wife Laxmi Kabir (who was later known as Savita Ambedkar) is astonishing. He wrote:

> I entirely agree with you that Gandhi should have not met his death at the hands of a Maharashtrian. May I go further and say that it would have been wrong for anybody to commit such a foul deed...
>
> *My own view is that great men are of great service to their country but they are also at certain times a great hindrance to the progress of their country.* There is one incident in Roman History which comes to my mind on this occasion. When Caesar was done to death and the matter was reported to Cicero, Cicero said to the messenger, 'Tell the Romans your hour of liberty has come.'
>
> While one regrets the assassination of Gandhi, one can't help finding in his heart the echo of the sentiments expressed by Cicero on

> the assassination of Caesar. Gandhi had become a positive danger to this country. He has choked all free-thought. He was holding together the Congress, which is a combination of all the bad and self-seeking elements in society who agreed on no social or moral principles governing the life of society except the one of praising and flattering Mr Gandhi. Such a body is unfit to govern a country. As the Bible says 'that sometimes good cometh out of evil,' so also *I think that good will come out of the death of Mr Gandhi.*[72]

It is surprising that this heartless statement is for that Gandhi who impressed upon Nehru to appoint Ambedkar as law minister! It is also surprising that what bothers him is that the killer was a Maharashtrian. He is critical of the Congress and minces no words expressing his disrespect for Gandhi but chooses to utter not a single word against *the ideology* that killed Gandhi. It is indeed strange that there is no mention of the gruesome violence against minorities in India as well as Pakistan and Gandhi's attempts to control that!

While the comparison between Mahatma Gandhi and Julius Caesar is surprising, this analogy from history is doubly cruel. After all, Cicero was pardoned by Caesar despite all his rebellions, but when Brutus invited him to join his cabinet, Cicero regretted that he was not invited to be a part of that conspiracy. The Bible says:

> The righteous perisheth, and no man layeth *it* to heart: and merciful men are taken away, none considering that the righteous is taken away from the evil *to come.* (Isaiah 57:1)

The Differences Between Nehru and Patel

The differences between Nehru and Patel, which Gandhi was worried about till the end, were also blurred by his death.

Patel had just entered home when Brij Krishna, one of Gandhi's associates, shouted from his car: 'Where is Sardar? Bapu has been shot. Bapu is dead.' At once, Vallabhbhai got into the car in which Brij Krishna had come. When they got to Birla House, the Gita was being recited around Gandhi's body, which lay on a carpet on the floor. The Mahatma's face seemed 'calm and serene' and forgiving to

Patel.[73] Nehru reached within minutes of his arrival and as Manuben remembers: 'And Panditji—Ah! One would not wish even one's enemy to fall upon such evil days—hid his face in Sardar Dada's lap like a little child and began to weep bitter tears of grief... At last, Sardar Dada, being a man of iron as he is, did not flinch in the least from passing through this most terrible of all ordeals. Of all men he alone consoled everybody.'[74] Mountbatten too reached Birla House in haste. The members of the cabinet were assembled in a room. Mountbatten entered the room and said that Gandhi in his last interview with him had said that his dearest wish was to bring full reconciliation between Nehru and Patel. On hearing this they embraced each other. Mountbatten also succeeded in getting Patel to broadcast a message at the same time as Nehru that fateful night.[75] Patel said in an emotional outburst:

> Friends, the occasion demands not anger but earnest heart searching from us all. If we give vent to our understandable anger, it would mean that we have forgotten our beloved master's teachings so soon after his death. And let me say that even in his lifetime we only haltingly followed our master.
>
> ... The mad youth who killed him was wrong if he thought that hereby he was destroying his noble mission. Perhaps God wanted Gandhiji's mission to fulfil and prosper through his death.[76]

Patel was severely criticized by people like Jayaprakash Narayan and Mridula Sarabhai. Stung, Vallabhbhai wrote out his resignation on 2 February. However, his associate Vidya Shankar succeeded in persuading him to not send it immediately. The next morning, he received a letter from Pandit Nehru. Reminding him of their long association and the final opinion of Gandhi, he wrote:

> When Bapu was alive we had hoped to meet him together and discuss various matters that had troubled us somewhat... Now, with Bapu's death, everything has changed and we have to face a different and more difficult world. The old controversies have ceased to have much significance and it seems to me that the urgent need of the hour is for all of us to function as closely and co-operatively as possible. Indeed, there is no other way.

> I have been greatly distressed by the persistence of whispers and rumours about you and me; magnifying out of all proportions any differences we may have... We must put an end to this mischief.
>
> In the crisis that we have to [face] now after Bapu's death I think it is my duty and, if I may venture to say, yours also to face it together as friends and colleagues. Not merely superficially, but in full loyalty to one another and with confidence in each other.
>
> I hoped to have a long talk with you, but we are so terribly pressed for time... Meanwhile I do not want to wait for this talk and hence this letter, which carries with it my affection and friendship with you.

Vallabhbhai reverted in a similar spirit on 5 February:

> I am deeply touched, indeed overwhelmed, by the affection and warmth of your letter of 3 February. I fully and heartily reciprocate the sentiment you have so feelingly expressed... I had good fortune to have a last talk with Bapu for over an hour just before his death... His opinion also binds us both and I can assure you that I am fully resolved to approach my responsibilities and obligations in this spirit.[77]

The previous day, addressing the Congress party in the Constituent Assembly, Vallabhbhai had publicly expressed his solidarity with, and loyalty to, Jawaharlal. Calling him, for the first time, 'my leader', Patel added, 'I am one with the Prime Minister on all national issues. For over a quarter of a century, both of us sat at the feet of our master and struggled together for the freedom of India. It is unthinkable today, when the Mahatma is no more, that we would quarrel.'[78] Differences remained, but the ice started melting in the true spirit of a democratic tradition.

But that death could not change the likes of Godse.

For some time, there was a hush and when the people present in the Birla House compound realized what had happened, the atmosphere was filled with grief and anger. A sergeant from the Royal Indian Air Force pounced upon Godse and gripped him by the wrist, swinging his arm up with one hand while raining blows on his face with the other. A moment later Raghu Mali, a gardener at Birla House, was grappling with him, and then there were about ten people attacking him. Police came to rescue him and took him in their custody. Soon, a rumour spread that the killer was a Muslim. Alan Campbell-Johnson wrote that 'Mountbatten was greeted by a scaremonger who told him, "It was a Muslim who did it." At that moment we still did not know the religion and the name of the assassin but Mountbatten, appreciating that if he was a Muslim we were lost anyhow and that nothing could then avert the most disastrous civil war, replied in a flash, "You fool, don't you know it was a Hindu!"'[79]

To lie seems a part of Nathuram's training. He did not reveal his name for a long time and then lied about his age.[80] Historian Y.D. Phadke's evaluation of Nathuram's actions leads him to write that the latter was 'a hardened liar who crushed the truth, a criminal'.[81] His behaviour in the court is testimony to this.

In response to a demand by Syama Prasad Mukherjee to release Hindu Mahasabha members like Mahant Digbijoy Nath and others, Sardar Patel wrote on 6 May 1948:

> I quite agree with you that the Hindu Mahasabha, as an organization, was not concerned in the conspiracy that led to Gandhiji's murder; but, at the same time, we can't shut our eyes to the fact that an appreciable number of the members of the Mahasabha gloated over the tragedy and distributed sweets. On this matter, reliable reports have come to us from all parts of the country. Further, militant communalism, which was preached until only a few months ago by many spokesman of Mahasabha including men like Mahant Digbijoy Nath, Prof Ram Singh and Deshpande, couldn't but be regarded as a danger to public security.[82]

In the mythological tradition of the Hindu religion, only *pishachas* are known to celebrate death. The humans of this great nation came to mourn the death of their beloved Bapu in an unprecedented number. Campbell-Johnson commented:

> The man who more than anyone else had helped to supersede the Raj was receiving in death homage beyond the dreams of any Viceroy.[83]

5. The Red Fort Trial

In his first action after the assassination of Gandhi, Nagarvala raided Savarkar Sadan. Some one hundred and fifty files and ten thousand papers were seized. When Nagarvala was asked by the Kapur Commission as to why V.D. Savarkar was not detained, his reply was that to arrest him after the bomb incident but before the murder would have set the whole of the Maharashtrian region of Bombay Province aflame.[1] Later, in an interview with Malgonkar after his retirement from the services, Nagarvala said, 'To my dying day I shall believe that Savarkar was the man who organized the Gandhi murder.'[2] Patel too wrote to Nehru on 27 February 1948, 'It was the fanatical wing of Hindu Mahasabha directly under Savarkar that [hatched] the conspiracy and saw it through.'[3]

The findings of the Kapur Commission finally proved them right. It's interesting that Malgonkar never mentions these findings in his book published in 1975.

Arrests

Nathuram kept repeating that he had carried out the murder alone, but the very first piece of evidence was found in his diary. He used to record his daily expenses in this diary and it had a mention of Rs 308 for an air ticket. This was twice the fare of an individual traveller. He had also kept a record of the money given to Badge and Gopal. This made it clear that there were others involved in the conspiracy and at least one of them travelled with him from Bombay. He made a further mistake and claimed that he stayed in Hotel Elphinstone from 20 January to 30 January and did not have any contact with anyone in Poona. An inquiry at the hotel revealed that he had stayed in the hotel from the 24th to the 27th and that he was not alone.

Working on the leads given by Madanlal, Nagarvala had passed an order to arrest Digambar Badge on 24 January. Not that he knew much about his involvement in the conspiracy, but he thought that the arms dealer might have some clue. It is an astonishing fact that the Poona Police took no action till Gandhi was murdered. Badge was at his house the whole time while the police claimed that he was hiding in the forests. After initial evasions, he soon narrated the whole story when he was confronted with Madanlal in Bombay; however, Madanlal did not give away much information. Gopal was next to be arrested from his village and brought to Bombay. Shankar, who had gone to see his mother in Sholapur, returned to Poona within a couple of hours after the arrest of his master. He decided to go to Bombay in search of him and reached Bhuleshwar to meet Dixit Maharaj. One of his servants took him to the CBI building and, thus, except Apte and Karkare, the whole gang was under detention by the first week of February.

Karkare and Apte were planning to flee to some foreign country with the help of some influential political leader from the Mahasabha[4] but they could find none and left for Bombay via Allahabad, where they stayed in Hotel Sea Green (North) for one night and then shifted to Elphinstone Annex. They went to meet G.M. Joshi on 2 February and caught a train to Poona on the morning of the 7th. They contemplated fleeing to Hyderabad or Goa, which were not parts of the Indian dominion till then, but finally decided to return to Bombay. On the morning of 11 February, they were back to Joshi's house, where they stayed for two days and then checked in to Hotel Apollo as N. Kashinath and R. Bishnu. Apte made a call to Manorama Salvi from the hotel's phone at about 10 p.m. on 14 February. Her phone had been put on surveillance and this ended their game of hide and seek. Parchure was also arrested the same day in Gwalior.

Nagarvala was appointed in charge of the case on the 17th, and with Badge turning approver, the conspiracy was laid bare.

Trial and Sentences

For the next two months, the police under Nagarvala collected enough pieces of evidence to fill the gaps. Waiters from hotels and restaurants where they stayed, ordered whisky, and dined; Bimba, the film actress; taxi drivers from Delhi and Bombay; Angchekar, who met Karkare in the train; Dixit and Dada Maharaj; the booking clerk at the Old Delhi railway station—there was no dearth of witnesses or evidence. Shankar had helped them with confiscation of the arms hidden in the forests behind the Hindu Mahasabha building and Badge had narrated every single detail. But it still took the police nearly five months to complete the investigation and declare the case ripe for trial.

The trial commenced on 22 June 1948, before Justice Atma Charan. He was a senior member of the judicial branch of the Indian Civil Service, appointed specially for the trial and given requisite jurisdiction, because the judge hearing the case had to deal with offences committed beyond his or her normal territorial jurisdiction. The proceedings inside the Red Fort were open to the public and the press, and were extensively reported. While Nathuram Vinayak Godse, Narayan Dattatreya Apte, Gopal Vinayak Godse, Madanlal Kashmirilal Pahwa, Vishnu Ramakrishna Karkare, Digambar Badge, Shankar Kistayya, Dattatreya Sadashiv Parchure and Vinayak Damodar Savarkar were present in the court, three others, namely Gangadhar Dandavate, Gangadhar Jadhav and Suryadeo Sharma, were absconding and were tried in absentia. The liberty to select their counsel was extended to all accused.[5] It is strange that none of the latter three were ever arrested or prosecuted. It is worth mentioning that all of them belonged to Gwalior and were involved in the procurement of revolvers; at least one of them, Dandavate, had been active with the Hindu Mahasabha.

This was the third historic trial in the Red Fort—ironically, the first one was held against Bahadur Shah Zafar after the failed rebellion of 1857; the second was against members of the INA who dreamt of unfurling the Indian flag from its ramparts under the leadership of the iconic Subhas Chandra Bose. This third one was being held against those brutal assassins who killed an unarmed Gandhi in their only exhibition of valour.

In this trial, Savarkar was present in the dock. It was the same Savarkar who had not only quoted Bahadur Shah Zafar in his book but had praised his 'grand and revered idol'.[6] Here was a man who vehemently opposed British power, went to prison, and then, due to his own weakness, bowed down before them and went on to become one of the most faithful servants of British imperialism. He was a father figure and master for everyone else present in the dock. Godse and his co-conspirators tried their best to save their master, but the master had already sent his proposal to the authorities on the seventeenth day of his arrest. He wrote to the Commissioner of Police, Bombay, on 22 February 1948:

> I am ready to give an undertaking that I shall refrain from taking part in any communal or political activities for any period Government may require in case I am released on that condition.[7]

While going through the report of the Kapur Commission, one wonders whether the authorities were complicit in the effort to save Savarkar! There is an incident involving Morarji Desai. He has mentioned it in his autobiography:

> The counsel for Mr Savarkar asked me a question which I do not remember now. The Judge told me that I am not bound to answer it. He also told me that if there is no merit to the question, you need not answer it. But I told the judge that I have no problem in answering this question. Please ask the accused whether he wants me to answer this question? When I said this the lawyer took this question back. Not only that, he even stopped his questioning after that.[8]

This question was excluded from the court proceedings, but a journalist noted it down. As per a news item published in the 1 September 1948 edition of *The Times of India*, the question which Morarji Desai forgot in his autobiography was: 'Did you have any other information about Savarkar, besides Professor Jain's statement for directing steps to be taken as regards him?'[9] One wonders why Desai needed Savarkar's nod before answering this question and why the chief prosecution counsel stopped questioning after that? Desai, as home minister of the state, must have been privy to confidential information regarding Savarkar and it is strange that he chose not to reveal it in the court!

Malgonkar has also done his best to twist the case. He has quoted Bhopatkar, who was an important leader of the Hindu Mahasabha and the counsel for Savarkar, from a 16 February 1989 publication of the Savarkar Memorial Committee, where he claims that the then law minister Dr Ambedkar met him and informed him that most of the members of the Nehru cabinet, including Patel, were against prosecuting Savarkar, but Nehru was adamant about it.[10] This clearly is a gambit to create a binary between Nehru and Patel and present Savarkar as a victim of it. Koenraad Elst has also tried to bring Ambedkar into the picture by narrating a story about Ambedkar meeting the lawyer of Nathuram and proposing the commutation of his sentence to lifetime imprisonment, which Nathuram rejected thereby earning the appreciation of Ambedkar.[11] Both stories are baseless and have no ground other than 'statements' by two staunch members of the cult of Savarkar. While Elst is not apologetic of his rightist agenda and shamelessly defends the assassins of Gandhi, Malgonkar tries to perform this duty under the garb of a liberal.

In response to the allegations by Syama Prasad Mukherjee that the prosecution of Savarkar was 'politically motivated' and because of his 'political convictions', Patel wrote on 6 May 1946 from Simla:

> As regards Savarkar, the Advocate General of Bombay, who is in charge of the case and other legal advisers, met me at a conference in Delhi before I came here. I told them quite clearly that the question of inclusion of Savarkar must be approached purely from a legal and judicial standpoint and political considerations should not be imported into the matter. My instructions were quite definite and beyond doubt and I am sure that they will be acted upon. I have also told them that, if they come to the view that Savarkar should be included, the papers should be placed before me before action is taken. This is, of course, in so far as the question of guilt be concerned from the point of view of law and justice. Morally, it is possible that one's commitment may be the other way about.[12]

It should be remembered here that Patel was himself a successful criminal lawyer before joining politics. Could he be any straighter forward in expressing his opinion and authority in this case? Most of the binaries between Nehru and Patel have been created for similar base objectives.

There is an interesting incident which helps understand the division of work between Nehru and Patel and their method of functioning.

A section of Gandhian leaders and social activists including Vinoba Bhave, Debeswar Sharmah, and G.V. Mavlankar started a campaign against the death penalty of Nathuram and Apte. Dr Ambedkar also gave a statement in the Constituent Assembly that he would much rather support the abolition of the death penalty. Two of Gandhi's sons, Manilal Gandhi and Ramdas Gandhi, actively participated and while Manilal sent a telegram from Durban, Ramdas wrote a letter to Nathuram on 17 May 1949.

In this letter he addressed him as 'Dear Sri Nathuram Godse' and wrote, 'I am sure, you will one day realise that you have only put an end to my father's perishable body, nothing more. Because, not only in my case, but in the case of millions all over the world, the spirit of my father still rules over their heart.' Arguing in favour of truth and non-violence he urged him to reflect on his acts. Nathuram, in his reply on 3 June, requested him to come to meet him personally and have a discussion. Ramdas accepted his proposal and wrote to Nehru for permission to meet him along with Vinoba Bhave and Kishorilal. In his reply, Nehru advised him against meeting Nathuram but left the final decision to his home minister. Sardar Patel, in his response to this, wrote on 16 June:

> I have now received the correspondence which has passed between Ramdas and Godse as also a copy of his letter to you. I adhere to my previous view that he should not see Godse. As it is, there is every likelihood of an attempt being made to treat him as a martyr. The discussion which Ramdas has proposed to have would invest the last days of Godse with a certain amount of glory. To me, it appears somewhat quixotic that any attempt should be made to convince a man who has done such a dastardly crime and takes pride in it.

Governor General Rajaji also echoed similar views and advised Ramdas to leave the case of Godse in the hands of the government. Many writers including Robert Payne have noted the abrupt end to this correspondence, but archival documents show that when Kishorilal met Patel with this request he expressed his views straightforwardly and told him to convey the same to Ramdas.* In a letter to Jawaharlal on 26 June, he wrote, 'As it has never been my intention to do anything that all the three of you may not like, I have decided to leave Godse's case in the hands of destiny. As it is destiny that impelled me to write both my letters to Godse.'

Patel also seems to have been quite disgusted by the campaign of senior Congress leaders for a pardon against the death penalty of Godse and Apte. In his correspondence with Rajaji in this regard, he regretted that the president of the Assam Congress and a member of the CWC, Mr Debeswar Sharmah was indulging in such nonsense. He further writes:

> The murder is certainly the most disgraceful and treasonable crime that has been committed in recent times. The whole world is shocked by it. The two prisoners have not during the trial or subsequently expressed the least sign of regret or repentance although by age and education they were quite fitted to realise the enormity if their crime... [T]here is therefore to be no question but that the law must take its course in both these cases.

Nehru does not appear to interfere in this entire episode.[13]

Idealism has its own naiveties. Ramdas was expecting a rational discussion on the basis of truth with the man who not only stuck to his lie that he alone had murdered Gandhi and that no other was part of the conspiracy, but taking advantage of court procedure, made a speech which was a vicious attempt to malign Gandhi. Madanlal followed suit and claimed that he alone was responsible for the attack of 20 January, and he did not intend to kill him but was only giving vent to the popular dissatisfaction with the policies of Gandhi!

The trial went on at its own pace. One hundred and forty-nine witnesses and thousands of pages of evidence were examined and cross-examined. Justice Atma Charan and government counsels received letters filled with threats. The sentence was pronounced on 10 February 1949 and while all the others were found guilty, Savarkar

* Also see the telegram sent by Kishorilal and its reply by Patel in *Sardar Patel's Correspondence*, vol. 6, p. 76.

was acquitted due to the lack of corroborative evidence to support the testimony of the government approver Digambar Badge.

The accused were given the option of appeal, and while others appealed for their innocence, Godse appealed to prove his contention that he was alone in the attempt. He knew well his destiny but used this opportunity to spread venom against Gandhi once again through the court of justice. The High Court bench of Justice Bhandari, Justice Achhuram and Justice Khosla upheld the verdict of the Red Fort trial in the case of all others but acquitted Shankar Kistayya, giving him the benefit of doubt, and Parchure, based on technical irregularities in his testimony before the magistrate in Gwalior. Nathuram's father had also filed a mercy petition before the Governor General, but it was rejected.[14]

15 November 1949 was fixed for the execution of Nathuram and Apte. Justice Khosla who was present at the time of execution gives an account of their hanging:

> The two condemned prisoners were led out of their cells with their hands pinioned behind them. Godse walked in front. His step occasionally faltered. His demeanour and general appearance evidenced a state of nervousness and fear. He tried to fight against it and keep up a bold exterior by shouting every few seconds the slogan '*Akhand Bharat*' (undivided India). But his voice had a slight croak in it and the vigour with which he had argued his case at the trial and in the High Court seemed to have been all but expended. The desperate cry was taken up by Apte who shouted '*Amar rahe*' (may stay forever). His loud and firm tone made an uncanny contrast to Godse's at times almost feeble utterance... It was said afterwards that Godse had, during his last days in gaol, repented of his deed and declared that were he to be given another chance he would spend the rest of his life in the promotion of peace and the service of his country.
>
> A single gallows had been prepared for the execution of both. Two ropes, each with a noose, hung from the high crossbar in parallel lines. Godse and Apte were made to stand side by side, the black cloth bags were drawn over their heads and tied at the necks. After adjusting the nooses, the executioner stepped off the platform and pulled the lever. Apte died almost at once and his still body swung

in a slow oscillating movement, but Godse, though unconscious and unfeeling, continued to wriggle and display signs of life in the shivering of his legs and the convulsing of his body for quite fifteen minutes.

The dead bodies were cremated inside the gaol. The ground where the pyres had been erected was ploughed up and the earth and ashes taken to the Ghaggar river and secretly submerged at a secluded spot.[15]

6. The Kapur Commission and Savarkar

> During the whole of the trial, I never saw Savarkar turning his head towards even Nathuram, who used to sit by him, in fact, next to him, much less speak with him... Savarkar sat there sphinx-like in silence, completely ignoring his co accused in the dock, in an unerringly disciplined manner...
>
> During the various talks I had with Nathuram he told me that he was deeply hurt by this—Tatyarao's [Savarkar's] calculated demonstrative non-association with him either in court or in Red Fort Jail during all the days of the Red Fort Trial. How Nathuram yearned for a touch of Tatyarao's hand, a word of sympathy, or at least a look of compassion in the secluded confines of the cells. Nathuram referred to his hurt feelings in this regard even during my last meeting with him at the Simla High Court.[1]
>
> —P.L. Inamdar, the defence lawyer for Parchure and Gopal Godse

This was so typical of Savarkar. In 1910, while bidding farewell to Madanlal Dhingra he told him sternly: 'Don't show me your face if you fail this time.' Dhingra had twice failed in the task, but this time succeeded in killing Curzon Wyllie. Savarkar was the mastermind behind this killing but stayed away from wielding any weapon. Vikram Sampath, while defending Savarkar, argues that he was needed as an intellectual 'strategist and mastermind'.[2] But he forgets to record that when such a leader sends apologies to his opponents and changes sides after his release, he hoodwinks the cause as well as those martyrs who laid their lives on his direction. When Dhingra was being tried, Savarkar was still an opponent of British rule and thus he not only supported Madanlal but went to meet him in prison after he was sentenced to death. The two had an emotional meeting with tears streaming down their cheeks. 'I have come to have a *darshan* (meeting) of a great patriot and martyr', Savarkar told Dhingra, to which the latter fell to his feet with tears of joy and gratitude.[3]

It is easy to celebrate the martyrdom of others and quite difficult to face it oneself. There are very few like Bhagat Singh who provided intellectual leadership to his organization, made plans, implemented them, and happily kissed the gallows. Subhas Chandra Bose never apologized to the British, even after the defeat of the INA in the Second World War. But Savarkar does not belong in this league. He couldn't face the hardships of the Cellular and surrendered before the enemy. This turned him from a revolutionary to a conspirator. Even R.C. Majumdar, who is one of the most renowned rightist historians, couldn't defend his act. He comments that, 'while Savarkar had changed his views, the Government view remained the same as before'. Savarkar was availing himself of special facilities as a foreman in the Andamans, but when other political prisoners demanded such facilities, he criticized them by saying that 'These political prisoners were at the beck and call for anything they [the authorities] needed and became very subservient—not to put it more bluntly—to the authorities.' Majumdar writes: 'This is a very serious insinuation against these political prisoners, and we have no means to determine how far Savarkar was justified in this assumption. He does not give any evidence or practical illustration.' Quoting *Jele Tirish Bochor*, a memoir by Trailokyanath Chakravarty, who was in the Cellular Jail between 1916 and 1920, Majumdar says that Savarkar and his brother Ganpat secretly encouraged other prisoners to call a strike but did not join it. His excuse was that if he had 'openly led them, his concessions would have been taken back, and he would have been sent to solitary confinement again'.[4] Sampath, however, omits this incident. These concessions were so important to him that he decided to bend before the British, and sent a similar proposal to the government of the day as soon as his name appeared in the Gandhi murder case. Thus, Godse could never find the affection that Dhingra had received before going to the gallows.

He was not convicted in the Red Fort trial in the absence of adequate and corroborative evidence. But during the investigations by the Kapur Commission, it was found that the evidence was always there, only it was not presented in the court due to reasons unknown.

Findings of the Kapur Commission

In a reception organized at Poona on 11 November 1964 to felicitate Gopal Godse on his release, G.V. Ketkar claimed that Nathuram used to discuss with him the outcomes of Gandhi's assassination, and that Badge had discussed future plans with him after the incident of 20 January 1948. Ketkar was Tilak's grandson and an ex-editor of *Kesari*. Ketkar also said that he had told this to a local leader of the Congress party, Balukaka Kanetkar, who had passed this information on to the then chief minister of Bombay state, B.G. Kher, and Morarji Desai.[5] An RSS leader N.G. Abhyankar was also present at this occasion, who compared Godse to Lords Krishna and Shankar. P.V. Davre and Shantabai Gokhle from the women's wing of the Hindu Mahasabha also praised Godse in this function.[6]

Gajanan Vishwanath Ketkar was an important member of Poona's right wing. While the sons of Lokmanya Tilak chose a progressive path and his grandson Jayantrao Tilak was elected as a member of parliament and later chairman of the Maharashtra Assembly from Congress, Ketkar joined that group of Tilakists which was squarely opposite to Tilak in its communal politics and only inherited his social fundamentalism. When a defence committee for legal help of the assassins was formed immediately after the murder of Gandhi, Ketkar took the responsibility of treasurer while Bhopatkar was appointed its president. He was also using *Kesari* as an editor to defend the killers. B.G. Khare and the secretary and chief whip of the Congress in the Maharashtra Assembly, Narhar Vishnu Gadgil, wrote separate letters to Patel and Nehru to inform them that Kesari was glorifying the killers in its editorials.[7] A fine of Rs 3,000 was imposed on Ketkar in this case.[8]

It was natural that this statement of Ketkar created a stir throughout the country. The union government constituted a commission on

22 March 1966 to inquire into his claims and their implications under the chairmanship of the seniormost advocate of Supreme Court, Mr Gopal Swaroop Pathak. But he was soon inducted into the cabinet and this responsibility fell to Justice Jivanlal Kapur on 21 November 1966. The Commission had the following terms of reference:

> (a) Whether any persons, in particular Shri Gajanan Vishwanath Ketkar, of Poona, had prior information of the conspiracy of Nathuram Vinayak Godse and others to assassinate Mahatma Gandhi;
>
> (b) whether any of such persons had communicated the said information to any authorities of the Government of Bombay or of the Government of India; in particular, whether the aforesaid Shri Ketkar had conveyed the said information to the late Bal Gangadhar Kher, the then Premier of Bombay, through the late Balukaka Kanetkar;
>
> (c) If so, what action was taken by the Government of Bombay, in particular by the late Bal Gangadhar Kher, and the Government of India on the basis of the said information?[9]

The range of these terms of reference before the Kapur Commission was so broad that over the next four years more than a hundred witnesses and innumerable pieces of evidence were scrutinized, including witnesses and evidence that were not included in the Red Fort trial. The commission examined the investigations of the Delhi and Bombay Police and went deep into those layers of this conspiracy which were not relevant for the court. Going through this 770-page report, one can clearly see that the persons who were responsible for the conspiracy to murder and the murderers of Mahatma Gandhi were Savarkarites belonging to the Hindu Rashtra Dal, who were blind followers of Savarkar whom they treated as the Fuehrer.*[10] In a letter to Jawaharlal Nehru on 27 February 1948, Patel wrote, 'It was the fanatical wing of Hindu Mahasabha directly under Savarkar that [hatched] the conspiracy and saw it through.'[11]

The second important finding is that the police departments of Ahmednagar and Poona did not take any prohibitive action in the

* Leader; a term used by the members of Nazi Party for Hitler.

wake of regular information about communal violence by this group. For example, a certain N.R. Athawale was arrested in Poona for carrying out a bomb explosion in a public library of Poona and during inquiry revealed that he was sent by Apte, but the police neither arrested him nor kept an eye on his activities.[12] In its comment on the Poona police, the Commission is quiet blunt: 'They could easily be deluded by the movement being given an anti-Muslim slant.'[13] One can't ignore the observation of Nehru in a letter to Patel on 26 January 1948: 'Many of these (RSS) people are in our offices and in the police.'[14]

Communalization of the police force had been one of the biggest obstacles in effectively controlling communal violence in independent India. The conspirators seem to have taken full advantage of it. As for as the Delhi and Bombay Police are concerned, the Commission found them 'guilty of lethargy and inefficiency'.[15] Since the then Delhi Police chief T. Sanjeevi had passed away, the Commission could not include his version, and thus accepted Nagarvala's statement that the officers from Delhi did not properly explain the testimony of Pahwa. However, the Commission commented:

> It is unfortunate that Mr Nagarvala was not allowed an opportunity to read and study Madanlal's statement, and it is surprising why he did not evince any interest in that statement and insist of [*sic*] reading it through to find out what Madanlal had disclosed. This action is quite at variance with his later action after the murder, when he got Madanlal over to Bombay and interrogated him at great length. No doubt, then he was the principal investigator and previously he was what he calls, working out an information. It might be that his inquiry was complementary to the investigation by the Delhi Police, but a study of Madanlal's statement should have been as helpful then as it was after the murder.[16]

Could Gandhi Be Saved?

Based on a news report of his attendance in the *urs* of Khwaja Qutubuddin Bakhtiyar on 27 January 1948 published in *Hindustan Times*, the Commission had concluded that Gandhi was careless about his security. However, we know it well that fear had never been a part of his philosophy and valour was integral to his understanding of non-violence. Be it South Africa, or Champaran, or Noakhali, he never cared for his security. The responsibility of his security was on those for whom he was putting his life at risk.

The Commission has made a very significant comment on his security arrangements. While it absolved Sardar Patel of the allegation regarding laxity in Gandhi's security,[17] at the same time, it raised very serious questions about flaws in the arrangements. Well-known law expert and a close associate of Gandhi, Purushottam Trikamdas said in his submission to the Commission that 'Mahatmaji should not have been asked about the search, because it was the duty of Government and the Police to protect him'.[18] The then DCP of Delhi Police submitted the response that 'if he had known about the conspiracy to murder Mahatmaji, he would have insisted on a meeting at a higher level to be called by Home Minister and that he would have stopped the prayer meeting whether Mahatmaji liked it or not, because his life was more important'.[19] It is strange that the Delhi Police could not anticipate a conspiracy even after the attack on 20 January and the arrest thereafter! The testimony of Madanlal and his repeated warning, '*Wah fir aayega*' (He will come again), should have been enough to understand that he was not alone. But the alertness of police can be gauged by the fact that Police Superintendent A.N. Bhatia was absent and Assistant Sub-Inspector Amar Nath came on duty at 4.30 p.m. on that fateful day![20]

The Commission found that after the murder of Mahatma Gandhi the Government of India became very alert regarding the security of the Prime minister and other members of the cabinet.[21] The Commission did 'not agree that the Mahatma's wishes or views as to prayer meeting being free to all could be ignored or treated unceremoniously. [But if] he objected to the search, that was the end of that protective measure and other modes should have been suggested and devised by the Police'.[22] On the basis of statements by G.K. Handoo, who was appointed chief of security to the ministers and senior police officers B.B.S. Jaitley and N.N. Kamat the Commission opined that for his security:

a) ...Police from Bombay should have been called in to act as watchers and spotters and others should have been stationed outside Birla House.

b) High ranking police officers should have been put in immediate charge of security as was done in the case of other V.I.P.s but after the murder.

c) Plain clothes police should have been deployed as if they were domestics and Congress volunteers to be flanking Mahatma Gandhi when he was going to the prayer meetings or returning therefrom.

d) Congress volunteers should also have been asked to flank Mahatma Gandhi if there was any strong objection to the presence of police flanking him. This was the practice which was generally followed before the partition in the Northern provinces.

e) At the Birla house the members of Mahatma's party were totally oblivious of the danger to his life even after the bomb incident and it appears that the Congress volunteers for that reason had become rather lax. [23]

The Commission concludes in this regard that:

> Knowing the conditions in Delhi and knowing the intensity of feelings against Gandhiji's post prayer speeches and with the warning of the bomb outrage the Police at Delhi should have been more alert. It is unfortunate that those in charge of security forgot about the existence of the blue print referred to by Mr. G.K. Handoo.[24]

However, this question is problematic as to whether Gandhi could have been saved by superior security arrangements. Leaders from Kennedy to Indira Gandhi have been killed around the world despite elaborate security arrangements. The Commission had also observed that:

> No one can be sure that even if this precaution could have protected the Mahatma or would have been sufficient for the purpose because it has been noticed that in other countries in spite of the elaborative arrangements and precautions taken, mishaps have happened.[25]

But as the commission puts it: 'That was no ground for not taking proper precautions which the experts had suggested.' The laxity on part of the police and administration was unfortunate at best and criminal at worst. It seems that either the Delhi Police was so ignorant that it was not expecting an attack so soon after the incident of 20 January 1948 or there were elements within the police who were not interested in saving Gandhi's life.

The Role of Vinayak Damodar Savarkar

Justice Atma Charan had found it 'unsafe' to pronounce Savarkar guilty in the absence of corroborative evidence. But going through the report one finds that there were enough testimonies to corroborate the statement of approver Digambar Badge that Godse and Apte had met Savarkar before leaving to kill Gandhi. It is strange that these pieces of evidence were never presented in the court, nor was an appeal filed in the Punjab High Court against the acquittal of Savarkar.

Savarkar had made following submissions in reply to the charges levelled against him:

> i. It is possible that Godse and Apte came to Savarkar Sadan on 14 January 1948, but they didn't meet me.
>
> ii. Godse and Apte didn't meet me on 17 January 1948. May be they came to meet some tenant who also resides on the first floor of the building.
>
> iii. I knew Nathuram Godse, Narayan Apte and Dattatreya Parchure as activists of Hindu Mahasabha. I only came to know about Badge when he wrote a letter to me. As far as other accused are concerned, I had no acquaintance with Shankar, Gopal and Madanlal, nor had I met them. Mr Apte and Pandit Godse introduced themselves to me as workers of the *Hindu Sabha* in Nagar and Poona and I was personally introduced to them later.

Godse, Apte and the other accused supported his statement. But this report notes that a person named N.V. Limaye was arrested by Bombay Police after the murder of Gandhi, who said that Savarkar must have been fully aware of the facts and Nathuram Godse must have consulted him before undertaking his mission. Another detenu W.B. Chavan told the police that Savarkar must have got the offence committed and that Godse must have been accompanied by his associate N.D. Apte because Godse never did anything without taking Apte with him. Thereafter, Savarkar's secretary Damle and bodyguard Kasar were interrogated and Savarkar's house was placed under strict surveillance. Others interrogated were Balraj Mehta, Rameshwar Singh Thakur, Trilok Nath Mehra, Fakir Chand Chopra, L.G. Thatte and Prahlad Dutt.[26]

Ramchandra Kasar, the bodyguard of Savarkar submitted before Bombay Police on 4 March 1948:

> i. Apte and Godse were frequent visitors of Savarkar since 1946 and Karkare also sometimes visited him. During the period when the Question of Partition of India was being discussed all these three used to visit Savarkar and discussed with him the question of the Partition and Savarkar advised them that they should carry on propaganda through the agency of the *Agrani* against the Congress and Mahatma Gandhi.[27]
>
> ii. In August 1947 when Savarkar went to Poona in connection with a meeting Godse and Apte were always with Savarkar and were discussing with him the future policy of the Hindu Mahasabha and told them that he himself was getting old and they would have to carry on the work.[28]
>
> iii. In the beginning of August 1947, on the 5th or 6th, there was an All India Hindu convention at Delhi and Savarkar, Godse and Apte travelled together by plane. At the Convention the Congress policies were strongly criticised. On the 11th August Savarkar, Godse and Apte and returned to Bombay together by plane.[29]
>
> iv. On or about 13th or 14th January, Karkare came to Savarkar with a Punjabi youth and they had an interview with Savarkar for about 15 or 20 minutes. On or about 15th or 16th Apte and Godse had an interview with Savarkar at 9.30 p.m. After about a week or so, may be 23rd or 24th January, Apte and Godse again came to Savarkar and had a talk with him at about 10 or 10.30 a.m. for about half an hour.[30]

Savarkar's secretary Gajanan Vishnu Damle submitted on the same day:

> i. He had known N.D. Apte of the *Agrani* for the last four years. Apte started a rifle club at Ahmednagar and also was an Honorary Recruiting Officer during the war. Apte was a frequent visitor to Savarkar's house and sometimes came with Godse. Savarkar had lent Rs 15,000 to Apte and Godse for the newspaper when security was demanded from the *Agrani*. That paper was stopped and the new paper called the *Hindu Rashtra* was started. Savarkar was one of its Directors and Apte and Godse were the Managing Agents. He knew V.R. Karkare who was a Hindu Mahasabha worker at Ahmednagar for about three years and occasionally visited Savarkar. Badge was also known to him for the last three years. He also used to visit Savarkar.[31]
>
> ii. In the first week of January 1948, Karkare and a Punjabi refugee boy came to see Savarkar and they both had an interview with Savarkar for about half an hour or 45 minutes. Neither of them came to see Savarkar again.[32]
>
> iii. Apte and Godse came to see Savarkar about the middle of January 1948 late at night. Last time that Badge paid a visit to Savarkar was in the last week of December 1947.[33]

These statements clearly corroborate the testimonies of Digambar Badge and film actress Bimba. Had these been presented in the court they would have been unassailable as corroborative evidence to 'safely' convict Savarkar. One wonders whether these were the facts which Desai chose to conceal in the court and 'forgot' in his autobiography! Were there people in Delhi who wanted Savarkar to be released? Was there a possibility of some more people being exposed in the conspiracy to assassinate Gandhi? These are questions that it is not possible to answer now, but repeatedly come up while reading the documents of the murder of the father of the nation.

The Commission opined that:

> The statements of both these witnesses show that both Apte and Godse were frequent visitors of Savarkar at Bombay and at conferences and at every meeting they are shown to have been with Savarkar. In January 1948 they were travelling with him both from Delhi to Bombay and back. This evidence also shows that Karkare was also well known to Savarkar and was also a frequent visitor.

> Badge also used to visit Savarkar. Dr Parchure also visited him. All this shows that people who were subsequently involved in the murder of Mahatma Gandhi were all congregating sometime or the other at Savarkar Sadan and sometimes had lone interviews with Savarkar. It is significant that Karkare and Madanlal visited Savarkar before they left for Delhi and Apte and Godse visited him both before the bomb was thrown and also before the murder was committed and on each occasion they had long interviews. It is specially to be noticed that Godse and Apte were with him at public meetings at various places in the years 1946, 1947 and 1948.[34]

In an earlier observation, the Commission says:

> The bundle of facts which were given to Mr Nagarvala were destructive of any theory, but the theory of conspiracy to murder Mahatma Gandhi by Savarkarites.[35]

The Commission concluded that a group of Poona Savarkarites was conspiring to kill Gandhi and had the statement of Madanlal been shared in detail with Nagarvala and had he been appointed the chief investigator at that time, the conspiracy could have been unearthed in time.

The Commission said in no uncertain terms, 'All these facts taken together were destructive of any theory other than the conspiracy to murder by Savarkar and his group.'[36]

Ketkar, Kanetkar, Desai and the Findings

The Commission was quite clear in its finding that G.V. Ketkar knew about the conspiracy to kill Gandhi since October–November 1947. Badge had talked to him about this on 23 January 1947. But Ketkar didn't share it with the then chief minister B.G. Kher, nor did he inform him through Baḷukaka Kanetkar.[37]

It needs to be mentioned here that both Kanetkar and Kher had passed away and this conclusion was based on the statement of Morarji Desai, who said that 'I cannot remember if I ever saw the letter but as far as I can recollect no names were mentioned by Balashib Kher'.[38] This should be seen with two more facts.

In an article written in a magazine called *Purusharth*, after the death of Gandhi, Kanetkar claimed that he had informed Desai and Kher about Nathuram Godse. Desai denied having seen this article before the Commission.[39] Strangely, the Bombay secretariat could not find of copy of Kanetkar's letter in its archives at the time of inquiry![40] B.G. Bhagwat, who was an Ex-Chief Officer of the Municipal Corporation of Poona and a close associate of Kher, also claimed that Kanetkar had informed Kher and Patel about this conspiracy, but no one trusted him.[41]

The second fact is the statement of Ketkar:

> At a public meeting in July 1947 to protest against the acceptance of the partition of India, Nathuram Godse, who was subsequently convicted and hanged for the murder of Mahatma Gandhi, stated. 'Gandhiji says he would live for 125 years—yes, if anybody allows him to live.' At that meeting Balukaka Kanetkar who was a very honest Congress worker of Poona was also with me. He was my friend. He said to me, 'What is that man talking about? It is a dangerous thing and we should let this Government know.'[42]

Even if we were to set aside this debate about whether Ketkar suggested to him to write or he wrote to Kher himself, it is difficult to believe that Kanetkar would not name Godse in a letter written after this incident. It is astonishing that DSP Angarkar, who was in the Intelligence Branch as an inspector had no such recollection![43] Such hypomnesia can be natural as well as affected, but while going through this report, one invariably feels a tinge deep within.

The Commission submitted its report on 30 September 1969, three years after the passing away of Savarkar. Ketkar was not prosecuted, and the file went into oblivion in the dark chambers reserved for government reports.

PART THREE

Godse Lied in the Courtroom

Nathuram Godse was caught red-handed in the act of murdering Gandhi with a gun, witnessed by hundreds of people. This was a straightforward case of cold-blooded murder. He accepted in the courtroom: 'I took courage in both my hands and I did fire the shots at Gandhiji on 30th January 1948, on the prayer-grounds of Birla House.'[1] He further states, 'There was no legal machinery by which such an offender (Gandhi) could be brought to book and it was therefore that I resorted to the firing of shots at Gandhiji as that was the only thing for me to do.'[2] If the same antiquated sense of justice that Godse believed in was to be applied to him, he would have been killed there and then. Fortunately for him, the people who ran the affairs of the country then had far more faith in democratic rights and the rule of law. Hence the law took its course wherein he was supplied with legal aid at government expense, and most of his demands during his stay in jail were fulfilled. On the second day of his hearing while asking for extra water, Godse acknowledged that he was surprised by the civility shown to him in detention.[3]

He then proceeded to utilize the legal procedure to his full advantage. On 8 November 1948, when permitted by the court to argue his case, he read out a ninety-two-page hand-written statement.

Thereafter, when the rest of his co-accused moved an appeal in the Punjab High Court, Godse moved one along with them as well, ostensibly to state that there was no conspiracy in Gandhi's murder, but in effect to seek an opportunity to read out the statement again. It is surprising to note while going through the records of the court proceedings that an accused of a daylight murder could be permitted to list out reasons for it and justify the killing. No allegation levelled at Gandhi could have legally remitted the punishment. A statement filled with baseless charges against Gandhi and the hate-filled propaganda countering which a secular state had just been founded could very well have been kept out of the court proceedings. One of the judges in the three-judge bench of the Punjab High Court, Justice Khosla, did indeed try to stop the recording of the statement citing its irrelevance to facts of the case, but the other two judges seemed mesmerized by the melodrama.[4] Douglass, in this connection, makes a pertinent remark:

> The fact that Judge Atma Charan allowed Nathuram Godse, Gandhi's confessed assassin, to speak for nine hours, in an ideological assault on Gandhi and a judicial defence of Savarkar, shows just how much the court was subservient to the political power of Gandhi's murderers.[5]

Although Savarkar never even once turned his gaze towards Godse in the courtroom, there is a widely held scholarly view that he had in fact either wholly written or applied finishing touches to the statement.* Savarkar had done this before, in the case of Madanlal Dhingra forty years ago, although the judges of the Old Bailey court in London did not permit Dhingra to read it out.[6]

This statement by Nathuram was published by Gopal Godse in a Marathi book titled *Gandhi Hatya Ani Mi* or 'Gandhi's Murder and I' subsequent to his release from jail. Before its publication as a book, the statement had already been serialized in a Marathi magazine called *Painjan*. On 6 December 1967, its publication was banned. Gopal Godse filed a writ against the ban in the Bombay High Court and a three-judge bench in its verdict on 6 August 1989 lifted the ban.[7]

---

* For example, see *Let's Kill Gandhi* by Tushar Gandhi.

Not only has this book continued to be published, but versions with different names and all kinds of alterations are also widely publicized and sold.

To cite an example, a 'Bhagat Singh Vichar Manch' published a version in 2019 titled *Maine Gandhi Vadh Kyon Kiya* ('Why I Killed Gandhi'). The book, apart from Nathuram's statement in the court, contains 'glimpses' of his supposed correspondence (whose sources cannot be verified) and a separate section to demonstrate the innocence of Savarkar in the matter. This particular section, aside from several unverified instances, broadly repeats the facts as put out by Malgonkar. Interestingly, the high praise of Savarkar here has inadvertently verified the allegation that he used to cross-check the statements made by Godse. The anonymous editor writes:

> Nathuram himself wrote what he had to say in Marathi which later would be translated into English. Nathuram had a wish that Savarkar would contribute some parts. Savarkar ji would reply—I do not need to write anything on your behalf. Show me what you write and if need be, I shall suggest changes.[8]

The editor, letting his imagination run riot, has concluded that Godse could not speak English, when in fact all his statements to the court are in English.[9]

The version published by Hind Pocket Books, titled *Gandhi Vadh Kyon* ('Why the Gandhi Murder') could be considered the most authentic. This version is copyrighted by Gopal Godse and I have used the same for the basis of my arguments. There is another version, published under the same title by Rashtrahitaishi Prakashan, Chennai. That book, claiming to be 'completely authentic' has neither an ISBN number, nor a year of publication, nor any address to contact the publishers. The last three chapters of the book contain the same misinformation against Gandhi and Jawaharlal Nehru using certain photographs that form the content of WhatsApp forwards these days. The book mentions a certain Purushottam Nagesh Oak as a reference for 'true history'. The Internet Archive (archive.org) also has a book named *Why I Killed Gandhi*, which mentions Nathuram Godse as the writer and copyright holder. The publication year is 1949, the year when he was hanged, and bears no ISBN or publisher's name!

These are of course just some instances of the forces that have inherited the legacy of Nathuram Godse using the statement he gave in court—which was an attempt to attack Gandhi ideologically after wounding him mortally—to further their anti-democratic ends by means of false allegations and made-up stories. Lying was a matter of habit for Godse who had not only concealed the role of Savarkar in the whole affair but denied that there ever was a conspiracy in the murder. His allegations against Gandhi reveal a mind brainwashed by constant training of a kind that can make one accept canards as logic. Those allegations have subsequently been used to poison the minds of generation after generation, and repeatedly result in sectarian violence and hatred.

1. The 'Fifty-Five Crores' Lie

Godse claimed in court that 'The decision to with-hold the payment of Rs 55 cores to Pakistan was taken up by our Government which claims to be the people's Government. But this decision of the people's Government was reversed to suit the tune of Gandhiji's fast.'[1]

Since then, the issue of these fifty-five crore rupees has been repeated countless times as a tale where Gandhi sat on a fast to compel the Indian government to pay Pakistan that sum of money as a present, which enraged Godse and gang who then assassinated him. This is in fact a classic strategy borrowed directly from Goebbels who excelled in turning a lie into truth through constant repetition. Malgonkar claims that Nathuram decided to kill Gandhi after receiving the news of the disbursal of this amount of fifty-five crores.

The fact is, Ketkar had known from October 1947 that Godse was planning to kill Gandhi. Nathuram had been openly declaring in public speeches that he would not allow Gandhi to live 125 years, a reference to the wish the latter had publicly voiced, at a time when the issue of these payments to Pakistan were not even an issue. For years he had been involved in attempts on Gandhi's life in Panchgani and other places and the fifty-five-crore issue was a ruse and an afterthought to justify the criminal act.

The Truth Behind the Payment of Fifty-Five Crores

Firstly, the fifty-five crore amount was not a gift, alms or charitable donation. This was a natural outcome of the partition of India. Just as a division in a household may lead to an equal distribution of the movable and immovable property on top of monetary wealth, so was the case with the money held in the Reserve Bank of India at the time of Partition. It is worthwhile to note that it had been pre-decided that the RBI would continue to play the role of central bank for both India and Pakistan up till October 1948. A six-member committee was constituted to lay down the conditions for equitable distribution which included from the Pakistani side Ghulam Mohammed, Zahid Hussain and I. Qureshi, and from the Indian side, K.G. Ambegaonkar, Sanjiv Rao and M.V. Rangachari. On the recommendations of the said committee, out of the 400 crore rupees deposited in the Reserve Bank, seventy-five crores were to be allocated to Pakistan. None of this was decided by Gandhi. The agreement was signed by Nehru and Sardar Patel on the Indian side and the first instalment was handed over right at the start, with a further agreement to transfer the rest of the fifty-five crores as and when Pakistan asked for it.[2]

It is important to remember that this was an agreement signed between two independent nations as per international law. No pre-condition had been attached to the agreement. Two hours after the agreement was signed, India did put forth a condition that the agreement was dependent on the two nations also arriving at an agreement on Kashmir. Pakistan, however, did not reply on this matter.[3] It is crystal clear that the agreement which had already been signed by the leadership of the two countries would hold precedence in international legal terms.

Even before Pakistan could raise the demand, the then governor of the Reserve Bank Sir C.D. Deshmukh, at the end of 1947, advised the Indian government to release the sum in short instalments of three crore rupees each. The Reserve Bank was obviously following the law as it existed. The finance ministry, however, declined to release any amount at that moment.[4] In October, the conflict over Kashmir had precipitated tensions between the two neighbours. When Pakistan demanded the release of the money, Nehru and Patel declined to release it for the time being. The cabinet in its meeting on 7 January unanimously agreed to withhold the money.[5]

The Pakistani finance ministry did not waste time reminding the Reserve Bank of its role as the central bank of both countries. It threatened to initiate legal action in case the bank failed to discharge its functions as a responsible institution.[6]

It is worthwhile for us to think and reflect. Had Pakistan decided to approach the international community with a written agreement signed by India foreswearing any pre-condition for the transfer of the money, how would we be seen? How could we have been able to defend such a position legally, and what would have been the impact on India's image on the world stage?

The Fast

When Gandhi decided to go on a fast on 12 January, the issue of these fifty-five crores was never there before him, and neither had he given any advice to anyone in this regard. The pre-conditions issued by him before the commencement of the fast did not mention the fifty-five-crore matter either. The prayer meeting of 12 January, in which the fast was declared, also did not have any mention of the matter. Stating his reason for the fast as the continuing violence on both sides of the border, he in fact said the following:

> That destruction is certain if Pakistan does not ensure equality of status and security of life and property for all professing the various faiths of the world and if India copies her. Only then Islam dies in the two Indias, not in the world. But Hinduism and Sikhism have no world outside India. Those who differ from me will be honoured by me for their resistance however implacable. Let my fast quicken conscience, not deaden it.[7]

His letter to his son Devdas regarding the cause of his fast did not mention anything related to the money either.[8] One wonders how Nathuram, then cooling his heels in Poona, got wind of the fact that Gandhi was fasting to give fifty-five crore rupees to Pakistan!

Gandhi went to meet Mountbatten immediately after the 12 January prayer meeting. Mountbatten here described the cabinet decision to withhold the money as politically tenuous and having little good sense—as 'unstatesmanlike and unwise' and India's 'first dishonourable act'. He said the same thing to Patel on meeting him the next day. Patel was extremely annoyed by such a stance and made his reservations clear to the Viceroy. However, Mountbatten only obliged so far as to remove the word 'dishonourable' and sent the amended advice to Gandhi.[9]

In the prayer meeting of 14 January there was no mention of the fifty-five crore rupees either. He said, 'What has happened in Karachi? Innocent Sikhs were murdered, and their properties looted. Now I understand the same thing has happened in Gujarat. There was a caravan coming from Bannu or somewhere. They were all refugees running away to save their lives. They were waylaid and cut down. I do not want to relate this grim tale. I ask the Muslims if in their name this kind of thing continues in Pakistan, how long the people in India will tolerate it.'[10] It is obvious that Gandhi was sticking to his stated aim of bringing an end to the violence and carnage through this fast.

On 15 January, another Cabinet was convened where everyone agreed that any further withholding of the money would invite legal sanctions and hence the remaining amount be released in the interest of India's image abroad. The decision was unanimous, endorsed by Patel as well as Syama Prasad Mukherjee. Patel wasn't entirely happy with the outcome[11] but understood the consequences of a decision otherwise. The intervention of Gandhi saved India from certain disgrace. In his thousands of letters written since the release of the money till his death, Patel didn't once mention the amount of fifty-five crores ever again. However, those who stayed away from the freedom struggle, suddenly found their patriotism awakened, to the extent that they worried more about the money than Patel, Nehru and Gandhi!

Had Gandhi's fast been about the money, it would have concluded after the payment was made. The fast continued after this decision on 15 January. On the same day, a journalist inquired of Gandhi regarding the purpose of the fast and received this reply:

> From all I have known of the powers and peoples outside India, I make bold to say that the fast has created only a healthy impression. Outsiders who are able to take an impartial and unbiased view of what is happening in India cannot distort the purpose of the fast, which is meant to bring sanity to all those who inhabit both the Union and Pakistan.[12]

The only people who could rake up the issue of the payment of fifty-five crores to Pakistan and blame Gandhi for the matter would be those who were prejudiced against him to the extent that they ignored historical facts in their determination to project him a villain. And only Godse and people of his kind could consider this payment of fifty-five crore rupees as treason, as they neither have a sense of history nor polity or diplomacy. They mistake their immorality for courage and ultimately insult the very purpose for which they claim to be fighting.

It is sometimes the duty of men of experience to advise young when they venture on a rash course of action. Gandhi had many a time given such advice to Nehru and Patel. However, when they did not agree with him, he would merely place his dissent and rest his case. This time they did agree to his advice. On 16 January 1948, Patel opined: 'We take a short-range view while he (Gandhi) takes a long-range one.'[13] It would also be disrespecting the wisdom of Nehru and Patel to say that they agreed to release the amount under pressure. It would have been a great calamity for any Indian government to be humiliated at the United Nations before the payment was made. Our epic, the *Mahabharata*, holds up the shining example of Karna, who could forego his life, but not go back on the word he had given to somebody. Godse considered himself an emissary of the same Indian culture and tradition which places commitment before life, but he had only acquired the lesson of deceit from the great epic, while Gandhi and his friends derived lessons of morality, courage and propriety.

It was the same sense of courage and conviction which carried Gandhi on to fast until 18 January 1948, when representatives of all major religions signed a promissory note to end the violence. Had the bullets of a cowardly Godse not pierced his body, Gandhi would have definitely gone to Pakistan to stop the atrocities against the minorities there with the same zeal as he had earlier gone to Noakhali.

2. Gandhi Was Not Responsible for the Partition

> Those who have shouted loudest of *Akhand Bharat*, the present Jana Sangh and its predecessors of the curiously un-Hindu spirit of Hinduism, have helped Britain and Muslim League partition the country, if the consequences of their acts and not their motivations are taken into account. They did nothing whatever to bring the Muslim close to the Hindu within a single nation. They did almost everything to estrange them from each other. Such estrangement is the root cause of partition. To espouse the philosophy of estrangement and, at the same time, the concept of undivided India is an act of grievous self-deception, only if we assume that those who do so are honest men.
>
> —Ram Manohar Lohia,
> *Guilty Men of India's Partition*[1]

It is worthwhile to ponder the Partition and its causes with an open heart. In a household, for instance, two sets of relatives think of separation when they deem it impossible to live together due to continued conflict. The key to averting separation is to diffuse tensions to the extent that the two parties drop the idea. One party trying to forcibly keep the other in the house by use of force would not do, as the other would resist and clamour for separation until it inevitably happens.

The same may be said to hold true for a nation. It was in fact a necessity for a diverse country like India that people belonging to different faiths, linguistic communities and regions live with a sense of an equal stake in the country and with mutual respect and cooperation. The first Great War of Indian Independence in 1857 was precisely the manifestation of such a feeling, where Hindus and Muslims united, fought against the oppressive British imperialism. Even Savarkar in his earlier days generously praised the inter-faith unity of Hindus and Muslims in his book *1857 ka Swatantrya Samar* (the *Indian War of Independence* is its English version). There he writes:

> [How] British rule lay shattered and Swadeshi rul[ers] re-established with the mutual consent of Hindus and Muslims. [How] the enemy was made to realise that no lesson learnt by their historians and administrators about the mutiny was as important as the warning that a revolution is possible where Brahmins and the Shudras, and Hindus and Mussalmans stand organized as one against us. [And] it is a folly to believe that the tranquillity and stability of our rule can rely on a landmass which has these different castes and creeds, because they understand each other and respect each other's traditions.[2]

The British had obviously learnt their lesson, and after the tragic failure of the 1857 revolt, actively worked to tear this unity to shreds. As I have already pointed out, the Governor of Bombay Lord Elphinstone noted at a meeting held on 14 May 1859, '[The old Roman motto] *Divide et Impeta*…should [now] be ours.'[3] Anyone with a rudimentary knowledge of history is now aware of this British tactic, which was aided and abetted by sectarian organizations within both the Hindus and Muslims. And yet, ninety years later, Godse was to hold Gandhi and the Congress responsible for the Partition. He said, 'Gandhi is being referred to as the Father of the Nation. But if that is so, he had failed his paternal duty in as much as he has acted very treacherously to the nation by his consenting to the partitioning of it. I stoutly maintain that Gandhi has failed in his duty.'[4]

Since its foundation in 1885, the Indian National Congress had a secular policy outlook and professed to champion Indian, rather than Hindu or Muslim, interests. Both communities meanwhile saw the growth of fundamentalist groups with active British support, committed to deepening communal discord. Neither the Muslim

League, nor the Hindu Mahasabha or the RSS ever participated in the freedom struggle and, in fact, in the name of community interest, set out to protect *elite* interests within these communities. It is neither a surprise nor a coincidence that the 1942 Quit India movement saw both the Muslim League and the Hindu Mahasabha standing rock solid with the British regime even as millions took to the streets and were imprisoned and incarcerated. The Mahasabha and the League sought to form coalition governments in both Bengal and Sindh after the resignation of the Congress ministries. The Sindh assembly headed by the Muslim League passed a resolution in support of Pakistan with the Hindu Mahasabha declining to oppose it, while the perennial Gandhi-baiter Jinnah stood silent as Savarkar proposed accepting Dominion Status. Neither did Savarkar nor his disciples make an attempt on Jinnah's life, and neither did the Direct Action of the League ever hurt Savarkar or his organization. It is for us to observe that the two forces were united in their vehement and vicious opposition of Gandhi.

The British regime through its various acts, namely the Partition of Bengal, the Morley–Minto Reforms, the Montague–Chelmsford Reforms and other measures, did everything to broaden the divide. Tilak's compromise with the Muslim League in 1916 was meant to bridge those divisions and Gandhi moved forward in the same tradition. In fact, he moved a step ahead by openly challenging social orthodoxies rooted centuries in the past. The only way to avert Partition was to assure all the religious minorities, Dalits, Adivasis and linguistic nationalities from east to west and north to south, that they would enjoy equal rights and dignity within an independent India. This was the central condition which could bring people together and make them fight for independence with one voice and all their strength. Respect for all religious beliefs, uncompromising struggle against untouchability, encouraging inter-caste marriages, encouraging an all-encompassing and inclusive Hindustani, instead of the Sanskritized or Persianized versions, and getting other languages equal status were some of the steps Gandhi actively took in order to achieve this unity. That is precisely why in Noakhali he worried about the minority Hindus and in Delhi about the plight of Muslims. Let alone supporting Partition, even after Partition became a fact, up until his last breath, Gandhi believed that India and Pakistan would again be one. For him they had in fact never been separated. That is why, while he tried to stop the mayhem in Delhi, he decried the violence in Pakistan as well and desired to go and do something about it. Gandhi was hence an inconvenience for all kinds of divisive forces who had been responsible for the Partition.

The people who were directly responsible for the partition of the country are in fact those who spared no effort in poisoning the relations between Hindus and Muslims. No Hindu could accept a *Nizam-e-Mustafa* and similarly no Muslim could accept *Hindu Rashtra*—conceptions of the nation with second-class status for minorities and majoritarian rule.

Gandhi, in the prayer meeting of 22 October 1947, clearly said:

> Are you going to annihilate all the three-and-half or four crore Muslims? Or would you like to convert them to Hinduism? But even that would be a kind of annihilation. Supposing you were so pressurised, would you agree to become Muslims? Supposing you were forced to read the Kalma and threatened with death if you refused? I would be the first person to say that they might rather cut our throats than suggest this. We must have at least that much courage. It is senseless to ask Muslims to accept Hinduism like this. I don't want such Hindus. Am I going to save Hinduism with the help of such Hindus? I want Hindus who can exercise restraint. Why should I be so arrogant and ruthless? One cannot become a tyrant and follow dharma at the same time.[5]

Perhaps Gandhi had in mind this shloka describing the antecedents of dharma:

> *Dhriti kshama damo'steyam shauchamindriyanigraha:*
> *Dhirvidya satyamakrodho dashakam dharmalakshanam*
> (Fortitude, forgiveness, [self-]control, non-stealing, purity, withdrawal of senses, intelligence, learning, truth, non-anger: [these] ten qualities constitute the characteristics of 'Dharma')

Bhagat Singh, though he was an atheist, had also talked about the need to accept the moral aspect of religion while staying away from the ostentation.[6] So did Gandhi, decrying the reactionary aspects of the *Manusmriti*, but utilizing the ethical aspects of such shlokas to our good. In this connection, we might mention a couplet of the medieval saint Kabir, which loosely translates to: the sages use the essence of religion, while deceitful people use sacred words and twist their meanings. Godse could be considered a classic example of the latter.

The Partition: Some Facts

Even a cursory analysis of the facts and circumstances leading up to Partition can make it clear that not only was Gandhi dead against the idea of dividing the country on sectarian grounds and resisted it till the end, but also that he accepted the outcome with a heavy heart after realizing that it had become virtually impossible for the two communities to coexist given the poison and divisiveness of that time.

It is useful to remind readers of the Congress Working Committee meet of 25 June 1946 to decide on the proposals of the Cabinet Mission, and Gandhi's response where he said, 'I accept defeat. You all should act as you deem fit.' Gandhi was quite apprehensive about the long-term success of the Constituent Assembly without sorting out the immediate issue of the formation of the interim government. However, Patel had already committed to the members of the Cabinet Mission in a meeting held on 2 June that he would get the 'May 16th Proposals', which cleared the way for interim government formation, ratified by the CWC. He had also convinced Nehru and Maulana Azad regarding the same. But when he went to ask Gandhi whether he was satisfied, Gandhi replied, 'On the contrary my suspicion has deepened.'[7] However, since virtually every important leader in the CWC had accepted the proposals, Gandhi had to concede.

Gandhi did not have to wait long to see his prophecy proved right when the joint Congress–Muslim League ministry was formed in the backdrop of tremendous upheaval. Patel was rigid on keeping the home portfolio, which he eventually did, while Liaquat Ali Khan from the League got finance.[8] He perhaps thought that control over the home ministry would help him implement the policies of the Congress. The arrangement backfired on the Congress as Liaquat put hurdles at every step by any Congress minister. Congress ministers were unable to obtain the finance ministry's approval even for recruiting a clerk. The fact of the matter was that the Muslim League ministers refused to recognize Nehru and Patel as leaders from day one and formed a cabinet within a cabinet to create deliberate logjams.[9] As the Direct Action programme approached, the Muslim League used its position within and outside government to increase pressure for a concession on Pakistan. A League minister Raja Ghazanfar Ali Khan declared openly that they were entering government to get a foothold to fight for their cherished goal of Pakistan.[10] Maulana Azad, a member of that cabinet wrote:

> The League Members of the Executive Council were thwarting us at every step. They were in Government and yet against it. In fact, they were in a position to sabotage every move we took. The powers of Finance Member were being stretched to the limit and a new shock awaited us when the Budget for the next year was presented by Liaquat Ali… Sardar Patel and Sri Rajagopalachari were violently opposed to his budget, for they felt that Liaquat Ali was more concerned with harassing industrialists and businessman than in serving the interests of the country.[11]

The British had a tacit internal understanding with the League and, eventually at a meeting in London, ruled in favour of the latter on the matter of 'the right to opt out of a group'. Patel wrote an angry letter to Sir Stafford Cripps on 15 December in which he stated: 'You know when Gandhiji was strongly against our settlement; I threw my weight in favour of it. You have created a very uncomfortable situation for me. All of us here feel that there has been a betrayal…'[12] Nehru also understood the scenario now. At the end of November, addressing a public meeting in Meerut, he said categorically, 'There is a silent understanding between the Muslim League and the British officials.'[13]

In the meantime, communal incidents rapidly escalated. Even as Gandhi was dousing the flames of Noakhali, seven thousand Muslims perished in Bihar and another thousand in Garhmukteshwar.[14] Reports of killings also started trickling in from other parts of the country. The difficulties of the interim government also multiplied where Jinnah kept up the boycott of the Constituent Assembly. Matters came to a head and Patel and Nehru requested Lord Wavell to drop League ministers from the cabinet. Wavell, however, refused, even when the Congress threatened to walk out of the ministry if the League ministers were not sacked. When Atlee announced British government withdrawal from India latest by June 1948, the party took back its decision.[15]

Patel and Nehru were now convinced that it was virtually impossible to have any coordination with the League. Even if Britain were to extend the deadline for independence on account of the prevailing law and order situation or the unsuccessful run of the Constituent Assembly, there was all likelihood of a bloody civil war and eventually a bloodier partition. Neither the League nor Hindu right-wing forces were ready to stop the violence in their spheres of influence. Gandhi, on whose every word the country used to hang onto, was now more and more isolated within and outside his own party. Patel had reluctantly concluded by the end of December that partition was the only possible option. His biographer Rajmohan Gandhi cites the diary of Manuben, his daughter, to point out that V.P. Menon had proposed the creation of Pakistan through partitioning Punjab and Bengal on 25 December 1946, which Patel agreed to.[16] This was much more acceptable than the demands of Jinnah in relation to the size of Pakistan. Jinnah in fact as early as November had made it clear in his conference with Lord Wavell, 'However small, the Muslims of India shall have their own nation.'[17] He did not stay quiet thereafter. While the League had majorities in Sindh and Bengal, Punjab was ruled by a coalition of the Congress, Akali Dal and most notably the Unionist Party (representing the landed gentry of Muslims, Sikhs and Hindus) headed by the latter's Malik Khizar Hayat Tiwana* which opposed the League and partition. Similarly, the North-West Frontier Province had a Congress government. The League started on a campaign with the slogan of 'Islam in Danger', to unseat these

* Khizar Hayat Tiwana remained defiantly against the Partition up till the bitter end. He believed that Punjab represented a pluralistic culture of Muslims, Sikhs and Hindus, and hence, in the event that partition was inevitable, Punjab should be an independent nation. The Pakistani administration seized a lot of his property and he immigrated to the United States. After the breakup of East and West Pakistan and the creation of Bangladesh, in 1975, three years from his death, he reiterated: 'this proves the fallacy of the two-nation theory propagated by Jinnah'.

governments hostile to its cause, and communal rioting resumed. In March, Khizar Hayat was forced to resign, and a fresh bout of killings raged in the Punjab. When Mountbatten assumed charge as Viceroy, Punjab had seen 2,049 deaths and more than a thousand injured as per official figures.[18]

Everyone was now mentally prepared for the division of the country, save Gandhi. In the beginning of March, the *Hindustan Times* printed Patel's affirmation to the plan for partitioning Bengal and Punjab. In Noakhali, on 22 March, Gandhi asked Patel, 'If you can, please explain your resolution about the Punjab. I cannot form any judgement.'[19] Patel replied, 'It is difficult, in a letter, to explain the Punjab resolution. It was arrived at after great deal of reflections, not in haste or without thought. We have gathered from newspapers that you have expressed your opinion against it. You have of course the right to say and do what you feel right.' Gandhi did not know that on 4 March. Four days before the Punjab resolution, Vallabhbhai conveyed his acceptance to a truncated Pakistan to Jinnah's close friend Kanji Dwarkadas. 'If the League insists on Pakistan,' Patel had written, 'the only alternative is the division of the Punjab and Bengal.'[20] It is quite often assumed that whatever Gandhi desired, happened inevitably. We can clearly infer from the course of events that while Gandhi was free to air his views, at least at this hour, Nehru and Patel barely listened to him.

When Mountbatten invited Gandhi for a meeting at the end of March, he was in Bihar.[21] He accepted, and immediately on his return to Delhi, met the Viceroy on 31 March 1947. When the latter asked Gandhi about his views on ending the violence, Gandhi said:

> He was now prepared under Mountbatten's umpireship—not as Viceroy but as man—to invite Jinnah to form a government of his choice at the centre and to present his Pakistan plan for acceptance even before the transfer of power. The Congress could give its whole-hearted support to the Jinnah Government. At the same time since the Muslim League would now be the Government, it would have no further excuse for continuing the movements of organised lawlessness, which it had launched in some of the provinces. These must be called off. Further, since the Viceroy had declared that he

> was out to do justice only and nothing would be yielded to force, if the League did not accept the offer, the same offer mutatis mutandis should be made to the Congress. The old policy of trying to please both the parties must be given up.[22]

Mountbatten knew that Patel would never agree to such a proposal, and hence talked of taking assent from Nehru and Maulana Azad. However, Menon got wind of it ahead of time and Patel rejected it outright in a face to face with Mountbatten. Nehru and Azad were also not in favour of the proposal.[23] Gandhi, however, persisted and on 4 April presented a draft.[24] On 10 April, he prepared an amended draft which contained proposals to nullify anti-Hindu ordinances in Sindh and prevent pro-League newspapers from spreading communal propaganda and hatred.[25] However, none except the Frontier Gandhi agreed to it. Resigned to fate, Gandhi wrote to Mountbatten on 11 April, 'I had several short talks with Pandit Nehru and an hour's talk with him alone, and then with several members of the Working Committee last night about the formula I had sketched before you, and which I had filled in for them with all the implications. I am sorry to say that I failed to carry any of them with me except Badshah Khan.'[26]

Thousands of pages have been written on the technicalities of the partition of India and thousands may in the future. But no example can be cited where Gandhi had agreed to the division. He was now increasingly alone, within his party and among the masses. The country which would rise on his every word had now changed. In the prayer meeting of 2 April 1947, he acknowledged the grim reality:

> No one listens to me anymore. I am a small man. True, there was a time when mine was a big voice. Then everyone obeyed what I said; now neither the Congress nor the Hindus nor the Muslims listen to me. Where is the Congress today? It is disintegrating. I am crying in the wilderness.[27]

Gandhi made a last-ditch effort on the day when the Congress Working Committee was to ratify the Partition proposal. Ram Manohar Lohia, who was an invitee to the meeting, wrote:

> Two of us socialists, Mr Jayprakash Narayan and I, were specially invited to this meeting... Barring us two and Khan Abdul Gaffar

> Khan, none spoke a single word in opposition to partition… Maulana Azad sat in a chair throughout the two days of this meeting in a corner of the very small room which packed us all, puffed away his endless cigarettes, and spoke not a single word… Gandhiji turned to Mr Nehru and Sardar Patel in mild complaint that they had not informed him of the scheme of partition before committing themselves to it. Before Gandhiji could make out his point fully, Mr Nehru intervened with some passion to say that he had kept him fully informed. On Mahatma Gandhi's repeating that he did not know of the scheme of partition, Mr Nehru slightly altered his earlier observation. He said that Noakhali was so far away and that, while he may not have described the details of the scheme he had broadly written of partition to Gandhiji… Keeping turned towards Messrs Nehru and Patel Gandhiji made his second point. He wanted the Congress Party to honour the commitments made by its leaders. He would therefore ask the Congress to accept the principle of partition. After accepting the partition, the Congress should make a declaration concerning its execution. It should ask the British government and the Viceroy to step aside, once Congress and the Muslim League had signified their acceptance to partition. The partitioning of the country should be carried out jointly by the Congress party and Muslim League without the intervention of a third party. This was, I thought so at that time and still do, a grand tactical stroke… It was not considered.[28]

Had the proposal to not involve the British in the actual process of partition been accepted, it could have been postponed for some time and Gandhi could have campaigned to avert it. At least the needless carnage and brutalities that resulted from the haste of Mountbatten and Cyril Radcliffe, a stranger to it all, could have been stopped. Alas! History doesn't care much for could-have-beens and retrospective presumptions.

The bitter sectarian conflict had forced the associates of Gandhi to weigh in on the choice between partition and civil war. Patel had said to Gandhi, 'It is a question of civil war or partition. As of civil war, no one can say where it will start and where it will end. True, the Hindus might win in the end but only after paying an unpredictable and huge price.' Gandhi gave in.[29]

The mutual distrust between the League and Congress meant that both had more faith in Mountbatten. Nehru and Patel hence decided to concede in order to save the country from a violent internal conflict and ensure that whatever remained of India could live in peace. It is utterly ludicrous to allege that these men were more concerned with power. Nehru and Patel had established their credentials as leaders of the independence struggle as well as succeeded in the previous elections, and it was certain that they would have been chosen by the people to lead an independent India. If they had given up trying to stop the partition, it was due to the persistent efforts of forces whose propagation of hate and violence had plunged the country into the hellish fire of civil conflict. To charge Gandhi, Nehru or Patel with Partition is sheer hypocrisy, and the ploy to show Patel as being on the side of Godse a brazen display of shamelessness.

And Hence, Some Questions For Godse and His Ilk

It is worthwhile to ask those who increasingly feel good about displaying their proud association with Nathuram Godse: why did he or anyone supporting him never attack Jinnah? Why not go after Savarkar when he described Hindus and Muslims as separate nations in multiple Hindu Mahasabha meetings? Why hide the fact that the Hindus of Sindh had overwhelmingly supported separation from Bombay Province in 1915?[30] Selective attention is given to Jinnah taking advantage of the Congress resigning from the ministries in 1939, but it was the Mahasabha that strengthened Jinnah's hand by forming coalition governments with the League. Why hide this fact? Nathuram in fact pulled the trigger for the advantage of those who had tacitly supported Jinnah. Were not leaders of the Hindu Mahasabha like Syama Prasad Mukherjee very much responsible for suppressing the 1942 Quit India movement? Wasn't it a fact that by aligning with the League, the Hindu Mahasabha and its follower Nathuram Godse became traitors? The concern for '*Vande Mataram*' did not go far enough for Nathuram to prefer being hanged by the British as other revolutionaries did. He must also answer the charge: Why did he not ask the RSS why they needed another nationalistic song,

'*Namaste Sada Vatsale*', when '*Vande Mataram*' already existed? The most decisive question, however, is: what did Godse or his followers do to stop the Partition?

The answers are obvious; the talk of keeping India as one was a lie, a smokescreen. Nathuram and his mentor Savarkar were both frustrated because of not getting a share of power despite their constant slavish subservience to the British. Savarkar was never interested in *Akhand Bharat*. He desired that Jinnah take away all the Muslim-inhabited regions so he could then lord over the rest of the country under the shadow of his colonial masters, which in fact had been his principal demand in exchange for cooperation during the Second World War. Dr Ambedkar makes a pertinent remark in this connection:

> Strange as it may appear, Mr Savarkar and Mr Jinnah, instead of being opposed to each other on the one nation versus two nations issue, are in complete agreement about it. Both agree, not only agree but insist, that there are two nations in India—one the Muslim nation and the other the Hindu nation. They differ only as regards the terms and conditions on which the two nations should live. Mr Jinnah says India should be cut up into two, Pakistan and Hindustan, the Muslim nation to occupy Pakistan and the Hindu nation to occupy Hindustan. Mr Savarkar on the other hand insists that, although there are two nations in India, India shall not be divided into two parts, one for Muslims and the other for the Hindus; that the two nations shall dwell in one country and shall live under the mantle of one single constitution; that the constitution shall be such that the Hindu nation will be enabled to occupy a predominant position that is due to it and the Muslim nation made to live in the position of subordinate co-operation with the Hindu nation…
>
> At the same time, it must be said that Mr Savarkar's attitude is illogical, if not queer. Mr Savarkar admits that the Muslims are a separate nation. He concedes that they have a right to cultural autonomy. He allows them to have a national flag. Yet he opposes the demand of the Muslim nation for a separate national home. If he claims a national home for the Hindu nation, how can he refuse the claim of the Muslim nation for a national home?[31]

The extent of Savarkar's commitment to a united India can be understood from the following instance. An intense Gandhi critic, the Diwan of the Travancore State, C.P. Ramaswamy, prevailed upon the ruler to decline acceding to India, and in fact in a further provocative act sent an ambassador to Pakistan. Jinnah reciprocated Ramaswamy's overtures and promised all possible assistance. When Patel was occupied with the difficult task of making princely states agree to accession in order to unite India, and the Congress party within Travancore faced repression for opposing the ruler's stance, any patriot would have opposed the steps taken by Ramaswamy which were prejudiced against the unity and integrity of India. Savarkar, contrary to expectations, sent an express telegram to Ramaswamy on 20 June 1947 and declared full support for an independent Travancore.[32]

It is true without a shadow of a doubt that along with Jinnah, people like Savarkar and Nathuram Godse were responsible for the Partition and hence should not be absolved.

3. Gandhi's Fasts: Sophisticated Weaponry of Non-Violent Resistance

> Had the Government then decided to take any military or police action against Hyderabad it would have been compelled to withdraw its decision just as was done as in the case of the payment of Rs 55 crores, for Gandhiji would have gone on fast unto death and Government's hands would have been forced to save the life of Gandhiji.
>
> —Nathuram Godse,
> *May it Please Your Honour*, pp. 153–54

Godse ridiculed Gandhi on his fasts more than once in his statement. Taking their cue from him, the right wing often ask why Gandhi did not undertake fasts on other occasions. To understand his philosophy of fasts I shall like to begin with a particular incident.

In the year 1918, the mill workers of an Ahmedabad textile firm went on strike demanding better pay and working conditions. The management was not ready for concessions and the list of owners included Gandhi's friend and associate Ambalal Sarabhai. Gandhi sided with the workers, stating that the demand for a fifty per cent wage increase was a reasonable one. The owners were undeterred despite the strike. The most intriguing aspect of this affair was that while Ambalal refused to concede to the demands, his own sister Anasuya Sarabhai distributed pamphlets written by Gandhi on the matter from house to house. The long duration of the strike, however, began to break the spirit of the impoverished workers. Gandhi got to know that people were talking about the privilege he and Anasuyaben enjoyed, and how nothing would happen to them since they moved about in a motor car. This set Gandhi thinking, and in one of his addresses to the workers he said, '[U]ntil the owners won't give workers reasonable terms, I shall not eat.'[1] Gandhi has often been accused of being conciliatory to capitalists, while this particular instance is often sadly ignored.

This was Gandhi's first fast in India. He had of course done it twice in South Africa. The first was in 1913 in his Phoenix Farm where an inmate of the ashram had violated its rules, which was morally unacceptable to Gandhi. Instead of meting out punishment to anyone, he decided to not eat for seven days. Likewise, in 1914 when another ashram inmate broke a promise made to him, Gandhi fasted for fourteen days. It is important to pause and reflect why Gandhi, who led political movements against the British regime in South Africa, would not use fasting as a tool to resist them. Why would he always fast when he saw something as morally reprehensible within his own ashram?

Gandhi elucidated his philosophy of fasting later. In 1924–25, Gandhi addressed a letter to the participants of a satyagraha for Dalit rights to enter temples in Vaikom, Travancore State (now in Kottayam district, Kerala):

> Fasting in Satyagraha has well-defined limits. You cannot fast against a tyrant, for it will be a species of violence done to him. You invite penalty from him for disobedience of his orders, but you cannot inflict on yourselves penalties when he refuses to punish and renders it impossible for you to disobey his orders so as to compel infliction of penalty. Fasting can only be resorted to against a lover, not to extort rights but to reform him, as when a son fasts for a father who drinks. My fast at Bombay and then at Bardoli was of that character. I fasted to reform those who loved me. But I will not fast to reform, say General Dyer, who not only does not love me but who regards himself as my enemy.[2]

His outlook on fasting is hence clearly demonstrated—it is not a pressure tactic or a tool for counter-violence, but a technique to reform. Fasting is different from a hunger strike. The first mention of the latter is found in *Satyagraha in South Africa*, in relation to the mistreatment by a jailor in Transvaal's Diepkloof Convict Prison, which prompted prisoners to go on strike. Gandhi writes, '[I]t was a completely legitimate strike… It was a struggle by the poor of a movement for the poor.' Gandhi, while expressing sympathy with the protest, called it a hunger strike rather than a fast since its objective was opposition to cruelty rather than reform.[3] He clarified the issue further in his prison notes of 1924:

> So one fine morning we heard that several Mulshi Peta prisoners were flogged for short task and that, as a protest against the punishment, many other Mulshi Peta prisoners had commenced a hunger strike. Two of these were well known to me. One was Devi and the other Dastane. Mr Dev had worked with me in Champaran, and had proved one of the most conscientious, sober and honest among the co-workers whom I had the privilege of having in Champaran. Mr Dastane of Bhusaval is known to everybody. The reader may therefore imagine my pain when I heard that Dev was among the party flogged and that he was also one of the hungerstrikers. Messrs Indulal Yagnik and Manzar Ali Sokta were at this time my fellow-prisoners. They were agitated equally with me. Their first thought was to declare a sympathetic hunger-strike. We discussed the propriety of such a strike and came to the conclusion that it would be wrong to do so. We were neither morally nor in any other way responsible for the floggings or the subsequent hunger-strike. As satyagrahis we were to be prepared for and to suffer cheerfully the rigours of jail life and even injustices including flogging. Such hunger-strike, therefore, with a view to preventing future punishment would be a species of violence done to the jail officials.[4]

Accusations directed at Gandhi as to why he sat on fast at particular occasions and not on others without understanding the philosophy behind his fast are not only senseless but deceitful. The conception of fasting for Gandhi emanated from religion. Just as the *upavas* or the *roza* is directed at God to seek blessings, ask forgiveness or for self-purification, Gandhi considered fasting a moral force to reach out to those he considered his own. In an article on 30 September 1926 in *Young India*, Gandhi said, '[M]y religion teaches me that whenever there is a sorrow that you cannot forego, you should pray and fast.'[5] The British regime in Africa would not fall in the category, but the inmates of his ashram would. Hence, he would fast for the purification of his and their souls. The jailor was neither his friend nor disciple, and hence the acts of tyranny, misbehaviour, and assault by him did not merit a fast. On the other hand, when one of his disciples, Appasaheb Patwardhan, sat on a hunger strike when the jail authorities in Yerawada Central Jail refused his demand to be allotted the work of a manual scavenger, Gandhi sat on one himself for two days to support his demand. The fine distinction made between hardship and punishment must be appreciated. Hence the protest against punishment within jail, which was an inevitable sacrifice of a satyagraha, was not supported. But when Appasaheb demanded and was denied permission to be allowed to clean all the latrines and drains, Gandhi endorsed the decision because not only was his disciple ready to endure more hardship, but he was also setting an example in the fight against untouchability. Gandhi in fact followed the example in 1934 by demanding the same work and going on a week's fast on being denied.

The declaration of the Ahmedabad fast mentioned above was accompanied by an explanation—that he was not undertaking the fast to build pressure on the mill owners, but to make them understand that their stand was unjust. We must remember that Gandhi could have easily got a wage increase through backroom negotiations since Sarabhai was his friend. But when the taunts by the workers moved him to fast, there were two clear purposes in his mind. The first was self-purification; when the workers and their families had to go hungry while they were on strike, not eating was a matter of ethics for Gandhi. Secondly, rather than negotiate, he sat out to transform the hearts of the mill owners who were either unmoved by their workers going hungry, or who could not remain unmoved if Gandhi went on a fast.[6] It is reasonable to suppose that the owners might have taken it as a pressure tactic since they were conditioned that way. Those who did not believe in the philosophy of non-violence could very well consider it a strategic manoeuvre, but Gandhi had made his intentions crystal clear through his pamphlets. The fast preceding the Poona Pact was also self-explanatory; it was in the interest of the Harijans who had given him tremendous affection. A lot of people can and would disagree with the outcome of the Poona Pact and not consider it to have been in the best interest of Dalits. But Gandhi ultimately believed that it would be wrong to push Dalits into the quagmire of competitive communalism and deem them comparable to Muslims and Sikhs. He believed firmly in the fight against untouchability, and it is a fact that he acquired massive support among Harijans. If elections are a benchmark, most Harijan votes went to Gandhi's Congress and the party of Dr Ambedkar failed to win in most of the reserved constituencies. It is hard not to see why Gandhi thought the Harijans loved him. None of his writings have shown any bitterness towards Dr Ambedkar which additionally leads us to conclude that, at least at the time, Ambedkar did not consider Gandhi an enemy.

That is why Gandhi went from house to house in Noakhali. At that juncture he could hardly consider the Muslim League an ally. He knew that the oppression meted out to the Hindus was done in full complicity with the League administration. That is why rather than fast, he went to the people. He decided to fast when Suhrawardy on his own account came to him in Calcutta. He knew that in Calcutta, people on both the sides held him in esteem. It is also why in Delhi he started his fast after humbly submitting his request to the Muslims and Hindus there. We must also note that the burden of guilt for not being able to stop the mayhem weighed heavily on his conscience. A Jawaharlal or a Patel could hardly stop the violence when there was a Jinnah and a Savarkar who categorically hated him. How could Gandhi have fasted when he knew that it would weaken the hand of Nehru and Patel? The only way Nehru and Patel could avert partition was to agree to the conditions Jinnah put to them with a heavy heart. Jinnah, who was now openly advocating violence to achieve his ends, could not care less if Gandhi lived or died. Those who question why Gandhi did not fast to prevent partition would need to reflect on the consequences of such an action.

It is in fact helpful to go through the list of fasts undertaken by Gandhi:

1. 1913: A seven-day fast at Phoenix Farm, South Africa, in consideration of an act committed by a disciple which he deemed immoral.

2. 1914: A fourteen-day fast again in Phoenix Farm after an ashram inmate broke a promise made to him.
3. 1918: Fast in support of the striking workers of Ahmedabad mills for three days (demands accepted on the third day).
4. 1921: Four-day fast post a controversy on the visit of the Prince of Wales and the boycott of his welcoming ceremony.
5. 1924: A twenty-one-day fast as penance after the recent Hindu–Muslim riots.
6. 1924: Fast for seven days after hearing the news of moral turpitude among students of Sabarmati Ashram.
7. 1932: Four-day fast at Yerawada Central Jail in solidarity with his disciple Appasaheb Patwardhan who fasted after being denied permission to clean toilets and drains.
8. 1932: Fast in opposition to the idea of giving Dalits a separate identity on the lines of Muslims, Sikhs, Buddhists and Anglo-Indians as minorities.
9. 1933: A twenty-one-day fast to support Harijans and for the penance of his associates.
10. 1934: A seven-day fast on being refused to clean the latrines in Yerawada Central Jail.
11. 1934: A seven-day fast for atonement after a Harijan was killed by a Sanatanist during the Harijan Yatra.
12. 1934: A four-day fast during the Rajkot Satyagraha.
13. 1942: A twenty-one-day fast in Agha Khan Jail during the Quit India movement.
14. 1947: A seventy-three-hour fast in Calcutta during sectarian killings there.
15. 1947: The last of Gandhi's fasts, in Delhi, to avert another bout of killings.

Those who fail to understand non-violent resistance, and cannot see anything in religion except ritual, would fail to appreciate that fasting for Gandhi was the demonstration of his philosophy, not a ploy to get what he wanted.

4. Godse and Bhagat Singh: The Contrast

One cannot become a Bhagat Singh merely by firing a gun or a Subhas Bose by wearing a military uniform. It is essential to remind Nathuram Godse and his followers that there is a difference between a revolutionary and a recalcitrant. There is also a difference between those who apologized to the British and remained their puppets and those who gladly went to the gallows. Perhaps Godse could have acknowledged the difference had he had the capacity to accept facts and not had his mind poisoned by communal fanaticism. But he had joined forces with those whom Bhagat Singh considered the biggest enemies of the nation. Perhaps Godse would have been filled with remorse had he known that his actions betrayed the ideals Bhagat Singh stood for, and he would not have used people like Bhagat Singh as tools to defend his criminal acts.

Bhagat Singh: A Legacy

Bhagat Singh can be considered the brightest star of the Indian revolutionary movement. It is not so simply because of the tales of grit and courage which are folklore, but also due to his clear ideological understanding and his dream of making India a nation free of sectarianism prompted by caste and creed, a nation of equals. Bhagat Singh's articles, letters, notes and pamphlets give us a glimpse into his thought. It is our great fortune that his writings, unlike those of many of his contemporaries, are widely and freely available.

In September 1987, a socialist literary society in Kanpur published some of his articles and letters in a book titled *Bhagat Singh ki Chuni Hui Kritiyan* ('Selected Writings of Bhagat Singh') which was edited by his erstwhile comrade Shiv Verma. The primary compilation contained twenty-nine of his writings/documents/letters and the appendix, ten documents of the Hindustan Socialist Republican Association, which surely he had a major role in drafting. Shiv Verma also wrote a long introductory note on the 'Ideology and History of the Revolutionary Movement' which provided precision and clarity regarding what Bhagat Singh thought. It is worthwhile to remind readers that Bhagat Singh was instrumental in getting the word 'Socialist' included in the amended name of the Hindustan Republican Association. Intriguingly, the two members who dissented to the addition of the word 'Socialist' also turned approvers for the government against Bhagat and his comrades later. Even a cursory reading of these documents makes it clear that Bhagat Singh and his comrades were the most modern and developed form of the revolutionary strand that passed from the Chapekar brothers and the Ghadar Party. They were the first in the Indian revolutionary movement to put out a clear stand on issues of caste, religious sectarianism, and other related matters.

In 1928, Bhagat Singh had the following to say as part of his article 'Religion and Our Freedom Struggle' published in *Kirati*:

> Isn't it true that religion creates discord even among those sharing a home? Does it not affect the goal of winning freedom for the country? Telling a child that god is omnipotent while man is merely a mould of clay is to render the child weak for eternity. It destroys his self-confidence and weakens his spirit.[1]

In his celebrated essay 'Why I Am an Atheist', written while he was in jail, he further writes:

> Go and oppose any institutionalized religion. Go and criticize a man who is considered great and hero worshiped, since he is supposed never to make an error of judgment, and the force of your logic will make the whole world call you arrogant and a know-it-all.[2]

At a time when, despite a strong Dalit movement in Maharashtra, there was a lack of consciousness to fight caste oppression among the

Congress and others fighting for independence, and when the Hindu Mahasabha of Godse sought to protect the varna order, Bhagat Singh's article 'The Problem of Untouchability', published in June 1928 in *Kirati*, was ground-breaking. He says:

> It is humbug to say that just because a man was born in a scavenger's house, he would have to clean dirt and not be entitled to develop himself. This is exactly how our forefathers, the Aryans treated them with contempt and unjustifiably condemned them to performing such lowly acts. There was also the concern that they may revolt, hence the propaganda of birth and rebirth was spread to tell them that it is the result of your sins in past lives and you can't do a thing about it. So be as you are! They gave sermons on patience and kept these people quiet. They committed a huge crime. They dehumanized living human beings by destroying their self-confidence and sense of entrepreneurship. There was suppression and there was injustice. It is time now for them to atone. You (the untouchables) should organize, stand up and challenge this rotten society. No one dare not give you your just rights. Do not be a pawn for others, nor beg anyone for help. But do not fall into the trap of the bureaucracy either. They do not want to help you, rather use you. This capitalist bureaucracy is the reason for your slavery and poverty. Do not join forces with them and beware of their conceit. Things would be fine thence. You are the real proletariat… Organize hence! It will not harm you, on the contrary your chains will break. Arise and revolt against the present system. Gradual reforms will not benefit you. Bring an upheaval through your social movement and be prepared for the impending political and economic revolution. You alone are the sons of the soil, and its true force. Lions asleep arise and revolt![3]

Those who consider him a romantic, excited by nihilistic ideas of death, would do well to read his letters to young political activists in which he extols them to go and work in the villages and in factories to lay the foundation of a transformed society. In a letter he writes: 'How does it matter if the head of the Indian government is Lord Irwin or Sir Purushottam Thakur Das? What would a poor peasant get by caring whether Lord Irwin is on the throne or Sir Tej Bahadur Sapru?' Bhagat Singh was not merely concerned with ridding India of its white rulers, but wanted to hand power to the workers, peasants and the marginalized sections and their struggles had ultimately attracted him to socialism.

Slogans are also crucial to understand what Bhagat Singh stood for. Moving on from '*Vande Mataram*' and '*Bharat Mata ki Jai*', he adopted '*Inqalab Zindabad*' (Long live the revolution) as the new slogan for the anti-imperialist struggle. In another popular essay 'What do we mean by *Inqalab Zindabad*' he not only gave a fitting answer to an editor mocking the slogan, but clarified his stand on the revolution: 'The word revolution signifies a belief and an aspiration for progress and change.'[4] This reflected a clear change of direction from anarchist beliefs towards socialism where he further writes: 'Arms and ammunition might be of use to the revolution time and again, but the sword of revolution can only be sharpened upon the stone of ideology. A revolution can not necessarily mean an armed struggle. Pistols and bombs are not synonymous with the revolution.'[5] Bhagat Singh followed the dictum himself by voraciously reading books as the struggle could not be won without ideological clarity.

His jail diary notes provide a further inkling into his thought where Marx, Lenin, Garibaldi and Mazzini had found a place and fired his dreams. It was not a coincidence that during his trial, he sent a letter to the Third Communist International on the death anniversary of Lenin. The letter contains another slogan: 'Death to Imperialism'. He did not merely object to British rule due to its foreign origin but was against the ideology of imperialism and a supporter of socialist thought.

The socialism he believed in signified equal opportunities for all castes, sects, and creeds. In the essay 'Communal Riots and Their Solutions' he writes:

> The present state of India is quite pitiable. Followers of one religion are sworn enemies of the other. It is now enough merely to be of a particular religion to be considered a foe of the other. The killings during the recent riots in Lahore were based entirely on whether somebody is a Hindu, a Sikh or a Muslim. A person could be killed by Muslims if he was a Hindu or a Sikh and likewise someone could be killed for being a Muslim. Only god can save this country if things continue this way.[6]

Nathuram and his ilk who believed in religious sectarianism were clearly enemies of the people in the eyes of Bhagat Singh and an impediment to the nation's freedom and progress. Such reactionaries from both religions defiled the legacy of martyrs like Bhagat Singh and, contrary to their wishes, divided the country. Their using the name of Bhagat Singh against Gandhi is hence nothing short of disrespect and the most heinous conceit.

Gandhi and Bhagat Singh

Bhagat Singh intended to establish socialism in India through an armed revolution whereas Gandhi wished to see swaraj through non-violence and satyagraha.

While they undeniably had ideological differences, there were similarities in their conceptions as well, most notably on the Hindu–Muslim question. While Bhagat Singh wished to achieve unity through atheism, Gandhi was studiously religious and believed he could achieve brotherhood through *sarva dharma sambhav* ('respect for everyone's faith'). While Bhagat Singh wanted to end all social and economic oppression through revolution, Gandhi believed in changing people's conscience. Their writings are testimonies to their differing ideologies, but also to their unflinching and unconditional stand against colonial rule. Neither of them ever apologized to the oppressors and both ultimately gave up their lives for the cause dear to them. They had ideological conflicts, but Bhagat Singh never dreamt of murdering Gandhi and the latter tried everything possible to save Bhagat from the gallows.

When the aims are just, there is always scope for expressing differences democratically without either party compromising on their ideals. On 23 December 1929, Bhagat Singh and his comrades tried to blow up the Viceroy's car, which resulted in Gandhi decrying the violence in an article titled 'The Cult of Bomb'. Bhagwaticharan Vohra and Bhagat Singh wrote a reply to it, 'The Philosophy of Bomb'. Despite his aversion to violent movements, Gandhi never shied away from praising the courage and sacrifice of the revolutionary youth from his first public meeting post return to India till the last. Bhagat

Singh and his comrades also had immense respect for stalwarts like Gandhi and Nehru despite their differing opinions. There is no mention of any revolutionary activity targeted at attacking Congress leaders, and definitely not the kind of vile abuse against Gandhi which was reproduced every day in Godse's newspaper. Ideological conflicts bereft of malice need no foul language, which is the reserve of those with sinister intentions. In order to examine the style of revolutionary critique, it is worthwhile to look at the essay 'New Leaders and Their Differing Ideas' by Bhagat Singh where he contrasts the thought of Nehru and Subhas Chandra Bose. He concludes thus:

> Today Subhash might quench the heart but cannot provide any other intellectual stimulation. The need of the hour is for the youth in Punjab to consolidate these monumental ideas. The Punjab urgently needs that intellectual diet which only Pandit Jawaharlal Nehru can offer. It does not mean however that one should be his blind supporter.

A revolutionary would never have blind faith in anyone but have the generosity to be respectful to ideological opponents. Arms and ammunition can easily be obtained by criminals as well, but they don't make them revolutionaries.

The Assembly Bombing Case Trial*

Bhagat Singh voluntarily handed himself over to the police on 8 April 1929 after exploding a bomb in the Central Legislative Assembly, where he never intended to kill anyone.[7] When the case went to court on 6 June, he declined to have a lawyer represent him and instead argued himself with the help of a legal expert. Batukeshwar Dutt, arrested with Bhagat in the same case, had him defended by the staunch nationalist Congressman Asaf Ali. The trial barely lasted a week and both men were sentenced for life. On 14 June, Bhagat Singh was transferred to Mianwali Jail while Batukeshwar was held in Lahore.

---

* For technical details of the case, please refer to A.G. Noorani, *The Trial of Bhagat Singh: Politics of Justice* (OUP, 2001).

Immediately thereafter, Hansraj Vohra and Jaigopal, who had been his comrades, testified against Bhagat Singh in the Saunders Murder Case. Hence, Bhagat Singh, Batukeshwar Dutt, Shiv Verma, Ajoy Ghosh, Jatin Das and Prem Dutt were charged and tried afresh.[8] Inside the jail, Bhagat Singh and his associates began a series of hunger strikes in true Gandhian fashion to demand the status of political prisoners and better facilities. Motilal Nehru came to the defence of the young men and said, 'They haven't gone on hunger strike for their own sake… The strike has a universal reason.' When the strikers were ignored, Jawaharlal Nehru went and met them along with a Congress delegation and later released a statement:

> I am deeply distressed by the condition of our heroes. They have put their lives on the line for the cause. They just want recognition and treatment as political prisoners. I am very hopeful that their sacrifice will be crowned with success.[9]

M.A. Jinnah raised the issue of Bhagat Singh in the Central Assembly and said, 'He is being given inferior food and life amenities as opposed to the standards at which Europeans are treated, on the grounds of his race.'[10] Note that till then Jinnah had not been afflicted by communalism. Jatin Das died after sixty-three days of the hunger strike. Subhas Bose arranged for the body to be brought back to Calcutta where his last wish was to be fulfilled: 'My last rites should not follow regressive traditions. Let every wall in Bengal be postered: "May my son be like Jatin Das".' The whole country was now in mourning. Punjab Congressmen Gopichand Bhargav and Mohammed Alam resigned from the Punjab Legislative Council. Motilal Nehru brought a resolution in the Central Assembly condemning the Punjab government's actions which were passed by majority vote.[11] While the rest of the HSRA group withdrew the strike, Bhagat Singh and Batukeshwar Dutt stood firm. Bhagat Singh only knew to keep himself at the front in the line of fire rather than leveraging his leadership position to use others as shields. Ultimately, his father and an active Congress member Sardar Kishan Singh brought him a resolution from the party requesting him to end the fast. The 116-day fast was ultimately brought to an end by Bhagat Singh and Batukeshwar Dutt on 5 October 1929 as a gesture of regard for Gandhi and the Congress.[12]

The Lahore trial of Bhagat Singh saw him defended in court by Gopichand Bhargav, Duni Chand, Barkat Ali, Aminchand Mehta, Bishan Nath, Amolak Roy Kapur, W.C. Dutt and Puranchand Mehta. The government, determined to sentence Bhagat Singh, held a show trial of sorts in contravention of all constitutional values. The revolutionaries, however, now had a massive public following, and celebrated activists from Motilal Nehru to Rafi Ahmed Kidwai and the Raja of Kalakankar met them in prison. The government responded by hurriedly transferring the case from the court of Justice Shadilal to a tribunal with unlimited powers and whose decision could not be challenged in any higher court. Bhagat called it out for what it was, a farce. He promptly refused to have a lawyer argue his case on government expense. The revolutionaries would shout '*Inqalab Zindabad*' and '*Down with Imperialism*' and obstruct the trial proceedings. As a consequence, almost the entire trial was held in their absence. On 7 October 1930, the tribunal sentenced Bhagat Singh, Rajguru and Sukhdev to death; Kishorilal, Mahavir Singh, Vijay Kumar Sinha, Shiv Verma, Gaya Prasad, Jaydev and Kamalnath Tiwari were deported to the Andamans; and Kundanlal and Prem Dutt were sentenced for seven and five years, respectively.[13]

The Hanging and Gandhi

The debate about whether Gandhi tried his best to save Bhagat Singh or not persists to this day.

If we were to ignore what Godse and people with similar ideologies think, most people who ask this question tend to believe two things. One, that Gandhi was so powerful that he could get the British to do what he wanted. Second, he was magnanimous and his heart would bleed even at his fiercest ideological opponent being hanged in such a way. The first is an illusion, the second absolute truth.

It is necessary to point out that Gandhi was aware of every detail of Bhagat Singh's trial, which exposes the lie that he somehow had a personal grudge against the revolutionaries. The following excerpt from an article by the researcher Chander Pal Singh's underlines this:

> A false impression has been created that Gandhi became interested in Bhagat Singh's fate only a few weeks before his execution. As far back as 4 May 1930, a day before he was arrested, Gandhi had written to the Viceroy strongly criticizing him for the creation of the special Tribunal to try the revolutionaries in the Lahore Conspiracy Case: 'You have found a short cut through the law's delay in the matter of the trial of Bhagat Singh and others by doing away with the ordinary procedure. Is it any wonder if I call all these official activities a veiled form of Martial Law?' On 31 January 1931, he spoke at Allahabad on the subject of Bhagat Singh's execution. 'Those under a death sentence should not be hanged. My personal religion tells me not only that they should not be hanged but also that they should not even be kept in prison. However, that is my personal opinion and we cannot make their release a condition.'[14]

The most talked about is the Gandhi–Irwin Pact. It is assumed that had Gandhi put a condition for the release of Bhagat Singh, it would have happened. In fact, had he done so there would be no pact. One instance suffices to prove the same. Gandhi tried to include a clause in the pact to constitute a commission of inquiry into police excesses and acts of cruelty against Congress activists and members of the public during the Civil Disobedience movement. Many of his associates had pressed him on it. Irwin, however, flatly refused and Gandhi was forced to take back his demand. The reason was that seven governors of provinces including the powerful governor of Bombay Sir Frederick Sykes threatened to resign if such a commission were constituted.[15] It is also pertinent here to remember suppression by the police under the same Irwin administration during the Salt Satyagraha about which the *New York Telegram* correspondent Web Miller wrote: 'In eighteen years of reporting in twenty-two countries during which I have witnessed innumerable civil disturbances, riots, street-fights and rebellions, I have never witnessed such harrowing scenes as at Dharsana.'[16]

While Bhagat Singh for Indians is a hero and occupies pride of place as one of the brightest stars in its history, for the British State he was the exact opposite. He was a criminal who murdered a police officer and threw a bomb inside the Central Assembly. What would constitute acts of bravery for Indians were acts of terror for them—the foremost being the conspiracy to blow up the Viceroy's car which was nothing short of a declaration of war on British rule in India. The Punjab Police in particular was determined to settle scores for the murder of two of their men. Even as Gandhi was being beseeched to press for Bhagat Singh's release, senior police officers of the Punjab threatened mass resignation if Lord Irwin considered any reprieve to the hanging. A close associate of Irwin and a senior correspondent of the *News Chronicle*, Robert Bernays, who was then in India, wrote in his diary: 'It was an extremely difficult situation for the Viceroy. The mention of Bhagat Singh might have driven India back into disorder... he might well have been faced with the resignation of every head of the police force.' Another newspaper, *The People*, wrote on 22 March 1931: 'Perhaps it goes without saying that some Punjab officials were pressing Lord Irwin to let the condemned be executed. It is said that some police officials even threatened to resign if the sentences were commuted.'[17] Irwin was already in the line of fire from his government back home for the decision to release Gandhi and his associates and could expect no help from London. It was virtually impossible for him to agree to Gandhi's persistent requests. We would do well to note the contents of a fortnightly government report of that time: 'The failure of Mr Gandhi to save Bhagat Singh and his associates verifies the opinions of some that his win in Delhi is not as large as made out to be.'[18]

The most important fact for our consideration is whether Bhagat Singh himself wanted a reprieve. When the tribunal held his trial, Bhagat fiercely resisted the formation of a defence committee at the initiative of his father. He was firmly of the opinion that having waged war against British rule, he deserved to be shot dead as a prisoner of war. Unlike Savarkar, he was dead against the idea of an apology even as he was condemned to the gallows.

Gandhi was also not in a position to defend the revolutionary method outright—having been an advocate of non-violence all his life—as it would paint him a hypocrite. He did try to do all he could to commute the death sentence on humanitarian grounds. On 18 February 1931, he told Irwin:

> He is undoubtedly a brave man but I would certainly say that he is not in his right mind. However, this is the evil of capital punishment, that it gives no opportunity to such a man to reform himself. I am putting this matter before you as a humanitarian issue and desire suspension of sentence in order that there may not be unnecessary turmoil in the country. I myself would release him, but I cannot expect any Government to do so. I would not take it ill even if you do not give any reply on this issue.[19]

He didn't relent even then, as verified by an excerpt from the memoirs of Irwin—'Gandhi greatly feared unless I could do something about it [the death sentence], the effect would be to destroy our pact, and I said I should regret that no less than he. It was impossible for me from my point of view to grant him [Bhagat Singh] reprieve.'[20]

It is to be noted that as soon as the charges of the murder of policemen were brought, Gandhi stopped receiving any support on the issue beyond Congress circles. Jinnah who had hitherto backed Bhagat Singh on the issue of equal treatment in jail during the Assembly case fell silent as soon as the charges were added. Rabindranath Tagore, who had returned his knighthood in protest at the shootings in Jallianwala Bagh kept quiet for the same reason. Periyar and Ambedkar did publish sympathetic articles post the hanging in their respective newspapers[21] but were silent throughout the trial. The most ardent supporter of the revolutionaries, Motilal Nehru, had died by this time and due to the limited reach of the revolutionary movement, no significant upheaval was noted outside Punjab. Gandhi wrote his last letter on the matter on the fateful date of 23 March:

> It seems cruel to inflict this letter on you, but the interest of peace demands a final appeal. Though you were frank enough to tell me that there was little hope of your commuting the sentence of death on Bhagat Singh and two others, you said you would consider my submission of Saturday. Dr Sapru met me yesterday and said that you were troubled over the matter and taxing your brain as to the proper course to adopt. If there is any room left for reconsideration, I invite your attention to the following. Popular opinion rightly or wrongly demands commutation. When there is no principle at stake, it is often a duty to respect it. In the present case the chances

> are that, if commutation is granted, internal peace is most likely to be promoted. In the event of execution, peace is undoubtedly in danger.
>
> Since you seem to value my influence such as it is in favour of peace, do not please unnecessarily make my position, difficult as it is, almost too difficult for future work. Execution is an irretrievable act. If you think there is the slightest chance of error of judgment, I would urge you to suspend for further review an act that is beyond recall.
>
> If my presence is necessary, I can come. Though I may not speak,* I may hear and write what I want to say.
>
> 'Charity never faileth.'†[22]

The colonial government had nevertheless decided its course and Bhagat Singh, Rajguru and Sukhdev were hanged even as the letter was being written.

One wonders what else Gandhi could do.

One of Bhagat Singh's close associates, Chamanlal happened to be in a train to Karachi with Gandhi and peppered him with insults throughout the ride which Gandhi heard out with a smile. He later turned a monk and wrote a memoir in which he says: 'Gandhi said to me, "I did what I could, but Irwin was under immense pressure from Punjab."' Towards the end he concludes: 'It is important for the people of India and her historians to know that this was not a failure of Gandhi.'[23] The truth is that the real culprits in sending Bhagat Singh to the gallows were the comrades turned traitors in his organization who gave him away.

And Again, Some Questions

It is quite surprising to see no questions asked of Vinayak Damodar Savarkar, always a votary of violent means, as to what he did to save Bhagat Singh's life. Not even a statement was issued on Savarkar's behalf

---

* Monday was a day of silence for him.

† This was a quote from the Bible. Gandhi knew that Irwin was a religious man and this was an indirect appeal to his faith to get him to commute the sentence.

in support of the revolutionaries. Godse, who used his newspaper to vilify Gandhi, did not write a single article in support, let alone launch a campaign in Maharashtra. Similar questions could be asked of Syama Prasad Mukherjee, Hedgewar, Moonje and Golwalkar who silently saw 'Hindus' like Bhagat Singh hanged before them. Godse never published a photo of Bhagat Singh in his newspaper (that of Savarkar was published on the header), but he did use his name during the courtroom trial to attack Gandhi.

5. The Lies on Kashmir*

> The main difference between a cat and a lie is that a cat only has nine lives.
>
> —Mark Twain

The above quote assumes great significance with respect to the lies peddled about Gandhi since Godse's statement in court. Truth requires fact-checks, references, and preparation, while a lie needs nothing more than a nefarious design. Godse could very well have called Savarkar a martyr or proclaimed himself a comrade of Bhagat Singh—even proved himself Subhas Bose reincarnated. The only reason he refrained from attacking Nehru and Patel in his statement was the knowledge that his mentor Savarkar had to continue living under their government post his hanging.

Hence Gandhi also took the blame for whatever transpired in Kashmir. Godse claimed that 'About Kashmir, Gandhiji again and again declared that Sheikh Abdullah should be entrusted the charge of the state and that the Maharaja of Kashmir should retire to Benares for no particular reason than that the Muslims formed the bulk of the Kashmir population'.[1]

The only thing Gandhi was spared blame for was the intense humidity experienced in the year 1947–48.

---

* There are many books to understand the history of Kashmir, including one of my own, *Kashmirnama: Itihas aur Samkal* ('A Tale of Kashmir: Past and Present'), whose English translation is forthcoming.

Gandhi's Kashmir Visit

Gandhi visited Kashmir for the first and only time on 1 August 1947. In fact, it was Nehru who, seeing the delay in Sheikh Abdullah's release and the continuing uncertainty in Kashmir, wanted to go, but Mountbatten advised him otherwise to forestall any tensions in the region. The Maharaja of Kashmir was disinclined to see Nehru come and hence Mountbatten requested Gandhi to go.[2] Gandhi's visit saw the people of Srinagar decorate the city in festive lights. Gandhi stayed there at the house of Lala Kishorilal.[3] Sheikh Abdullah's wife Akbar Jahan was among those in attendance at Gandhi's prayer meeting.[4]

It is a matter of speculation as to what exactly transpired between the Maharaja and Gandhi in the meeting, but we can conclude for certain that Gandhi requested him to honour the people's wishes and release Sheikh Abdullah. He categorically stated to a delegation of Hindus in Jammu that the people should be able to determine their own future. While leaving for the refugee camp in Rawalpindi he told the press that the matter of Kashmir needed to be peacefully settled by India, Pakistan, the Maharaja and the people of Kashmir, but that could not be possible without the release of the biggest popular leader, Sheikh Abdullah.[5] Although Gandhi described the visit as apolitical, it was impossible in those times for it not to have political ramifications. Gandhi knew that while the Maharaja was deliberately postponing his decision and in fact still clinging onto the dreams of an independent Dogristan, Sheikh Abdullah had expressed the wish to accede to India in no uncertain terms. The extent of suppression under the Maharaja is described by Balraj Puri, active in the region at the time, who states that the ruler was imprisoning pro-India voices even in Jammu. His prime minister Ramchandra Kak was actively engaged in secret negotiations with Pakistan and Sheikh Abdullah was thrown behind bars. Gandhi tried hard to pull the people of Kashmir towards India through his advocacy of Abdullah and spoke to Hari Singh regarding accession. *The Times* wrote on 25 October 1947:

> Indications are that the Hindu Maharaja of Kashmir, Sir Hari Singh, has lately been much influenced by representations made by Mr Gandhi who visited Kashmir three months ago.[6]

The first impact of Gandhi's visit was the dismissal of the much-hated Ramchandra Kak as prime minister. All sources point out that Gandhi had slammed Kak in no uncertain terms. Thereafter, at first Janak Singh was appointed in Kak's place, followed by the Indian representative to the boundary commission and a judge of the East Punjab High Court, Mehr Chand Mahajan, who it is believed was appointed on the Indian side's suggestion. Consequently, efforts were made to improve communications with India through telegraph, road, and rail. Towards the end of September 1947, when the chief of the kingdom's armed forces Henry Lawrence Scott retired, Patel recommended the name of an Indian army lieutenant colonel Kashmir Singh Katoch in his place to the kingdom's defence minister Baldev Singh. This appointment was bound to be in India's favour and its acceptance by the Maharaja an arm extended to India. These events made clear to the Maharaja that in the event of him foregoing his enmity with the Congress on account of the latter's friendship with Sheikh Abdullah, and by giving Sheikh an honourable place in the state's politics post accession to India, his own interests would be taken care of.[7] Gandhi's note post his return from Kashmir said the following:

> Bakshi [Ghulam Mohammed] was most sanguine that the result of the free vote of the people, whether on the adult franchise or on the existing register, would be in favour of Kashmir joining the Union provided of course that Sheikh Abdullah and his co-prisoners were released, all bans were removed and the present Prime Minister was not in power. Probably he echoed the general sentiment. I studied the Amritsar treaty properly called 'sale deed'. I presume it lapses on the 15th instant. To whom does the State revert? Does it not go to the people?[8]

The importance of Gandhi's Kashmir visit is underscored by the fact that Jinnah too was continuously attempting to come to the state. He sent a number of messages to Hari Singh expressing his intent to stay in Srinagar to improve his health. The Maharaja, however, politely declined stating that he was unable at that hour to put arrangements in place for welcoming the head of state of an important neighbour.[9]

Hari Singh's Dither and the Pakistani Invasion

Hari Singh, in line with his perennial indecision to a rapidly escalating situation didn't heed to the release of Sheikh Abdullah or other demands, and two days before the independence of India and the cutoff date decided by Mountbatten for accession to either nation, sent a proposal of a Standstill Agreement on 13 August to both India and Pakistan through his then prime minister Janak Singh. This was a contingency arrangement in the event of no decision on accession, to keep things as they were with both countries. On 15 August, Pakistan accepted the proposal which brought all centrally administered affairs pertaining to Lahore Circle under Pakistani control. Hence, the postal and telegraph services of the state came under Pakistani administration for the time being with their offices displaying Pakistani flags. The Indian side, however, pressed for a long-term treaty before a standstill, in line with its stated policy which the ruler didn't react to, and there was no agreement.[10] India's only exception to this policy was a standstill agreement with Hyderabad, which was much later in November 1947, but there had been a number of treaties signed before that.[11] Lord Birdwood, citing Abdullah as a source, informs us that India was not ready to sign any agreement with the Maharaja without gauging the people's mood and without Sheikh's involvement.[12] There is consensus on the point, however, that the agreement was just an arrangement to keep things as they were rather than a precursor to accession, as is often claimed.[13] However, A.G. Noorani, through his access to archival documents from London, does inform us that the text of the draft agreement wasn't similar as sent to both countries. Whereas Pakistan was proposed status quo in matters of communication, supplies, postal and telegraph services, India was in addition asked to maintain status quo on foreign affairs, security and control of armed forces. The government of India committed to sending a minister to finalize details. Before this could be done, the tribal invasion commenced.[14]

Indecision could not be maintained for eternity considering the rising communal temperature in the rest of the country. Kashmir was not immune to the developments. It is to be emphasized here that within the Kashmir valley where Sheikh Abdullah had influence and the National Conference had fought for communal harmony, there was no major communal incident. Neither did any Muslim go to Pakistan nor were Sikhs or Hindus thrown out of the Valley. However, Jammu had turned into a cauldron of sectarian hate thanks to the Rashtriya Swayamsevak Sangh and the Muslim Conference holding sway over their respective communities. It is a matter of great surprise that neither serious researchers like Alastair Lamb, nor diplomat writers like Lord Birdwood or Joseph Corbel show awareness of the differences between Jammu and the Valley in terms of history, culture, and traditions. It was precisely this difference that led to the message of religious harmony propagated by the National Conference holding sway in the Kashmir valley and communalism of all kinds in Jammu. Any retaliatory measure for the anti-Muslim violence in Jammu would have been a nightmare for the Pandits in the Valley.

Jammu had become the hotbed of communal consolidation thanks in particular to the activities of the Jammu Praja Parishad, an allied organization of the local branches of the RSS and Hindu Mahasabha. The Parishad played a key role in vitiating the atmosphere by continuous rumour-mongering and provoking the Hindu refugees coming to Jammu from West Punjab and the Frontier Province. The state of Jammu according to the 1941 census had a population of two million out of which roughly 1.2 million were Muslims. In the city of Jammu, out of a population of fifty thousand, some sixteen thousand were Muslim. By the end of September, a majority of Muslims from border areas such as Bishrah, Akhnoor and RS Pura had migrated to Pakistan. According to Ved Bhasin, a student leader active in Jammu at that time, Udhampur, Chenani, Ramnagar, Resai and Bhadarwah saw large-scale killings of Muslims and abduction and rape of Muslim women. Despite the tempest, the Kashmir valley stood calm, prompting Gandhi to call it a 'ray of hope' in such dark times. The hope, for Gandhi, was the protection of minorities in all areas irrespective of their religion.

Minds filled with sectarianism and a distorted sense of history may never be able to comprehend that Gandhi never stood for one religion, but for minority rights. He knew that the Hindus, the majority in the rest of India were a minority in Noakhali, most of Punjab and the Kashmir valley, while Muslims were a minority in the rest of India except places like these. If a majority killed the minority at one place, it was well-nigh impossible to stop retaliatory carnage somewhere else. Hence, saving one community was the only option to save the other.

It is clear hence that those who murdered Muslims in India were directly responsible for the murder of Hindus in Pakistan and those who killed Hindus were responsible for the murder of Muslims. The most succinct example is Bahawalpur where no Hindu or Sikh was harmed up till 15 August, when incoming Muslim refugees narrated their tale of atrocities, and the district went up in flames.

Meanwhile, Gandhi's trust in the people of Kashmir was rewarded when they resisted together the Pakistani invasion in the guise of an attack by tribesmen.

Kashmiri People's Resistance

Hari Singh moved to Delhi on the advice of Patel's principal secretary, V.P. Menon. He did not forget to retrieve all his valuables including jewellery, costly paintings and carpets which were transported in forty military trucks. Whereas his own state was now in urgent need of motor vehicles to repel the invaders, he did not forget to bring with him the entire quota of the state's petrol.[15] He signed the instrument of accession on the very same day which also included the provision to ratify the accession according to the wishes of the state's people as and when things normalized. The Maharaja did form an interim government before leaving and gave its reigns to Sheikh Abdullah.[16] While Mahajan was still technically the prime minister, Sheikh had been appointed Director General of the administration and had full control and responsibility.[17] The operation to save Srinagar commenced under Bakshi Ghulam Mohammed. Muslims, Hindus, Sikhs, men, women and children—all of them showed bravery and courage in defending the city despite most of them not being professional soldiers. Their tale of courage and sacrifice is best illustrated through the martyrdom of Mir Maqbool Sherwani, as told by Margaret Bourke-White:

> In Baramula the townspeople told me of a young Muslim shopkeeper who had sacrificed his life rather than recant in his creed of religious tolerance. His martyrdom had taken place almost under the shadow of the convent walls. And in memory of the devoted Kashmiris he was fast assuming the stature of a saint.
>
> In the democratic movement, and like Abdullah he had preached the need for religious unity in the fight for people's rights. He must have been a sort of Robin Hood character, from the stories the townspeople told me.
>
> When tribesman invaded Kashmir and terrorized the countryside, Sherwani, who knew every footpath in the Valley, began working behind the lines, keeping up the morale of the besieged villagers, urging them to resist and to stick together regardless of whether they are Hindu, Sikh or Muslim, assuring them that help from the Indian Army and People's Militia was on the way. Three times he skilfully planted rumours [and] decoyed bands of tribesman and got them surrounded and captured by Indian infantry. But the fourth time he was captured himself.
>
> The tribesman took Sherwani to the stoop of a little apple shop in the town square of Baramula, and the terrified townspeople were driven into the square in front of him with the butts of rifles. Knowing Sherwani's popularity with the people, his captors ordered him to make a public announcement that joining Pakistan was the best solution for Muslims. When he refused, he was lashed to the porch posts with ropes, his arms spread out in the shape of a cross.
>
> It was a curious thing that the tribesman did the next. I do not know why these savage nomads should have thought of such a thing, unless their sight of these sacred figures in St Josef Chapel on the hill just above had suggested it to them. They drove nails through the palms of Sherwani's hands. On his forehead they pressed a jagged piece of tin and wrote on it: 'The punishment of a traitor is death.'
>
> Once more Sherwani cried out, 'Victory to Hindu–Muslim unity', and fourteen tribesmen shot bullets into his body.[18]

Sherwani was honoured as a hero whose sacrifice is remembered every day by the Indian Army; he also has a memorial hall dedicated to him in Baramulla. A documentary on him was produced by the Films Division of India. The well-known Indian English novelist Mulk Raj

Anand published *Death of a Hero* in his honour in 1955. Similar is the story of the Baramulla school teacher Master Abdul Aziz who, seeing non-Muslim women being raped, held the Quran in his hand and pledged that he would not allow this to continue till he was alive. He later died at the hands of the invaders.[19]

On 27 October, the Indian Army landed in Srinagar in a uniquely improvised operation involving civilian aircrafts but had scarce transport to move any further on land. Bakshi Ghulam Mohammed arranged buses and the army under the command of Lt Col Diwan Ranjit Rai sought direct engagement. By evening, the Indian troops formed a line of defence sixteen miles ahead at Pattan, losing Rai in the process. The air force battalion arrived the very next day and under the command of Brigadier L.P. Sen along with Major General Balwant Singh, Major General Thimaiyya, Major General Atma Singh and Vice Air Marshall S. Mukherjee and others, the Indian side captured Baramulla on 8 November and pushed back the invaders. The Indians also took control of Uri, Tanmarg and Gulmarg by 14 November.

The prompt response and counterattack by the Indian Army took Pakistan by complete surprise. Alastair Lamb and other researchers have continued to repeat the allegations by the Pakistani establishment that India had made advance preparations for the attack, despite V.P. Menon's diary giving a minute-by-minute account of the operation.[20] Jinnah asked the Pakistan army chief General Sir Douglas Gracy to mount a full-scale assault citing Indian involvement. However, the supreme commander of the Indian and Pakistani armies Claude Auchinleck on being informed of the matter told Jinnah that he would remove all British officers from both armies in that event. This was part of an already existing directive from him during the transfer of power for British officers to stand down both armies to forestall Britons fighting against each other in the event of war. Jinnah, thus, couldn't involve the Pakistani army openly,[21] which did make the task of the Indian soldiers somewhat easier.

Patel was right in stating that 'Gandhi takes the long-range view'. He knew that Kashmir couldn't be integrated without taking the most popular leader of Kashmiri Muslims, Sheikh Abdullah, on their side. Gandhi's non-violence did not propagate cowardice but courage of the highest order. In a prayer meeting of 29 October, citing the news from Kashmir he said:

> All that would happen would be that Kashmir would belong to the Kashmiris. I fully agree with Sheikh Abdullah who says that Kashmir belongs to the Kashmiris and not to the Maharaja. But the Maharaja has given all powers to Sheikh Abdullah, leaving it to the Sheikh's discretion to do whatever should be done and save Kashmir if he can. After all, Kashmir cannot be saved by the Maharaja.
>
> If anyone can save Kashmir, it is only the Muslims, the Kashmiri Pandits, the Rajputs and the Sikhs who can do so. Sheikh Abdullah has affectionate and friendly relations with all of them.
>
> It is possible that while saving Kashmir, Sheikh Abdullah would have to sacrifice his life, his Begum and his daughter would have to die and all women of Kashmir would have to die. And, if that happens, I am not going to shed a single tear. If we are fated to have a war, there will be a war. God alone knows, if it is going to be a war between the two only or others too would be involved. If the aggressors have no support or encouragement of Pakistan, I do not know how they can hold on. Maybe, there is no such encouragement. If the people of Kashmir die in the fighting, who would be left behind? Sheikh Abdullah would have gone, because his lion-heartedness consists in dying while fighting and saving Kashmir to his last breath. He would have saved the Muslims and also the Sikhs and the Hindus.[22]

Gandhi's non-violence did not teach him cowardice or unconditional surrender to an oppressor. It did not teach him to turn his back on battle either, though he knew that ultimately wars were futile. Gandhi was proud of being a Hindu as can be evidenced from his writings. But his religion did not teach him to hate another. He had learnt the lesson quite clearly in his long public life. Thus he says at the end of the same prayer meeting speech:

> I believe that there are good people among all, Hindus and Muslims and Sikhs. And it is due to these good people that the world goes on—not due to the people carrying arms.[23]

The whole Kashmir saga of those days can be summed up by an instance from 1944. Savarkar, on a visit to Kashmir, tried actively to enlist support for a Hindu Rashtra among the local Kashmiri Pandits. The leader of the Sanatan Dharam Yuvak Sabha, Pandit Shiv Narayan Fotedar was blunt: 'Hindu sectarianism is as alien to Kashmir as Muslim sectarianism.' That is the same year when Sheikh Abdullah categorically asked Jinnah to leave Kashmir empty-handed.[24]

6. Godse: A Revolutionary or a Coward?

> What makes Godse's confident statements in court a sad documentary is the fact that there is not even a sense of self-doubt, let alone atonement. This is what makes him an ideological killer. Godse was neither insane nor a fundamentalist, but the insight into the effects of ideology on the mind is easily gained standing at the place where Gandhi fell.
>
> —Krishna Kumar, *Shanti Ka Safar*, p. 26

Had Gopal Godse any semblance of moral courage, he could very well have confessed that his bravery was accidental. That in the heat of passion he went to kill Gandhi but could not pull the revolver's trigger, and when his elder brother cleverly planned to entrap Digambar Badge and the innocent servant Shankar, he joined in. That he ran away when the plan failed and went back to his job. That when his elder brother went to kill Gandhi for a second time, he came back after handing him the weapon, living life as if nothing had ever happened. That he tried desperately to escape sentencing in court but could not.

Sans the moral courage, Gopal Godse turned out an apologist for a criminal act using the tag of bravery he was accorded by a stroke of luck. His attempts to valorize the murderer of Gandhi are juvenile, and the lies can be seen exposed in the preceding chapters.

Nathuram's Perverse Allegations

Godse's courtroom statement shows a raw idealistic mind poisoned by Savarkar to such an extent that he considered everything told to him as gospel truth. He seemed intoxicated by the same poison we see today on social media, which is spat out by youth who have been made to substitute it for historical fact. He claimed to have read world history and ideologies such as Marxism, but none of it is apparent in his statement. It appears his strategy was to emulate Bhagat Singh by using the court as a stage to project an image of a revolutionary and the illusion of being erudite and noble. He had obviously no consonance with the fact that Bhagat Singh led his life as a revolutionary and died opposing imperialism, while he had reduced his life's purpose to murdering an individual. Bhagat Singh's jail diary displays his ardent quest for truth, which led him to conclude that bombs and pistols were not the necessary tools of revolution, and that the real task at hand was to go organize at the village and factory level. Nathuram on the contrary had reduced himself to a tool of his mentor's perverse hatred.

For instance, he also raises the issue of language. He goes on to accuse Gandhi of being pro-Muslim, with his promotion of Hindustani, which in his view was tilted towards Urdu rather than Sanskritized Hindi. To quote him: 'Everybody in India knows that there is no language called Hindustani; it has no grammar; it has no vocabulary; it is a mere dialect; it is spoken but not written. It is a bastard tongue and a crossbreed between Hindi and Urdu and not even the Mahatma's sophistry could make it popular.' The irony of the matter is that Godse and his mentor Savarkar wrote all their lives in Marathi and English, while Gandhi, despite being a Gujarati, both spoke and wrote in Hindi. Both the newspapers published by Godse were Marathi. Meanwhile, Gandhi wanted neither a Sanskritized nor Persianized tongue, but one which could be understood by the masses irrespective of their creed. Replying to similar criticism in June 1916, he wrote:

> In fact, neither Urdu nor Hindi is to be termed Hindustani. Though not in vogue today, Hindustani is a wise mixture of the two. If newspaper and other critics will exercise a little forbearance they will presently see that it is not difficult to understand what is Hindustani as distinguished from Hindi and Urdu. I admit that those who write for *Harijan Sevak* are still struggling but they are determined to reach the desired goal. Readers must bear kindly

> with what may today seem a hotchpotch of the two forms. If God spares my life I hope to prove to the readers of *Harijan Sevak* that Hindustani can be as sweet as either Urdu or Hindi. The seeming quarrel of today will shortly disappear when it is realised that the two forms are sister and that through their joint effort will come into being a stately language which will serve the crores of India.[1]

The challenge before Gandhi was to establish a language for administration and communication in a multi-linguistic country. Gandhi never once imagined Partition and hence had to factor in Urdu which was prominent in a large area from Kashmir to Punjab. The foremost Hindi story writer Premchand had started out with Urdu and the Hindi he wrote was closer to the Hindustani Gandhi spoke of. Such a language could not be nurtured by parochialism, as is evidenced by the difficulty of very many people to fully understand Sanskritized Hindi. The conversational Hindi used today is in fact the happy amalgamation of Sanskrit, Urdu and regional dialects. We are left to wonder at the wisdom of a Nathuram Godse conversant only in Marathi and patchy English, to question a man well versed in Hindi, Sanskrit, Gujarati, Urdu and Sanskrit, but still finding time to practise the Bengali taught to him by Prof Nirmal Bose till his dying day.

Gandhi's stand on language and script is further clarified through a peek into his conversation with a Ramesh Chandra of Shillong on 3 January 1948:

> Question: Whether the national language is called Hindi or Hindustani, is not a very controversial matter. In daily conversation current Hindustani will be used. Nobody denies that for advanced literature, science and similar subjects new terms will have to be borrowed from Sanskrit. Will there be any harm if this is made clear to all?
>
> Answer: The first part of this question is all right. If everybody takes a word in the same sense, there is no trouble. It is not the name but its use that matters. If there is unanimity on usage, all objections to different names are futile.
>
> Why should the words for advanced literature and science be drawn from Sanskrit alone? One should not be dogmatic on this score. A small committee can collect a vocabulary of current words.

> Suppose an English word is currently used in Hindustani. Why should we replace it by a pure Sanskrit word? For chair shall we coin a Sanskrit word, *chatuspad-pithika* (four-legged seat), or unhesitatingly accept the current word *kursi*? Such instances can be multiplied.[2]

We all know the disastrous consequences for Hindi that have resulted from the use of an unheard-of Sanskrit vocabulary in science, administrative work and literature, ignoring Gandhi's counsel. I personally find the version of Hindustani suggested by Gandhi far more convenient to reach out to my readers. And they may judge for themselves how opposing this language could be called patriotism.

But that is not all. Godse claimed to be well read in the very beginning of his statement, but it seems that he hadn't even read his mentor's book, *Hindutva*. Else he must have known that Savarkar had himself accepted—

> Hindusthani is *par excellence* the language of Hindusthan. The attempt to raise Hindi to the pedestal of our National tongue is neither new nor forced... A sadhu or a merchant from Rameshwaram and proceeding to Hardwar, could make himself understood in all parts of India through this tongue. Sanskrit might have introduced him to the circle of Pandits but Hindusthani was a sure passport to Rajsabhas as well as to Bazaars. A Nanak, a Chaitanya, a Ramdas could and did travel up and down the country as freely as they would have done in their own provinces teaching and preaching in this tongue.[3]

Did the 'bazaar' with a 'z' in this sentence not come from Urdu? Was this 'Hindusthani' any different from what Gandhi was proposing?

Godse also accused Gandhi, who during the Second World War proclaimed 'Do or Die' and '*na denge ek pai, na denge ek bhai*' (neither a penny, nor my brother), and was jailed because of non-cooperation with the British, of siding with them. In fact, it was his own younger brother Gopal Godse who fought with the British in the war while his associate and partner in crime, Narayan Apte, was a recruitment officer enlisting able-bodied men for the British army. Savarkar, his mentor, had famously campaigned for recruitment for the British. The ludicrous nature of such charges requires no further explanation or answer.

The allegation of Gandhi's alleged mistreatment of Subhas Chandra Bose also merits counter questions. For example, did Savarkar clarify to the men he recruited for the British that they shouldn't fight the Indian National Army? Gopal Godse also had the option of enlisting for Subhas's army which wanted to free India, which he failed to exercise and so did Narayan Apte. The allegation is a matter of the pot calling the kettle black.

As with Bhagat Singh, the ideological differences between Gandhi and Subhas were accompanied by mutual respect. Subhas Bose in fact named the brigades of the Indian National Army after Gandhi, Nehru and Azad rather than Savarkar. The INA contained men and women of all religions. It was in fact Subhas who after the death of Kasturba in 1944 referred to Gandhi as 'Mahatma' for the first time. Sarat Bose, the elder brother of Subhas, remained in the Congress till 1947 and was a great favourite of Gandhi. Gandhi stood with Sarat, contrary to Congress party policy, on the proposal of a united Bengal. While in Noakhali, Gandhi appealed for the release of Haridas Mitra, the husband of Bela Mitra, Subhas's niece, who was herself imprisoned for alleged pro-Japanese conspiracy. Haridas was consequently released.[4] We have already seen the efforts Gandhi made for the release of INA prisoners. The speech Gandhi gave, a week before he died, on Subhas's birth anniversary, suffices to underline his respect for the latter.

The Idea of India and Its Cowardly Opposition

The mutual respect between people like Gandhi, Bhagat Singh, Nehru, Patel, Subhas Bose and Tilak stems from the fact that their primary aim was to fight the unjust British rule. They were men of clear conscience who dreamt of a better future for India. Gandhi's only opposition to Subhas was on account of the latter's wish to take the Congress in a radical direction in direct opposition to Gandhi's non-violence. His proposal to nominate Nehru as the Congress president and therefore the head of the interim government was not simply a matter of personal preference. Patel had begun his political career as a protégé of Gandhi and despite the former's sometimes bitter denunciations (because of policy differences rather than malice) bringing tears to his eyes, Gandhi never said a word against him. Patel saw the 'forgiveness' in Gandhi's placid eyes after death, which reminded him how, despite his strong words leaving Gandhi feeling insulted in a CWC meeting on 14 January, the latter remained quiet and chose to praise Patel in a public meeting the next day.[5] The only reason he wanted Nehru to lead was because Nehru had studied at Harrow and Cambridge which could come in handy in steering India internationally in such tenuous times.[6] Patel acknowledged the same and the overstatement of differences between Nehru and Patel was more the work of malicious rumour mills and far removed from the mutual respect the two men had.

Savarkar didn't fit in that league. He could not gain the respect of any of these men and hence could not reciprocate either.

It is also, in our last passages, perhaps right to ask the difficult question: Subhas Chandra Bose stood against communalism and sectarianism all his life, but ended up joining forces with a man like Hitler; would Nazi xenophobia have been any better than British imperialism?

In fact, the most important lesson we may draw is that no one is divine and hence beyond critical scrutiny. Everyone committed mistakes during the freedom struggle, which is only natural. If we were to have a cynical reading of events, Bhagat Singh's movement was destroyed by the treachery of some of his associates; Subhas's impatience ruined the prospects of the INA; Gandhi's entire life, devoted to the principle of non-violence, came to naught when his own followers attacked Brahmins in Maharashtra after his assassination.

History dictates its own pace and determines who turns out to be a hero and who doesn't. The fact of the matter is that different and sometimes contesting strands made our freedom struggle more vibrant and laid the foundation of the great 'Idea of India', which promised communal harmony, democratic rights and an end to caste oppression—the cornerstones of our Constitution.

Gandhi's killers stand opposed to that idea. Their hatred of him stems from the cowardice that prevented them from being an opposition to the British Empire.

Epilogue

It has been more than seven decades since Gandhi was murdered in cold blood, and as I try to pen this epilogue, the larger part of the globe is slipping into the grip of fundamentalist forces. Gandhi's dream of swaraj is being shattered day by day with jingoistic slogans and an attempt to create a theocratic nation. Not only *fringe* elements, but lawmakers can be seen openly praising Nathuram. Temples dedicated to him are being built and the slogan, '*Bharat Mata ki Jai*' (Hail Mother India), is being used to shelter crimes as severe as rape. Going by the findings of the V-Dem Institute at the University of Gothenburg,* India is now an electoral autocracy!

This is a time when 'secularism' is being reduced to a bad word and 'nationalism' is turning into a synonym for racism. This hate-driven ideology is turning enthusiastic and idealistic youths of all religions into killers. Be it Hindu Nationalism or Pan-Islamism or the beliefs of the Ku Klux Klan, these ideologies are based on the sinister ideals of racist supremacy, which create a futile division between 'us' and 'others' and inject people with an irrepressible hatred. Therefore, any answer to the question 'Who were they?' cannot be answered in terms of their identities. One must delve deeper into their inspiration which turned them into predators.

Let us deal with the primary question. Where does this jingoistic fervour lead? We have enough examples in history. Hitler's Germany

---

* 'Autocratization Turns Viral: Democracy Report 2021', Gothenburg: V-Dem Institute, University of Gothenburg, 2021 (available online: https://www.v-dem.net/files/25/DR%202021.pdf, last accessed on 8 December 2021).

is a famous one. Everyone knows that his theory of racial supremacy shattered his own country, humiliated its masses, and killed millions around the world. The worst part is that it could not bring any glory to the people it claimed to be representing. The Jews migrated to Palestine and they created their own theory of historical enmity and racial supremacy. That converted the Arab world into a war zone. Those who were victims in Germany and elsewhere became executioners in Palestine.

Let us also look at Pakistan. While the idea of India emerged through the ideals of secularism, brotherhood and co-existence, the idea of Pakistan was based solely on the theocratic two-nation theory, which rejects the possibility of co-existence between two religions. The socio-political development process of Pakistan and India can be analysed as a case study for a comparison of these two theories. Pakistan couldn't hold East Pakistan and the very creation of Bangladesh proved Jinnah and his two-nation theory wrong. It proved that religion cannot be the only unifying factor for any modern nation. Regional, linguistic, and other aspirations can't be suppressed under this garb for long. Despite obvious faultlines, India has flourished as a multi-lingual, multi-religious and multi-cultural country under its secular-democratic constitution while Pakistan paid a heavy price in terms of socio-political instability for its authoritative structure, at least till the time of Zia-ul-Haq.

As we have discussed earlier, the theory of Hindutva of Savarkar and Golwalkar is a Hindu carbon copy of this principle of non-co-existence and racial supremacy. Their claim to nationalism is basically an endeavour to establish a nation based on upper-caste supremacy; their call for Hindu unity is not only to reduce minorities to second-class citizens but to establish a caste hierarchy which would render second-class status on Dalits and women as well. Let us ask one more question: Would it benefit the so-called upper caste? It depends on your perception of benefit. Did Hitler's policy help its advocates? Did Zia's jingoism help Muslims in Pakistan? Yes and no. In the short run they may feel empowered. But this cannot be the case for long. An ideology based on hatred is bound to be self-destructive. It must seek new enemies to survive. Once the outsiders are gone, they will be chosen from within. The definition of 'others' will be updated. The basis for this new 'other' may be region, language, food habits or any such thing. A part of the mainstream of today will be outsiders tomorrow and socio-political tensions within that small, privileged group will give rise to new equations.

At the same time, a section of the citizenry reduced to second-class status is bound to bounce back and demand their rights with increased fervour and intensity. Their repression will lead to a series of bloody repercussions including further revolts. That is exactly what has happened throughout history all over the world. That is what is taking shape in many parts of India. Be it minorities or farmers, they are coming forward in large numbers despite brutal repression. You cannot simply remove eighty-five per cent of your populace from the mainstream. This will either lead to a bloody revolt or to further partition of the country, as happened in the case of Bangladesh.

The unity and prosperity of any country ultimately depend on its capacity to adapt and co-exist. Developed Western nations provide an apt example of this phenomenon. The philosophy of Gandhi is a torch to lead this path, while that of Savarkar can only create barriers. Gandhi attempted to imbibe the higher human values of Hinduism and apply them to the polity in such a way that it could co-exist with all the other religions of the world. There is famous couplet from the great saint and reformer, Kabir: *Sadhu aisa chahiye, jaisa soop subhay / saar-saar ko gahi rahe, thotha dei udaay* (A saint should be like a crucible that can separate the essence from the trivial elements). The edifice of Hindutva was built on the trivial elements while Gandhi chose substance for realizing his dream of swaraj.

Religious fundamentalism will lead to destruction while inclusiveness will lead to prosperity. The Constitution will lead to unity while racial supremacy will lead to disintegration. The choice is ours, and these choices will decide our future as a nation and civilization.

Bibliography

Books and Articles

Abdullah, Sheikh. *Flames of the Chinar.* Translated by Khushwant Singh. New Delhi: Penguin, 1993.

Ambedkar, Bhimrao. *Pakistan, Athwa Bharat Ka Vibhajan.* [In Hindi.] Translated by Dhammamitra Satyaprakash. Delhi: Samyak Prakashan, 2018.

Andrews, C.F. *Mahatma Gandhi's Ideas.* London: Henderson & Spalding, 1949.

Azad, Maulana Abul Kalam. *India Wins Freedom.* New Delhi: Orient BlackSwan, 2020.

Birdwood, Lord Christopher. *Two Nations and Kashmir.* London: Robert Hale Ltd, 1956.

Bose, Nirmal Kumar. *My Days With Gandhi.* Calcutta: Nishan, 1953.

Bourke-White, Margaret. Halfway to Freedom: A Report on New India in the Words and Photographs of Margaret Bourke-White. Bombay: Asia Publishing House, 1949.

Campbell-Johnson, Allan. *Mission with Mountbatten.* Delhi: Jaico Publishing House, 1951.

Chaman Lal, ed. *Bhagat Singh ke Sampoorna Dastavez.* [In Hindi.] Panchkula: Aadhar Prakashan, 2005.

Chandra, Bipan et al. *India's Struggle for Independence.* Delhi: Penguin Random House India, 2016.

Dayal, John. *A Matter of Equity: Freedom of Faith in Secular India.* Delhi: Anamika Publishers, 2007.

Desai, Morarji. *Maaru Jeevan Vrittanṭ.* [In Gujarati.] Ahmedabad: Navjivan Prakashan Mandir, 2014.

Douglass, James W. *Gandhi and the Unspeakable.* New York: Orbis Books, 2012.

Dutt, V.N. *Gandhi and Bhagat Singh.* Delhi: Rupa, 2008.

Elst, Koenraad. *Gandhi and Godse: A Review and a Critique.* New Delhi: Voice of India, 2001.

———. *Why I Killed the Mahatma: Uncovering Godse's Defence*. Delhi: Rupa, 2018.

Fischer, Louis, ed. *The Essential Gandhi*. New York: Vintage Spritual Classic, 2002.

———. *Mahatma Gandhi: His Life and Times*. London: Jonathan Cape, 1951.

Ganachari, Arvind. *Gopal Ganesh Agarkar: The Secular Rationalist Reformer*. Mumbai: Popular Publication, 2005.

Gandhi, M.K. *Collected Works of Mahatma Gandhi*. 98 vols. [eBook.] New Delhi: Publications Division, Government of India, 1999.

Gandhi, M.K. *Satyagraha in South Africa*. [eBook.] New Delhi: Publications Division, Government of India.

Gandhi, Manuben. *Antim Jhanki*. [In Hindi.] Kashi: Akhil Bharat Sarva Seva Sangh, 1960. Translated in English as *Last Glimpses of Bapu* (Delhi: Shivlal Agarwal and Co, 1962).

———. *Kalkatte ka Chamatkar*. [In Hindi.] Ahmedabad: Navjivan Prakashan Mandir, 1956.

Gandhi, Rajmohan. *Gandhi: The Man, His People, and the Empire*. Berkeley: University of California Press, 2008.

———. *Patel: A Life*. Ahmedabad: Navjivan, 2017.

———. 'Independence and Social Justice: The Ambedkar-Gandhi Debate'. *Economic & Political Weekly*, vol. 50, no. 15 (11 April 2015).

Gandhi, Tushar. *Let's Kill Gandhi*. Delhi: Rupa, 2009.

Godse, Gopal. *Gandhi Vadh Kyon*. [In Hindi.] Delhi: Hind Pocket Books, 2015.

Godse, Nathuram. *Maine Gandhi Vadh Kyon Kiya*. [In Hindi.] Anonymous editor. Delhi: Sakshi Prakashan, 2019.

———. *May it Please Your Honour*. Delhi: Surya Prakashan, 1987.

Golwalkar, M.S. *We, or Our Nationhood Defined*. Nagpur: P.N. Indurkar, 1939.

Gupta, Virendra, and Alok Bansal, eds. *Pakistan Occupied Kashmir: The Untold Story*. Delhi: Manas Publiction, 2016.

Hasnain, F.M. *Freedom Struggle in Kashmir*. Delhi: Rima Publishing House, 1988.

Inamdar, P.L. *The Story of the Red Fort Trial*. Bombay: Popular Publication, 1979.

Islam, Shamsul. *Muslims Against Partition of India*. New Delhi: Pharos, 2018.

Jain, Dr Jagdish Chandra. *I Could Not Save Bapu*. Banaras: Jagran Sahitya Mandir, 1948.

Keer, Dhananjay. *Veer Savarkar*. Bombay: Popular Publications, 1966.

Khan, Yasmin. *The Great Partition*. London: Yale University Press, 2017.

Khosla, G.D. *The Murder of the Mahatma*. Bombay: Jaico Publishing House, 1965.

Kumar, Krishna. *Shanti Ka Safar*. [In Hindi.] Delhi: Rajkamal Prakashan, 2008.

Lamb, Alastair. *Kashmir: A Disputed Legacy, 1846–1990*. Hertfordshire: Roxford Books, 1991.

Lester, Muriel. *Entertaining Gandhi*. Richard Clay and Sons Ltd, 1932.

Lohia, Ram Manohar. *Guilty Men of India's Partition*. Delhi: B.R. Publishing Corporation, 2020.

Maclean, Kama. *A Revolutionary History of Interwar India*. New Delhi: Penguin Books, 2015.

Mahajan, Sucheta. *Independence and Partition*. New Delhi: Sage, 2000.

Majumdar, R.C. *Penal Settlements in Andamans*. New Delhi: Gazetteers Unit, Department of Culture, Government of India, 1975.

Malgonkar, Manohar. *The Men Who Killed Gandhi*. Delhi: Roli Books, 2019.

Menon, A. Sreedhara. *Triumph and Tragedy in Travancore: Annals of Sir CP's Sixteen Years*. Kottayam: DC Books, 2019.

Menon, V.P. *The Story of the Integration of the Indian States*. Calcutta: Orient Longman, 1955.

Mookerjee, Syama Prasad. *Leaves from a Dairy*. New Delhi: Oxford University Press, 1993.

Moraes, Frank. *Jawaharlal Nehru: A Biography*. Mumbai: Jaico Books, 2013.

Nanda, B.R. *Gandhi and His Critics*. Delhi: Oxford University Press, 1997.

Nayyar, Kuldip. *Shaheed Bhagat Singh: Kranti Ke Prayog*. [In Hindi.] Meerut: Samvad Prakashan, 2004.

Noorani, A.G. *The Kashmir Dispute, 1947–2012*. 2 vols. New Delhi: Tulika Books, 2015.

______. *Savarkar and Hindutva*. Delhi: LeftWord, 2017.

Pandey, Ashok Kumar. *Kashmir Aur Kashmiri Pandit*. [In Hindi.] Delhi: Rajkamal Prakashan, 2020.

______. *Kashmirnama: Itihas Aur Samkal*. [In Hindi.] Delhi: Rajpal and Sons, 2018.

Payne, Robert. *The Life and Death of Mahatma Gandhi*. Delhi: Rupa, 1969.

Phadnis, Jagan. *Gandhi Ki Shahadat*. [Translated from Marathi to Hindi.] Varanasi: Sarva Seva Sangh Prakashan, 2010.

Polak, H.S.L. et al. *Mahatma Gandhi*. London: Odhams Press Ltd, 1948.

Polak, Milie Graham, *Mr. Gandhi: The Man*. [eBook.] Available online: https://www.gandhiashramsevagram.org/pdf-books/gandhi-the-man.pdf, last accessed 8 December 2021.

Prakash, Virendra. *Hindutva Demystified*. New Delhi: Virgo, 2002.

Prasad, Shabu. *Assassination of Mahatma Gandhi: Neglected Chronologies*. Kochi: Kurukshetra Publication, 2017.

Puri, Balraj. *Kashmir: Insurgency and After*. 3rd ed. New Delhi: Orient Longman, 2008.

Pyarelal. *Mahatma Gandhi: The Last Phase*. Ahmedabad: Navjivan, 1958.

Sagar, Daya. *Jammu and Kashmir: A Victim*. Delhi: Ocean Books Pvt Ltd, 2015.

Sampath, Vikram. *Savarkar: Echoes from a Forgotten Past, 1883–1924*. New Delhi: Penguin, 2019.

Savarkar, Vinayak Damodar. *1857 Ka Swatantrya Samar.* [Translated to Hindi.] Delhi: Prabhat Prakashan, 2018.

———. *Hindutva.* Bombay: Veer Savarkar Prakashan, 1923.

———. *Savarkar Samagra.* [In Hindi.] Poona: Samagra Savarkar Wangmay Prakashan Samiti, Maharashtra Prantik Hindu Sabha, 1963–65.

———. *Hindu Rashtra Darshan.* Poona: Maharashtra Prantik Sabha.

Schofield, *Victoria. Kashmir in Conflict: India, Pakistan and the Unending War.* London: I.B. Tauris, 2003.

Setalvad, Teesta, ed. *Beyond Doubt.* Delhi: Tulika Books, 2018.

Singh, Neerja, ed. *Nehru-Patel, Agreement within Differences.* Delhi: National Book Trust, 2010.

Srivas, Anuj. 'The Messy Partition of the Reserve Bank of India', *The Wire*, 14 August 2017.

Tendulkar, D.G. et al., eds. *Mahatma: Life of Mohandas Karamchand Gandhi.* 8 vols. Bombay: Karnatak Publishing House, 1954.

———. *Gandhi: His Life and Work.* Bombay: Karnatak Publishing House, 1944.

Vaidya, Chunnibhai. 'Assassination of Gandhi: The Facts Behind'. Available online: https://www.mkgandhi.org/assassin.htm, last accessed 8 December 2021.

Wolpert, Stanley. *Gandhi's Passion.* New York: Oxford University Press, 2001.

Documents

Report of the Jeevan Lal Kapur Commission of Inquiry into the Conspiracy to Murder Mahatma Gandhi

Papers related to the murder of Mahatma Gandhi, National Archives of India

Proceedings of Godse's Trial at Red Fort

Notes

The Guilty Men of Red Fort

1 Manohar Malgonkar, *The Men Who Killed Gandhi*, pp. 46–47.
2 A.G. Noorani, 'Savarkar's Mercy Petitions', *The Outlook*, 8 April 2005 (https://frontline.thehindu.com/the-nation/article30204154.ece, last accessed on 8 December 2021).
3 Malgonkar, *The Men Who Killed Gandhi*, p. 57.
4 Dhananjay Keer, *Veer Savarkar*, p. 219.
5 Ibid., p. 221.
6 Malgonkar, *The Men Who Killed Gandhi*, p. 58.
7 Ibid., p. 63.
8 Arvind Ganachari, *Gopal Ganesh Agarkar*, p. 29.
9 Dayanesh Jathar, 'Apte Was a British Agent', *The Week*, 12 November 2017 (https://www.theweek.in/theweek/cover/apte-was-a-british-agent.html, last accessed on 8 December 2021).
10 Malgonkar, *The Men Who Killed Gandhi*, p. 76.
11 Ibid., pp. 81–84.
12 Dr Jagdish Chandra Jain, *I Could Not Save Bapu*, p. 7.
13 Ibid.
14 Tushar Gandhi, *Let's Kill Gandhi*, p. 37.
15 Saira Menezes, 'I Regret I Wasn't The Man To Kill Gandhi', Outlook, 2 February 1998 (https://www.outlookindia.com/magazine/story/i-regret-i-wasnt-the-man-to-kill-gandhi/204997, last accessed on 8 December 2021).
16 Jain, *I Could Not Save Bapu*, pp. 8–12.
17 Gandhi, *Let's Kill Gandhi*, p. xxi.
18 Malgonkar, *The Men Who Killed Gandhi*, p. 124.
19 'Nathuram Godse never left RSS, says his family', The Economic Times, 8 September 2016 (https://economictimes.indiatimes.com/news/politics-and-nation/nathuram-godse-never-left-rss-says-his-family/articleshow/54159375.cms?from=mdr, last accessed on 8 December 2021).
20 See 3 May 1923 issue of Gwalior newspaper *Jayaji Pratap* (available in the National Archives).
21 Result published in *Jayaji Pratap*, 21 June 21 1923.
22 G.D. Khosla, *The Murder of the Mahatma*, p. 25.

The Gandhi Murder: A Chronology

1 Chunnibhai Vaidya, 'Assassination of Gandhi: The Facts Behind' (accessed at https://www.mkgandhi.org/assassin.htm).
2 Shabu Prasad, *Assassination of Mahatma Gandhi*, chapter 4.

1. Poona, the Peshwa Capital, Chitpavan Brahmins and the Dream of a Hindu Rashtra

1 Jagan Phadnis, *Gandhi ki Shahadat*, pp. 15–16.
2 Koenraad Elst, *Gandhi and Godse*, p. 10.
3 Ibid., pp. 10–11.
4 Phadnis, *Gandhi ki Shahadat*, p. 5.
5 'Gopal Hari Deshmukh and his Contribution to Maharashtra', India Study Channel (https://www.indiastudychannel.com/resources/147327-Gopal-Hari-Deshmukh-and-his-Contribution-to-Maharashtra.aspx, last accessed on 8 December 2021).
6 Pyarelal, *Mahatma Gandhi: The Last Phase*, vol. X, pt. 2, p. 915.
7 Ganachari, *Gopal Ganesh Agarkar*, p. 19.
8 Ibid., pp. 21–22.
9 Phadnis, *Gandhi ki Shahadat*, p. 6.
10 Ganachari, *Gopal Ganesh Agarkar*, pp. 125–31.
11 Ibid., p. 139.
12 Ibid., pp. 151–54.
13 Sudheendra Kulkarni, 'Why Tilak's Pact with Jinnah Is Relevant for Indo-Pakistan Peace', *The Quint*, 1 August 2021 (https://www.thequint.com/voices/blogs/tilak-why-his-pact-with-jinnah-is-relevant-for-india-pakistan-peace, last accessed on 8 December 2021).
14 Phadnis, *Gandhi ki Shahadat*, p. 19.
15 Quoted in ibid., p. 20.
16 M.K. Gandhi, *Satyagraha in South Africa*, pp. 52–53.
17 'Investigation into the Assassination of Mahatma Gandhi and other things about assassination', Digitized Private Papers, Sardar Patel, File no. 2/233 of 1948, held by the National Archives of India (available online: https://indianculture.gov.in/archives/investgation-assasination-mahatma-gandhi-and-other-things-about-assassination-0, last accessed on 8 December 2021).
18 Kulkarni, 'Why Tilak's Pact with Jinnah Is Relevant'.
19 V.D. Savarkar, *Savarkar Samagra*, pt. 6, p. 296.
20 Nathuram Godse, *Maine Gandhi Vadh Kyon Kiya*, p. 93.
21 Report of the Jeevan Lal Kapur Commission of Inquiry into the Conspiracy to Murder Mahatma Gandhi (hereinafter Kapur Commission Report), pt. 2, p. 301, para 25.97.
22 A.G. Noorani, *Savarkar and Hindutva*, p. 41.
23 V.D. Savarkar, *Hindutva*, pp. v–vi.

24 Ibid., p. iv.
25 Ibid., p. 3.
26 Ibid.
27 Ibid., p. 13.
28 Ibid., p. 83.
29 Ibid, p. 84.
30 Ibid.
31 Virendra Prakash, *Hindutva Demystified*, p. 33.
32 'Historic Statements by Savarkar', savarkar.org (available here: http://savarkar.org/en/encyc/2017/5/23/2_12_15_55_historic_statements_by_savarkar.v001.pdf_1.pdf, last accessed on 8 December 2021).
33 Ibid.
34 M.S. Golwalkar, *We, or Our Nationhood Defined*, pp. 47–48.

2. Non-Violence and a Fearless Life: Attempts on Gandhi Before January 1948

1 B.R. Nanda, *Gandhi and His Critics*, p. 153.
2 *Collected Works of Mahatma Gandhi* (hereinafter *CWMG*), vol. 91, p. 349.
3 James W. Douglass, *Gandhi and the Unspeakable*, pp. 29–30.
4 Louis Fischer, *Mahatma Gandhi*, p. 142.
5 Shamsul Islam, *Muslims Against Partition of India*, p. 205.
6 Bipan Chandra et al., *India's Struggle for Independence*, p. 301.
7 Phadnis, *Gandhi ki Shahadat*, p. 70.
8 Kama Maclean, *A Revolutionary History of Interwar India*, chapter 7.
9 Douglass, *Gandhi and the Unspeakable*, pp. 1–2.
10 Louis Fischer (ed.), *The Essential Gandhi*, p. 343.
11 Gandhi, *Satyagraha in South Africa*, p. 63.
12 Milie Graham Polak, *Mr. Gandhi*, pp. 61–62.
13 Pyarelal, *Mahatma Gandhi: The Last Phase*, vol. X, pt. 2, p. 914.
14 Robert Payne, *The Life and Death of Mahatma Gandhi*, p. 151.
15 Douglass, *Gandhi and the Unspeakable*, pp. 8–10.
16 Payne, *The Life and Death of Mahatma Gandhi*, p. 164.
17 Ibid.
18 Ibid., p. 180.
19 Douglass, *Gandhi and the Unspeakable*, p. 14.
20 Ibid., p. 24.
21 Ibid.
22 Ibid., p. 36.
23 Payne, *The Life and Death of Mahatma Gandhi*, p. 288.
24 Ibid., p. 142.
25 Douglass, *Gandhi and the Unspeakable*, p. 36.
26 Payne, *The Life and Death of Mahatma Gandhi*, pp. 297–98.
27 Fischer, *Mahatma Gandhi*, p. 153.
28 Payne, *The Life and Death of Mahatma Gandhi*, p. 300.

29 Muriel Lester, *Entertaining Gandhi*, pp. 160–61.
30 *CWMG*, vol. 5, pp. 50–52.
31 Rajmohan Gandhi, 'Independence and Social Justice: The Ambedkar-Gandhi Debate', *Economic & Political Weekly*, vol. 50, no. 15 (11 April 2015).
32 Fischer (ed.), *The Essential Gandhi*, p. 280.
33 Ibid., p. 282.
34 Ibid., p. 281.
35 Lester, *Entertaining Gandhi*, pp. 47–48.
36 *CWMG*, vol. 16, p. 139.
37 Rajmohan Gandhi, 'Independence and Social Justice'.
38 Payne, *The Life and Death of Mahatma Gandhi*, p. 439.
39 Lester, *Entertaining Gandhi*, p. 41.
40 C.F. Andrews, *Mahatama Gandhi's Ideas*, p. 29.
41 Payne, *The Life and Death of Mahatma Gandhi*, p. 294.
42 Ibid., p. 439.
43 *CWMG*, vol. 48, p. 298, or vol. 54, p. 154.
44 Payne, *The Life and Death of Mahatma Gandhi*, p. 442.
45 Fischer (ed.), *The Essential Gandhi*, p. 280.
46 Ibid., p. 281.
47 *CWMG*, vol. 51, p. 154.
48 Payne, *The Life and Death of Mahatma Gandhi*, p. 44.
49 Rajmohan Gandhi, 'Independence and Social Justice'.
50 Uday Balakrishnan, 'Ambedkar and the Poona Pact', *The Hindu*, 13 April 2020 (https://www.thehindu.com/opinion/op-ed/ambedkar-and-the-poona-pact/article31333684.ece, last accessed on 8 December 2021).
51 Rajmohan Gandhi, 'Swatantrata aur Samajik Nyay: Ambedkar-Gandhi Vimarsh', Swadheen (blog), 23 November 2015 (https://swaadheen.blogspot.com/2015/11/blog-post_23.html?m=1, last accessed on 8 December 2021).
52 D.G. Tendulkar et al. (eds.), *Mahatma: Life of Mohandas Karamchand Gandhi*, pt. 8, p. 3.
53 Rajmohan Gandhi, 'Independence and Social Justice'.
54 *CWMG*, vol. 91, p. 139.
55 Teesta Setalvad (ed.), *Beyond Doubt*, pp. 154–55.
56 Fischer (ed.), *The Essential Gandhi*, p. 285.
57 Keer, *Veer Savarkar*, p. 180.
58 Ibid., p. 226.
59 V.D. Savarkar, *Hindu Rashtra Darshan*, pp. 63–64.
60 Setalvad (ed.), *Beyond Doubt*, pp. 87–88.
61 Fischer (ed.), *The Essential Gandhi*, p. 285.
62 *CWMG*, vol. 77, p. 298.
63 D.G. Tendulkar et al. (eds.), *Gandhi: His Life and Work*, pp. 467–70.
64 Fischer (ed.), *The Essential Gandhi*, p. 346.
65 Payne, *The Life and Death of Mahatma Gandhi*, pp. 493–95.
66 Vikram Sampath, *Savarkar: Echoes from a Forgotten Past*, pp. 458–59.
67 Savarkar, *Hindu Rashtra Darshan*, p. 63.
68 John Dayal, *A Matter of Equity*, p. 443.

69 Pyarelal, *Mahatma Gandhi: The Last Phase*, vol. IX, pt. 1, p. 123.
70 Savarkar, *Hindu Rashtra Darshan*, pp. 68–71.
71 Syama Prasad Mookerjee, *Leaves from a Dairy*, p. 179.
72 Pyarelal, *Mahatma Gandhi: The Last Phase*, vol. IX, pt. 1, p. 112.
73 Stanley Wolpert, *Gandhi's Passion*, p. 205.
74 Tushar Gandhi, *Let's Kill Gandhi*, p. 172.
75 Setalvad (ed.), *Beyond Doubt*, p. 159.
76 Kapur Commission Report, pt. 1, p. 124, para 9.36 and 9.37.
77 Pyarelal, *Mahatma Gandhi: The Last Phase*, vol. IX, pt. 1, pp. 128–29.
78 Kapur Commission Report, pt. 1, para 10.6.
79 Kapur Commission Report, pt. 1, p. 126, para 10.8.
80 Kapur Commission Report, pt. 2, p. 3, para 18.14.
81 Kapur Commission Report, pt. 1, p. 126, para 12.61.
82 Payne, *The Life and Death of Mahatma Gandhi*, p. 488.

3. Last Days: Delhi, Noakhali, Delhi

1 *CWMG*, vol. 91, p. 203.
2 Sucheta Mahajan, *Independence and Partition*, p. 144.
3 Lester, *Entertaining Gandhi*, p. 129.
4 Wolpert, *Gandhi's Passion*, p. 183.
5 Payne, *The Life and Death of Mahatma Gandhi*, p. 512.
6 Wolpert, *Gandhi's Passion*, p. 212.
7 Chunnibhai Vaidya, 'Assassination of Gandhi'.
8 Wolpert, *Gandhi's Passion*, p. 212.
9 Ibid., p. 210.
10 Mahajan, *Independence and Partition*, p. 59.
11 Ibid., p. 62.
12 Ibid., p. 220.
13 Nandini Rathi, '1945 INA trials: a rare glimpse from the lens of photojournalist Kulwant Roy', *The Indian Express*, 29 August 2017 (https://indianexpress.com/article/research/ina-trials-from-the-lens-of-photojournalist-kulwant-roy-4819120/, last accessed on 8 December 2021).
14 Payne, *The Life and Death of Mahatma Gandhi*, p. 514.
15 Wolpert, *Gandhi's Passion*, p. 232.
16 Mahajan, *Independence and Partition*, p. 145.
17 *CWMG*, vol. 91, p. 193.
18 Ibid., p. 194.
19 Ibid., p. 152.
20 Mahajan, *Independence and Partition*, p. 218.
21 *CWMG*, vol. 90, p. 22.
22 Yasmin Khan, *The Great Partition*, pp. 33–34.
23 Bipan Chandra et al., *India's Struggle for Independence*, p. 493.
24 *CWMG*, vol. 90, p. 66.
25 Khan, *The Great Partition*, p. 61.

26 Wolpert, *Gandhi's Passion*, pp. 221–22.
27 *CWMG*, vol. 91, p. 329.
28 Ibid., vol. 92, p. 436.
29 Ibid., vol. 91, pp. 325–26.
30 Ibid., vol. 91, pp. 31–32.
31 Ibid., vol. 90, p. 54.
32 Ibid., vol. 91, p. 142.
33 Ibid, p. 147.
34 Khan, *The Great Partition*, p. 41.
35 Tushar Gandhi, *Let's Kill Gandhi*, p. 256.
36 Islam, *Muslims Against Partition of India*, pp. 209–11.
37 Tushar Gandhi, *Let's Kill Gandhi*, pp. 50–52.
38 *CWMG*, vol. 91, pp. 223–24.
39 Ibid., p. 334.
40 Karl Marx, 'A Contribution to the Critique of Hegel's Philosophy of Right', 1844 (https://www.marxists.org/archive/marx/works/1843/critique-hpr/intro.htm, last accessed on 8 December 2021).
41 Mahajan, *Independence and Partition*, pp. 223–23.
42 *CWMG*, vol. 91, pp. 342–43.
43 Mahajan, *Independence and Partition*, pp. 223–25.
44 Khan, *The Great Partition*, p. 63.
45 Mahajan, *Independence and Partition*, p. 226.
46 Nirmal Kumar Bose, *My Days With Gandhi*, p. 32.
47 *CWMG*, vol. 92, pp. 44–45.
48 Bose, *My Days With Gandhi*, p. 97.
49 Lester, *Entertaining Gandhi*, p. 101.
50 Payne, *The Life and Death of Mahatma Gandhi*, p. 519.
51 Bose, *My Days With Gandhi*, p. 34.
52 Mahajan, *Independence and Partition*, p. 235.
53 *CWMG*, vol. 92, p. 382.
54 Bose, *My Days With Gandhi*, p. 33.
55 *CWMG*, vol. 92, p. 432.
56 Bose, *My Days With Gandhi*, pp. 36–40.
57 *CWMG*, vol. 92, p. 435.
58 Ibid., p. 451.
59 Mahajan, *Independence and Partition*, p. 235.
60 Bose, *My Days With Gandhi*, p. 45.
61 Ibid., p. 47.
62 Tushar Gandhi, *Let's Kill Gandhi*, p. 271.
63 Bose, *My Days With Gandhi*, p. 140.
64 Ibid.
65 Douglass, *Gandhi and the Unspeakable*, p. 57.
66 Mahajan, *Independence and Partition*, pp. 238–39.
67 Tushar Gandhi, *Let's Kill Gandhi*, p. 271.

4. And He Was Killed...

1 *CWMG*, vol. 91, p. 220.
2 Malgonkar, *The Men Who Killed Gandhi*, pp. 90–100.
3 *CWMG*, vol. 96, pp. 230–34.
4 D.G. Tendulkar et al. (eds.), *Mahatma: Life of Mohandas Karamchand Gandhi*, pt. 8, pp. 95–96.
5 Wolpert, *Gandhi's Passion*, p. 235.
6 *CWMG*, vol. 96, pp. 298, 321.
7 Manuben Gandhi, *Kalkatte ka Chamatkar*, pp. 117–32.
8 Rajmohan Gandhi, *Patel: A Life*, p. 429.
9 Pyarelal, *Mahatma Gandhi: Purnahuti* [Gujarati edition], pt. 4, p. 43.
10 Ibid., p. 8.
11 Khosla, *The Murder of the Mahatma*, p. 27.
12 *CWMG*, vol. 98, p. 27.
13 Pyarelal, *Mahatma Gandhi: Purnahuti*, pt. 4, p. 17.
14 *CWMG*, vol. 98, p. 200.
15 Manuben Gandhi, *Last Glimpses of Bapu*, p. 105.
16 Malgonkar, *The Men Who Killed Gandhi*, p. 124.
17 Khosla, *The Murder of the Mahatma*, p. 28.
18 Malgonkar, *The Men Who Killed Gandhi*, p. 126.
19 Noorani, *Savarkar and Hindutva*, pp. 116–17.
20 Ibid., p. 131.
21 Ibid., p. 136.
22 Jain, *I Could Not Save Bapu*, pp. 8–17.
23 Khosla, *The Murder of the Mahatma*, p. 28.
24 *CWMG*, vol. 98, p. 238.
25 Ibid., p. 223.
26 Pyarelal, *Mahatma Gandhi: The Last Phase*, vol. X, pt. 2, pp. 857–58.
27 *CWMG*, vol. 98, pp. 225–26.
28 *CWMG*, vol. 98, p. 235.
29 Payne, *The Life and Death of Mahatma Gandhi*, p. 551.
30 Ibid., p. 561.
31 Pyarelal, *Mahatma Gandhi: The Last Phase*, vol. X, pt. 2, pp. 869–70.
32 Ibid., p. 878.
33 Ibid., pp. 878–79.
34 Malgonkar, *The Men Who Killed Gandhi*, p. 145.
35 Pyarelal, *Mahatma Gandhi: The Last Phase*, vol. X, pt. 2, p. 888.
36 Menezes, 'I Regret I Wasn't The Man To Kill Gandhi'.
37 Malgonkar, *The Men Who Killed Gandhi*, p. 145.
38 Manuben Gandhi, *Last Glimpses of Bapu*, pp. 214–16.
39 *CWMG*, vol. 98, p. 274.
40 Malgonkar, *The Men Who Killed Gandhi*, p. 184.
41 Pyarelal, *Mahatma Gandhi: The Last Phase*, vol. X, pt. 2, p. 914.
42 Malgonkar, *The Men Who Killed Gandhi*, pp. 183–84.
43 Menezes, 'I Regret I Wasn't The Man To Kill Gandhi'.

44 Manuben Gandhi, *Last Glimpses of Bapu*, p. 222.
45 Kapur Commission Report, pt. 2, p. 23, para 18.94.
46 Kapur Commission Report, pt. 2, pp. 24–24, para 18.95.
47 Case diary prepared by DSP Jaswant Singh. Digitized Private Papers, Sardar Patel, File no. 2/233 of 1948, NAI, p. 93.
48 Malgonkar, *The Men Who Killed Gandhi*, p. 191.
49 Kapur Commission Report, pt. 2, p. 356, para 26.112.
50 Digitized Private Papers, Sardar Patel, File no. 2/233 of 1948, NAI, p. 29.
51 Malgonkar, *The Men Who Killed Gandhi*, p. 192.
52 Jain, *I Could Not Save Bapu*, pp. 20–23.
53 Kapur Commission Report, pt. 2, p. 10, para 18.43.
54 D.G. Tendulkar et al. (eds.), *Gandhi: His Life and Work*, p. 335.
55 *CWMG*, vol. 98, p. 279.
56 Rajmohan Gandhi, *Patel: A Life*, p. 466.
57 Digitized Private Papers, Sardar Patel, File no. 2/233 of 1948, NAI, pp. 93–94. Case diary prepared by DSP Jaswant Singh.
58 Ibid., p. 104.
59 Kapur Commission Report, pt. 2, p. 356, para 26.111.
60 *CWMG*, vol. 98, p. 317.
61 Malgonkar, *The Men Who Killed Gandhi*, p. 230.
62 Allan Campbell-Johnson, *Mission with Mountbatten*, p. 319.
63 Manuben Gandhi, *Last Glimpses of Bapu*, p. 273.
64 *CWMG*, vol. 98, p. 329.
65 Manuben Gandhi, *Last Glimpses of Bapu*, p. 297.
66 Rajmohan Gandhi, *Patel: A Life*, p. 467.
67 Manuben Gandhi, *Last Glimpses of Bapu*, p. 308.
68 Douglass, *Gandhi and the Unspeakable*, p. 87.
69 From Nehru's address to the nation on the evening of 30 January 1948.
70 Rajmohan Gandhi, *Gandhi: The Man, His People, and the Empire*, p. 67.
71 Douglass, *Gandhi and the Unspeakable*, p. 88.
72 See Dr Surendra Ajnat (ed.), *Letters of Ambedkar*, 2nd ed., Jalandhar: Navchetna Publications, 2018, pp. 169–70.
73 Rajmohan Gandhi, *Patel: A Life*, p. 468.
74 Manuben Gandhi, *Last Glimpses of Bapu*, pp. 311–12.
75 Campbell-Johnson, *Mission with Mountbatten*, p. 318.
76 Rajmohan Gandhi, *Patel: A Life*, p. 468.
77 Neerja Singh (ed.), *Nehru-Patel, Agreement within Differences*, pp. 285–87.
78 Rajmohan Gandhi, *Patel: A Life*, p. 470.
79 Campbell-Johnson, *Mission with Mountbatten*, pp. 317–18.
80 *Hindustan Times*, 31 January 1948. Digitized Private Papers, Sardar Patel, File no. 2/233 of 1948, NAI, p. 114.
81 Setalvad (ed.), *Beyond Doubt*, p. 82.
82 See Durga Das (ed.), *Sardar Patel Correspondences*, vol. 6, Ahmedabad: Navjivan, 1973, p. 66.
83 Campbell-Johnson, *Mission with Mountbatten*, p. 322.

5. The Red Fort Trial

1 Kapur Commission Report, pt. 2, p. 354, para 26.105.
2 Malgonkar, *The Men Who Killed Gandhi*, p. 199.
3 Durga Das (ed.), *Sardar Patel Correspondences*, vol. 6, p. 56.
4 Malgonkar, *The Men Who Killed Gandhi*, pp. 321–22.
5 Khosla, *The Murder of the Mahatma*, pp. 13–14.
6 V.D. Savarkar, *1857 Ka Swatantrya Samar*, p. 110.
7 Noorani, *Savarkar and Hindutva*, p. 96.
8 Morarji Desai, *Maaru Jeevan Vrittant*, p. 234.
9 Noorani, *Savarkar and Hindutva*, p. 130.
10 Malgonkar, *The Men Who Killed Gandhi*, p. 199.
11 Koenraad Elst, *Why I Killed the Mahatma*, chapter 1, p. 176.
12 Digitized Private Papers, Sardar Patel, File no. 2/233 of 1948, NAI, p. 81.
13 Ibid., pp. 3–26, 46–50, 69–80.
14 *Hindustan Times*, 16 October 1948.
15 Khosla, *The Murder of the Mahatma*, pp. 47–48.

6. The Kapur Commission and Savarkar

1 P.L. Inamdar, *The Story of the Red Fort Trial*, p. 141.
2 Sampath, *Savarkar: Echoes from a Forgotten Past*, p. 161.
3 Ibid., p. 169.
4 R.C. Majumdar, *Penal Settlements in Andamans*, p. 232.
5 Kapur Commission Report, pt. 1, p. 62, para 5.22.
6 *The Indian Express*, 15 November 1948.
7 Digitized Private Papers, Sardar Patel, File no. 2/233 of 1948, NAI, pp. 1–2.
8 See *Gajanan Vishwanath Ketkar vs The State on 21 July, 1965*, AIR 1967 Bom 96 (https://indiankanoon.org/doc/383735/, last accessed on 8 December 2021).
9 Kapur Commission Report, pt. 1, p. 3.
10 Kapur Commission Report, pt. 2, p. 332, para 26.15.
11 Digitized Private Papers, Sardar Patel, File no. 2/233 of 1948, NAI, p. 87.
12 Kapur Commission Report, pt. 2, p. 346, para 26.74c.
13 Ibid., p. 348, para 26.82.
14 Digitized Private Papers, Sardar Patel, File no. 2/233 of 1948, NAI, p. 90.
15 Kapur Commission Report, pt. 2, p. p. 357, para 26.117.
16 Ibid., p. 361, para 26.122(xii).
17 Ibid., p. 359, para 26.122(v).
18 Ibid., pt. 1, p. 218, para 12H.7.
19 Ibid., p. 219, para 12H.10.
20 Ibid., p. 219, para 12H.11.
21 Ibid., p. 220, para 12H.17.
22 Ibid., p. 220, para 12H.14.
23 Ibid., pt. 2, p. 360, para 26.122(vii).
24 Ibid., pt. 1, p. 231, para 12I.23.

25 Ibid., pt. 1, p. 226, para 12H.35.
26 Ibid., pt. 2, p. 294, para 25.61.
27 Ibid., pt. 2, p. 317, para 25.161.
28 Ibid., pt. 2, p. 317, para 25.163.
29 Ibid.
30 Ibid., pt. 2, p. 317, para 25.166.
31 Ibid., pt. 2, p. 318, para 25.168.
32 Ibid., pt. 2, p. 317, para 25.169.
33 Ibid., pt. 2, p. 318, para 25.170.
34 Ibid., pt. 2, p. 318, para 25.173.
35 Ibid., pt. 2, p. 301, para 25.97.
36 Ibid., pt. 2, p. 303, para 25.106.
37 Ibid., pt. 2, p. 358, para 25.121(a) 1–3.
38 Ibid., pt. 2, p. 5, para 18.21.
39 Ibid., pt. 2, p. 5, para 18.22.
40 Ibid., pt. 2, p. 103, para 20.91.
41 Ibid., pt. 2, p. 103, para 25.92.
42 Ibid., pt. 2, p. 79, para 20.3.
43 Ibid., pt. 2, pp. 110–11, para 20.107–109.

Godse Lied in the Courtroom

1 Nathuram Godse, *Why I Killed Gandhi*, p. 6 (available online: https://ia903202.us.archive.org/11/items/why-i-killed-gandhi/why-i-killed-gandhi.pdf, last accessed on 8 December 2021).
2 Nathuram Godse, *May it Please Your Honour*, p. 157.
3 Tushar Gandhi, *Let's Kill Gandhi*, p. 541.
4 Khosla, *The Murder of the Mahatma*, p. 47.
5 Douglass, *Gandhi and the Unspeakable*, pp. 91–92.
6 Noorani, *Savarkar and Hindutva*, pp. 116–17.
7 See *Gopal Vinayak Godse vs The Union of India & Ors on 6 August 1969*, AIR 1971 Bom 56 (https://indiankanoon.org/doc/726232/, last accessed on 8 December 2021).
8 *Maine Gandhi Vadh Kyon Kiya*, Delhi: Bhagat Singh Vichar Manch, 2019, p. 226. The book mentions no editor.
9 Ibid., p. 227.

1. The 'Fifty-Five Crores' Lie

1 *May it Please Your Honour*, p. 152.
2 Anuj Srivas, 'The Messy Partition of the Reserve Bank of India', *The Wire*, 14 August 2017 (https://thewire.in/banking/Parttion-reserve-bank-of-india, lass accessed on
3 Rajmohan Gandhi, *Patel: A Life*, p. 461.

4 Anuj Srivas, 'The Messy Partition'.
5 Rajmohan Gandhi, *Patel: A Life*, p. 462.
6 Anuj Srivas, 'The Messy Partition'.
7 *CWMG*, vol. 98, p. 220.
8 Ibid., pp. 230–31.
9 Rajmohan Gandhi, *Patel: A Life*, p. 463.
10 *CWMG*, vol. 98, pp. 233 and 230–31.
11 Rajmohan Gandhi, *Patel: A Life*, pp. 462–63.
12 *CWMG*, vol. 98, pp. 233 and 239.
13 Rajmohan Gandhi, *Patel: A Life*, p. 464.

2. Gandhi Was Not Responsible for the Partition

1 Ram Manohar Lohia, *Guilty Men of India's Partition*, pp. 1–2.
2 Savarkar, *1857 Ka Swatantrya Samar*, p. 25.
3 Pyarelal, *Mahatma Gandhi: The Last Phase*, vol. IX, pt. 1, Page 112.
4 *Why I Killed Gandhi*, p. 6.
5 *CWMG*, vol. 97, pp. 139–40.
6 Chaman Lal (ed.), *Bhagat Singh ke Sampoorna Dastavez*, p. 150.
7 Rajmohan Gandhi, *Patel: A Life*, p. 367.
8 Maulana Abul Kalam Azad, *India Wins Freedom*, pp. 177–78.
9 Ibid.
10 Rajmohan Gandhi, *Patel: A Life*, p. 378.
11 Azad, *India Wins Freedom*, pp. 188–89.
12 Rajmohan Gandhi, *Patel: A Life*, p. 381.
13 Frank Moraes, *Jawaharlal Nehru: A Biography*, p. 346.
14 Rajmohan Gandhi, *Patel: A Life*, p. 378.
15 Ibid., p. 385.
16 Ibid., pp. 385–86.
17 Ibid., p. 387.
18 Moraes, *Jawaharlal Nehru*, p. 351.
19 *CWMG*, vol. 94, p. 168.
20 Rajmohan Gandhi, *Patel: A Life*, p. 390.
21 *CWMG*, vol. 94, p. 188.
22 Rajmohan Gandhi, *Patel: A Life*, p. 209.
23 Ibid., p. 392.
24 *CWMG*, vol. 94, pp. 228–29.
25 Ibid., pp. 275–76.
26 Ibid., p. 283.
27 Ibid., p. 217.
28 Lohia, *Guilty Men of India's Partition*, pp. 21–25.
29 Rajmohan Gandhi, *Patel: A Life*, p. 392.
30 Bhimrao Ambedkar, *Pakistan Athwa Bharat Ka Vibhajan*, p. 131.
31 Ibid., pp. 149–50.
32 A. Sreedhara Menon, *Triumph and Tragedy in Travencore*, p. 244.

3. Gandhi's Fasts: Sophisticated Weaponry of Non-Violent Resistance

1 Payne, *The Life and Death of Mahatma Gandhi*, pp. 323–25.
2 *CWMG*, vol. 27, p. 323.
3 M.K. Gandhi, *Satyagraha in South Africa*, pp. 210–11.
4 *CWMG*, vol. 28, pp. 1–2.
5 Fischer (ed.), *The Essential Gandhi*, p. 182.
6 *CWMG*, vol. 16, p. 337.

4. Godse and Bhagat Singh: The Contrast

1 Chaman Lal (ed.), *Bhagat Singh ke Sampoorna Dastavez*, p. 149.
2 Ibid., p. 256.
3 Ibid., pp. 158–61.
4 Ibid., p. 229.
5 Ibid., p. 152.
6 Ibid., p. 172.
7 Kuldip Nayyar, *Shaheed Bhagat Singh: Kranti Ke Prayog*, pp. 81 and 85.
8 Chaman Lal, 'Rare Documents on Bhagat Singh's Trial and Life in Jail', *The Hindu*, 15 August 2011 (https://www.thehindu.com/opinion/op-ed/rare-documents-on-bhagat-singhs-trial-and-life-in-jail/article2356959.ece, last accessed on 8 December 2021).
9 Nayyar, *Shaheed Bhagat Singh*, p. 103.
10 Ibid., p. 104.
11 Ibid., pp. 108–9.
12 Ibid., p. 113.
13 Ibid., p. 145.
14 See 'What Mahatma Gandhi Did to Save Bhagat Singh' by Chander Pal Singh on mkgandhi.org (https://www.mkgandhi.org/articles/bhagat_singh.htm?fbclid=IwAR3HdtSTcsp-212ZJ_v20UCtiIOclSgqVbMaJJ23pg98SkSe3vbhHf9Et_A, last accessed on 8 December 2021). The two Gandhi quotes are taken from vol. 42 (p. 391) and vol. 45 (p. 133) of the *Collected Works of Mahatma Gandhi*.
15 V.N. Dutt, *Gandhi and Bhagat Singh*, pp. 62–63.
16 Nanda, *Gandhi and His Critics*, p. 63.
17 Ibid., p. 64.
18 Maclean, *A Revolutionary History of Interwar India*, chapter 7.
19 *CWMG*, vol. 51, p. 155.
20 Dutt, *Gandhi and Bhagat Singh*, p. 44.
21 Krishna Kant, 'Bhagat Ke Siyasi Bhagat', *Tehelka Hindi*, 13 April 2016 (http://tehelkahindi.com/a-long-report-on-how-bhagat-singh-is-getting-politicized-in-current-times/2/, last accessed on 8 December 2021).
22 *CWMG*, vol. 51, p. 290.
23 Maclean, *A Revolutionary History of Interwar India*.

5. The Lies on Kashmir

1 *May it Please Your Honour*, p. 105.
2 *CWMG*, vol. 96, p. 438.
3 Ibid., p. 189.
4 Sheikh Abdullah, *Flames of the Chinar*, pp. 84–85.
5 F.M. Hasnain, *Freedom Struggle in Kashmir*, p. 145.
6 Lord Birdwood, *Two Nations and Kashmir*, p. 43.
7 Virendra Gupta and Alok Bansal (eds.), *Pakistan Occupied Kashmir: The Untold Story*, pp. 69–70.
8 *CWMG*, vol. 96, p. 194.
9 Ibid., p. 71.
10 Balraj Puri, *Kashmir: Insurgency and After*, p. 7.
11 Alastair Lamb, *Kashmir: A Disputed Legacy*, p. 10.
12 Lord Birdwood, *Two Nations and Kashmir*, p. 44.
13 Ibid.
14 A.G. Noorani, *The Kashmir Dispute*, vol. 1, p. 17.
15 Margaret Bourke-White, *Halfway to Freedom*, pp. 163–64.
16 Victoria Schofield, *Kashmir in Conflict*, p. 54.
17 Abdullah, *Flames of the Chinar*, p. 97.
18 Bourke-White, *Halfway to Freedom*, pp. 163–64.
19 Daya Sagar, *Jammu and Kashmir: A Victim*, p. 80.
20 V.P. Menon, *The Story of the Integration of the Indian States*, p. 361.
21 Schofield, *Kashmir in Conflict*, p. 97.
22 *CWMG*, vol. 97, p. 186.
23 Ibid.
24 Ashok Kumar Pandey, *Kashmir Aur Kashmiri Pandit*, p. 269.

6. Godse: A Revolutionary or a Coward?

1 *CWMG*, vol. 91, p. 117.
2 Manuben Gandhi, *Antim Jhanki*, pp. 29–30.
3 Savarkar, *Hindutva*, p. 41.
4 Bose, *My Days With Gandhi*, p. 100.
5 Rajmohan Gandhi, *Patel: A Life*, pp. 463–68.
6 Ibid., p. 370.